Presidents'
Most Wanted™

Other "Most Wanted™" Titles from Potomac Books

Italy's Most Wanted: The Top 10 Book of Roman Ruins, Wonderful Wines, and Renaissance Rarities, Luciano Mangiafico

Basketball Championships' Most Wanted: The Top 10 Book of March Mayhem, Playoff Performances, and Tournament Oddities, David L. Hudson, Jr.

Football's Most Wanted II: The Top 10 Book of More Bruising Backs, Savage Sacks, and Gridiron Oddities, Walter Harvey

Basketball's Most Wanted II: The Top 10 Book of More Hotshot Hoopsters, Double Dribbles, and Roundball Oddities, David L. Hudson, Jr.

Military History's Most Wanted: The Top 10 Book of Improbable Victories, Unlikely Heroes, and Other Martial Oddities, M. Evan Brooks

Presidents' Most Wanted™

The Top 10 Book of Extraordinary Executives, Colorful Campaigns, and White House Oddities

Nick Ragone

Potomac Books, Inc.
WASHINGTON, D.C.

Library of Congress Cataloging-in-Publication Data
Ragone, Nick.
Presidents' most wanted : the top 10 book of extraordinary executives,
colorful campaigns, and White House oddities / Nick Ragone. — 1st ed.
p. cm. — (Most wanted)
Includes bibliographical references and index.
ISBN 978-1-59797-074-7 (alk. paper)
1. Presidents—United States—Miscellanea. I. Title.
E176.1.R23 2008
973.09'9—dc22

2007015706

Printed in the United States of America on acid-free paper that meets the
American National Standards Institute Z39-48 Standard.

Potomac Books, Inc.
22841 Quicksilver Drive
Dulles, Virginia 20166

First Edition

10 9 8 7 6 5 4 3 2 1

For my mother and father,
because I sometimes forget to express
my love and gratitude

Contents

Illustrations

Acknowledgments

There are a dozen or so people I should thank for making this book possible, including my wonderful agent, Barb Doyen and editor Kevin Cuddihy. However, proper credit will have to wait for a future project. The truth is this book wouldn't have been possible without the unwavering support of my beautiful wife, Tyan, who months into this project gave birth to our second child, Mona Tan Ragone (to go along with Frank Tan Ragone). I'm still not sure where she found the energy to give birth, take care of the family, go back to work, and monitor my progress, but thankfully she kept this project on track—a task made doubly difficult given my unrelenting effort to fritter the summer away watching my beloved Mets enjoy a resurgent season. Quite simply, she did everything but put words on paper, and in every sense she is a full partner on this book. I wouldn't want it any other way.

Introduction

The presidency is a special office. Along with the vice president, the president is the only nationally elected official in the United States, and the office has come to symbolize American government both home and abroad. In many ways, the office is greater than the people who have occupied it.

In the two hundred-plus years of U.S. history, the presidency has grown and evolved dramatically—more so than any other office. With the exception of Abraham Lincoln and Andrew Jackson, the nineteenth-century officeholders exerted little executive power and mostly deferred to Congress on domestic affairs. Theodore Roosevelt began to change all that, and Franklin Roosevelt completed the transformation of the office with his New Deal program, laying the foundations for the modern presidency. With the onset of the Cold War, the "imperial" presidency was in full bloom, and after a brief lull in executive power following the Cold War, the current war on terror has led to new and unprecedented presidential powers. Undoubtedly, at the beginning of the twenty-first century, the presidency is not only the most powerful—and important—job in the United States but arguably in the world.

The purpose of *Presidents' Most Wanted* is to explore various aspects of the office and the people who have occupied it. This book is neither a complete history of the presidency nor the final word on the presidents. I will be happy if it simply entertains readers, provokes debate, and sparks an interest in learning more. This admonition holds particularly true for the chapters on ranking the presidents and vice presidents. Admittedly this endeavor is not an academic one; instead, it's a temporary truce between fact and opinion, with each side occasionally winning out. For those readers who bring a strong ideological preference or partisan bent, surely there will be much to find wrong or disagreeable.

Richard Nixon may have summed up best the inherent difficulty in placing the presidents in historical context: "History will treat me fairly. Historians probably won't because most historians are on the Left."

Firsts

Every president has been the first ever to do something, whether it is to use a telephone, throw out the first pitch at a baseball game, appear on television, or simply grow facial hair. Following are some interesting firsts.

1. THE MEDIA

William Henry Harrison was the first president to be photographed. James K. Polk delivered the first inaugural address transmitted by telegraph. In 1913, Woodrow Wilson became the first president to hold a press conference, while in 1961 John F. Kennedy was the first president to a hold a press conference on live television. Franklin Delano Roosevelt was known for his "fireside" chats broadcast over the radio, but Warren G. Harding was actually the first president to be heard on radio when a Baltimore radio station transmitted his 1922 dedication of the Francis Scott Key Memorial. Calvin Coolidge was the first to make a political speech on radio as well as the first to have his inaugural address and State of the Union speech broadcast live on radio. Roosevelt was the first to appear on television when he made an appearance at the opening ceremonies of the 1939 World's Fair. His successor, Harry S. Truman, made the first televised address from the White House in 1947 and was the first to have his inaugural address televised. Dwight D. Eisenhower and Adlai Stevenson ran the first television ads during the 1952 presidential campaign. In 2000, Bill Clinton became the first president to participate in an online chat and was the first to have an e-mail address (though he rarely used it).

2. TRANSPORTATION AND TRIPS

While Theodore "Teddy" Roosevelt (TR) was the first to ride in a plane (after he was president), Franklin Roosevelt was actually the first sitting president to travel by airplane when he took a Boeing Clipper to the 1943 Casablanca Conference. But he wasn't the first president to cross the Atlantic Ocean—that distinction belongs to Woodrow Wilson, who made the trip in 1919 to attend the Paris Peace Conference following World War I. Andrew Jackson was the first to ride a locomotive while James Monroe took the first trip on a steamboat. William McKinley was the first president to ride in an automobile, though TR was the first to actually drive one himself. Rutherford B. Hayes was the first president to visit the West Coast as well as the first to have a telephone in the White House. Herbert Hoover was the first president to have a telephone on his desk at the White House. Dwight Eisenhower was the first to use a presidential helicopter. Richard Nixon was the first president to visit all fifty states.

3. INAUGURATIONS

James Madison was the first president to have an inaugural ball and partied the night away in 1809. Martin Van Buren was the first president-elect to ride with the sitting president, Andrew Jackson, to the swearing-in ceremony, a tradition that continues to this day. James Buchanan was the first president to be photographed at his inauguration, and William McKinley's ceremony was the first recorded by motion picture cameras. President Harding was the first president to ride to and from his inauguration in an automobile. Franklin Roosevelt was the first president inaugurated on January 20 per the Twentieth Amendment; previously, inaugurations took place in March. Franklin Pierce was the first president not to kiss the Bible after the swearing-in ceremony, a tradition started by George Washington.

4. BASEBALL

In 1865, Andrew Johnson hosted the first White House visit by an organized team, and his successor, Ulysses S. Grant, hosted the first visit by a professional team, the Cincinnati Red Stockings. In 1892, Benjamin Harrison took in the first Major League Baseball (MLB) game as he watched the Reds defeat the Washington Senators, 7–4. In 1909, William Howard Taft became the first president to watch an MLB game outside of Washington, D.C., when he visited Pittsburgh. The following year, he became the first president to throw out a season-opening ceremonial first pitch. Since then, with the exception of Jimmy Carter, every sitting president has thrown out a first pitch. In 1915, Woodrow Wilson became the first president to attend a World Series game. In 1924, Calvin Coolidge became the first president to throw out the first pitch at a World Series game, and in 1937 Franklin Roosevelt was the first to do the same at the All-Star Game. In 1988, Ronald Reagan became the first and only president to do play-by-play announcing, which he did for two innings as the Pittsburgh Pirates defeated the Chicago Cubs 10–9 at Wrigley Field.

5. BIRTH

Martin Van Buren, the eighth president, was the first born in the United States of America; the previous seven presidents were born prior to the Constitution's ratification. Van Buren was also the first president of Dutch descent, and he spoke the language at home with his wife. Millard Fillmore, the thirteenth president, was the first born in the nineteenth century;

In 1924, Calvin Coolidge became the first president to throw out the first pitch at a World Series game. *New York Times*

John Kennedy, the first in the twentieth century; and Bill Clinton, the first after World War II. Abraham Lincoln was the first president born outside the thirteen original colonies (Kentucky), but Herbert Hoover was the first president born west of the Mississippi River. Andrew Jackson was the first of seven presidents born in a log cabin, while Jimmy Carter was the first president born in a hospital.

6. WHITE HOUSE
John Adams was the first president to reside in the White House; Washington was the only president to never have lived there. Thomas Jefferson was the first to open the White House to public tours. Franklin Pierce was the first to have a Christmas tree in the White House. Benjamin Harrison had electricity installed in the White House for the first time. Grover Cleveland was the first president to get married in a White House ceremony, though John Tyler was the first president to marry while in office. James Monroe's daughter was the first of many presidential offspring to marry in the White House.

7. STYLE
Thomas Jefferson was the first president to shake hands rather than bow. James Madison was the first president to wear full-length trousers instead of knee breeches. Abraham Lincoln was the first to wear a beard (Benjamin Harrison was the last), and Chester Arthur was the first to sport muttonchop sideburns. John Quincy Adams was the first and only president to skinny-dip in the Potomac River. James Buchanan was the only bachelor president, having never married. Ronald Reagan was the first to wear contact lenses. Gerald Ford was the first and only president to model clothing. George H. W. Bush was the first former president to go skydiving.

8. OCCUPATIONS
John Adams was the first lawyer to ascend to the White House,

while James Madison was the first member of Congress to win the office. James Monroe was the first former governor to be elected president. Zachary Taylor was the first person to win the presidency who had never held office of any kind. James Garfield was the first former schoolteacher to become president; Grover Cleveland is the only former sheriff turned president. Warren Harding was the first journalist—he was a newspaper editor—in the White House, while Jimmy Carter was the first and only peanut farmer to reside in the White House. Ironically, Ronald Reagan was the only union member (he belonged to the Screen Actors Guild) to become president.

9. AGE

Though John F. Kennedy at age forty-three was the youngest person elected president, Theodore Roosevelt was actually the youngest to serve as president—he was forty-two when he took over after William McKinley was assassinated. James Monroe was the first president who was younger than his vice president, and George Washington was the first president who was younger than his wife. At age seventy-seven when he left office in 1989, Ronald Reagan was the oldest man to have served in the office. Gerald Ford was the oldest living ex-president when he passed away at age ninety-three.

10. THEODORE ROOSEVELT

Not surprising, Theodore Roosevelt had a bunch of firsts. He was the first president to drive an automobile, submerge in a submarine, and fly on an airplane. In 1910 the Wright brothers took him for a spin once they had ironed out all the kinks in their flying machine. He was the first sitting president to travel outside the United States when he visited Panama to observe the construction of the canal. Perhaps most important, he was the first American to win a Nobel Peace Prize and the first president to invite an African American, Booker T. Washington, to dinner in the White House.

Advisers

While the cabinet plays an important role in presidential decision making, presidents also turn to West Wing staff and advisers for guidance and counsel. Over the years, this staff's role and influence have grown as the cabinet has receded in importance. It is often said real power in the West Wing comes from having the president's ear.

1. HARRY HOPKINS, AUGUST 17, 1890–JANUARY 29, 1946

Most Washington insiders considered one of the principal architects of Franklin Roosevelt's New Deal program, Harry Hopkins, or "Harry the Hop" as the president called him, the "deputy president" of the Roosevelt administration. In fact, he enjoyed such a unique and close bond with Roosevelt that he and his wife and daughter officially resided at the White House during the war years. A sickly man for most of his adult life, Hopkins spearheaded several critical tasks for Roosevelt, including publicizing and defending the New Deal programs, administering the Lend-Lease program, and acting as a back channel for communications between FDR and Winston Churchill with Joseph Stalin during World War II. When Wendell Wilkie, FDR's Republican opponent during the 1940 election, asked why he placed so much faith in Hopkins, Roosevelt responded that if Wilkie were to win the election, "you'll learn what a lonely job this is, and you'll discover the need for someone like Harry Hopkins, who asks for nothing except to serve you."

2. EDWARD MANDEL HOUSE, JULY 26, 1858–MARCH 28, 1938

Though he held no official title, the self-styled "colonel," as Edward House liked to be called, was Woodrow Wilson's closest adviser and confidant throughout his two terms in office. Born into a prominent Texas political family, House was regarded as a kingmaker in Texas politics when he and Wilson first met in 1911. House helped Woodrow Wilson win the presidency the following year and quickly established himself as President Wilson's most trusted adviser. Wilson once said of House, "He is my independent self. His thoughts and mine are one. If I were in his place, I would just do as he suggested." During the Wilson administration's first two years, House served as a liaison to administration officials, members of Congress, and other prominent Americans. In 1914, Wilson dispatched him to Europe to help prevent the outbreak of war and again in 1915 to spur peace talks and to offer a mediation plan. House also played a large role in crafting Wilson's "Fourteen Points" speech that he gave before Congress and helped draft the Treaty of Versailles and the Covenant of the League of Nations. After the Paris Peace Conference, Wilson and House had an abrupt falling out over the direction of the talks; Wilson believed House had negotiated away many of the "fourteen points" in his peace proposal. It was a bitter ending for the aide Wilson once called "my second personality."

3. CLARK CLIFFORD, DECEMBER 25, 1906–OCTOBER 10, 1998

Considered by many to be the first Washington "super lawyer," Clark Clifford occupies a unique place in presidential advising and governance, having served as a confidant and adviser to three presidents and as a secretary of defense to another. Clifford was a mainstay in Washington for more than fifty years—the ultimate "fix-it" man for Democratic administrations—though he spent only eight of those years actually in government service. He began his government career as a naval aide in the Truman White House and quickly worked his way to special counsel and speechwriter for the president. He participated in the creation of the Marshall Plan and the formation of the North Atlantic Treaty Organization (NATO), wrote the enabling legislation for the Central Intelligence Agency (CIA), and helped formulate the Truman Doctrine. Clifford also played a major role in Truman's "upset" victory over Thomas Dewey in 1948 with the "Give 'Em Hell, Harry" campaign. It is said that Clifford turned down opportunities to run for the U.S. Senate and sit on the Supreme Court so that he could return to his private law practice and "earn a living." In 1960, he led John F. Kennedy's presidential transition team and later was appointed chairman of the newly created Foreign Intelligence Advisory Board after the failed Bay of Pigs invasion. Caught in the throes of an increasingly unpopular war, Lyndon B. Johnson appointed Clifford as his secretary of defense in March 1968 in the hope of salvaging some kind of victory; instead, Clifford became an advocate for bombing reductions and peace negotiations and helped bring about the withdrawal process. He would go on to counsel Jimmy Carter and Bill Clinton, working well into his late eighties. "The mind is a muscle," he was fond of saying. "The more I use it, the better it gets."

4. KARL ROVE, DECEMBER 25, 1950–
Nicknamed "Bush's Brain" by Washington insiders and members of the press corps, Karl Rove has been considered by many pundits and historians to be the most powerful

presidential adviser in modern times. His relationship with George W. Bush dates back to 1978, when Rove advised Bush on his failed congressional race. He later orchestrated Bush's Texas gubernatorial victory over Ann Richards in 1994 and his lopsided reelection in 1998. Along with advisers Karen Hughes and Joe Allbaugh, the trio came to be known as Bush's "Iron Triangle" during the 2000 presidential campaign and tightly scripted the campaign's themes, messages, and images. During the president's first term, Rove served as a senior adviser, with a broad portfolio that included domestic policy, congressional relations, and political messaging. Rove is credited (perhaps too much so) with almost single-handedly orchestrating President Bush's reelection in 2004, and in his second term Rove picked up the additional title of deputy chief of staff. His portfolio grew to include foreign policy as well, and conventional wisdom had it that only Vice President Dick Cheney and former chief of staff Andy Card approached Rove in influence and power. As one commentator put it, Rove's real legacy may be that he "blends political hack and propeller head in a way no one has ever achieved."

5. SHERMAN ADAMS, JANUARY 8, 1899–OCTOBER 27, 1986

Sherman Adams served as senior counselor to Dwight Eisenhower from 1953 through 1958, fulfilling what turned out to be the first chief of staff role in the West Wing. Eisenhower liked Adams's fiscal conservatism and military-style orderliness and discipline with the staff. During his tenure in the White House, Adams had near total autonomy over White House operations and domestic policy and rankled even Republican loyalists with his tight-fisted control over access to President Eisenhower. Adams was forced to resign his position in 1958 after it was revealed that he took gifts from Bernard Goldfine, a friend and manufacturer who was being investigated by the Federal Trade Commission. Few were sad to see him leave.

6. DAVID GERGEN, MAY 9, 1942–

David Gergen stands alone in modern political times as being an official adviser to presidents of both political parties. Gergen began has career in Richard Nixon's White House as a speechwriter and continued in that role in Gerald Ford's administration. Ford later promoted Gergen to director of communications, where he oversaw presidential briefing books, speeches, and other communications, and served as a liaison to the Ford campaign committee. He was also responsible for debate preparation for the 1976 campaign. In the early 1980s, Gergen served as the director of communications for Ronald Reagan, where he played a large role in staging events and crafting the "Reagan image." After the Republicans won control of Congress in the 1994 midterm elections, Bill Clinton made the unusual move of bringing Gergen on as a senior adviser to help him re-chart his domestic agenda and reach out to the new Congress. Gergen held the position for a little more than a year. Prominent Web blogger Glenn Reynolds may have summed up Gergen best, saying that he "is pretty much the standard measurement unit for conventional wisdom" in Washington.

7. AMOS KENDALL, AUGUST 16, 1789–NOVEMBER 12, 1869

Amos Kendall was one of several influential advisers to Andrew Jackson. Their group came to be known as the "Kitchen Cabinet," the first such time that term *cabinet* appeared in politics. He began his career as a journalist, culminating as the co-owner and coeditor of the *Argus of Western America*, one of the most influential papers of its day. He supported Jackson's failed presidential bid in 1824 and upon Jackson's victory in 1828 was appointed the fourth auditor of the treasury (essentially the treasurer for the U.S. Navy). As President Jackson's most trusted member of the Kitchen Cabinet, Kendall was responsible for drafting many of Jackson's speeches and state papers, served as point man for the controversial re-chartering of the Bank of the United States, and was often called upon to vigorously defend the president's policies in newspapers. In 1935, Jackson appointed Kendall U.S. postmaster general, and he reorganized the badly mismanagement department. The writer Harriet Martineau once said of Kendall: "I was fortunate enough to catch a glimpse of the invincible Amos Kendall, one of the most remarkable men in America. He is supposed to be the moving spring of the administration; the thinker, planner, and doer."

8. TED SORENSON, MAY 28, 1928–
Described by John F. Kennedy as his "intellectual blood bank," Ted Sorenson served as a special assistant and speechwriter for President Kennedy, penning some of his most memorable speeches and formulating domestic policy. It has long been rumored that Sorenson also ghostwrote Kennedy's Pulitzer Prize–winning book *Profiles in Courage,* a charge Sorenson has steadfastly denied over the years. Though his primary responsibility was domestic affairs, Sor-enson became increasingly involved in foreign policy after the botched Bay of Pigs invasion and played an instrumental role in resolving the Cuban missile crisis. After serving briefly for President Johnson, Sorenson left the White House and wrote President Kennedy's biography. Many credit Sorenson with first creating, and then nurturing, the Kennedy "myth."

9. ELIHU WASHBURNE, SEPTEMBER 23, 1816–OCTOBER 22, 1887
One of four brothers to serve in Congress, Washburne was one of the founders of the Republican Party and was a trusted

counselor to Abraham Lincoln and Ulysses S. Grant. A radical abolitionist, Washburne played an important role in Lincoln's 1858 Senate race against Stephen Douglas—particularly the famous Lincoln-Douglas debates—and again in his 1860 presidential election, when he wrote the future president's official campaign biography. Undoubtedly, Washburne's greatest contribution was his aggressive championing of an unknown Ulysses S. Grant to President Lincoln. "About all I know of Grant I have got from you," Lincoln wrote Washburne in 1864. "I have never seen him. Who else besides you knows anything about Grant?" Washburne would go on to serve in Grant's administration, first as his secretary of state (for all of twelve days) and then as an ambassador to France.

10. **GEORGE STEPHANOPOULOS, FEBRUARY 10, 1961–**

George Stephanopoulos came to symbolize the youth, promise, and ambition of the Clinton administration, first as the spokesperson for Clinton's 1992 campaign and later as White House press secretary and senior adviser. Though President Clinton was famous for having an ever-expanding and contracting circle of advisers, George Stephanopoulos's influence stemmed, in part, from his celebrity status as Clinton's "boy wonder kid." Telegenic and charming, Stephanopoulos frequently took to the airwaves to promote the president's policies and defend against its critics. The term *Stephanopouli* was coined to describe the cadre of young staffers who held positions of prominence during Clinton's first term. It is said that Aaron Sorkin based his Lewis Rothschild and Sam Seaborn characters in *The American President* and *The West Wing,* respectively, on Stephanopoulos.

Distinguished Cabinet Members

Rarely do cabinet members make a dramatic difference in an administration's fortunes. Most toil in relative obscurity, and few Americans can name more than a handful throughout history. Every now and again, however, a few members push their president in a new direction.

1. ALEXANDER HAMILTON—WASHINGTON

Alexander Hamilton was the first ever secretary of the treasury and is still regarded as the greatest to ever hold that position. If George Washington is considered the "father" of our country, then Hamilton could be called the "father of our economy." Among the founding generation, no individual deserves as much credit for creating a national economy than Hamilton, especially regarding his vision, persistence, and political acumen. Hamilton and Thomas Jefferson—the two leading political theorists of the day—held competing beliefs when it came to the power of the federal government and the need for a national economy: Jefferson believed in a weak central government and strong states rights and thought the economy should remain primarily agrarian; however, Hamilton envisioned a manufacturing and industrial economy that would require a strong federal government. Hamilton advanced his vision by establishing a national bank and a national mint; by having the federal government assume state debt; by implementing a system of tariffs, levies, and duties to raise funds; and by creating the Coast Guard to strengthen the nation's defenses. During the five years he served as treasury secretary, Hamilton essentially converted the chaotic, prerevolution agrarian economy into a manufacturing- and industrial-based commercial economy. Among Hamilton's other achievements include coauthoring the *Federalist Papers,* arguably the most influential writings in American history, and founding the Federalist Party, which was the first political party in U.S. history and maybe in world history. He also held progressive beliefs when it came to slavery, becoming an outspoken abolitionist before the abolition movement had begun.

2. FRANCES PERKINS—F. ROOSEVELT AND TRUMAN

Frances Perkins is the answer to two trivia questions: Who was the first woman appointed to a cabinet position, and who is the longest tenured secretary of labor in history (having served in that post for twelve years under FDR and Truman)? Perkins was a key player in the suffragette movement when New York governor Al Smith tapped her to become the first woman on the New York State Industrial Commission in 1918, which she wound up chairing a few years later. She caught the attention of Governor Franklin Roosevelt, who made her the state's industrial commissioner (the top labor post in New York State). Following his defeat of Herbert Hoover in 1932, President Roosevelt named Perkins as his secretary of labor, a groundbreaking appointment at the time. During her years in that post she played a key role in writing and selling several landmark New Deal reforms, including a bill establishing a minimum wage, and helped draft the Social Security Act. Her crowning achievement came in 1938, when Franklin Roosevelt signed into

law the Fair Labor Standards Act, a bill she had championed, which created the framework for workers' compensa-
tion and workplace health and job safety rules. In 1945, Harry
Truman appointed her to the U.S. Civil Service Commission, where she remained until retiring from federal service
in 1952.

3. WILLIAM SEWARD—LINCOLN AND JOHNSON

Secretary of State William Seward was a towering political
figure of his day and arguably President Lincoln's closest
adviser. During the 1850s he rose to national prominence
as an outspoken critic of slavery, arguing that "moral law"
made slavery wrong and unjust; he even opened up his house
to the Underground Railroad to help transport escaped slaves
to northern territories. Seward all but predicted the slavery
issue would result in a civil war a decade before it happened.
During the early months of Lincoln's presidency, Seward
made several missteps, but over time he found his voice in
Lincoln's cabinet. Among other things, he worked diligently
to discourage European nations from diplomatically recog-
nizing the Confederacy, adroitly handled the Trent Affair and
thus avoided war with England, and helped rally northern public
opinion at a time when the Union was floundering. The same
night John Wilkes Booth assassinated Lincoln, one of Booth's
associates went to Seward's home and violently stabbed him
in the neck. He survived the attack and remained secretary
of state through Johnson's administration. Seward's legacy
from the Johnson years was the purchase of Alaska from
Russia for approximately $7 million. At the time, the press
ridiculed the deal as "Seward's Folly" or "Seward's Icebox,"
but time has proven it to be a wise decision.

4. GEORGE C. MARSHALL—TRUMAN

George Marshall holds the distinction of being the only man

who wasn't president to receive *Time* magazine's Man of the Year honor twice, first in 1943 and again in 1948. He also won the Nobel Peace Prize in 1953 for his years of public service. In anticipation of war breaking out in Europe, President Roosevelt appointed the career military man as U.S. Army chief of staff in 1939. In that position, Marshall oversaw both theaters of operation—Europe and Asia—and effectively set the strategy for the entire Allied effort. After expressing disappointment at being passed over for supreme Allied commander of the D-Day invasion, which went to Dwight Eisenhower, Roosevelt told him, "I couldn't sleep nights, George, if you were out of Washington." In 1947, President Truman made Marshall secretary of state, and in this role he helped put together a reconstruction plan for Europe, which came to be known as the "Marshall Plan." It entailed massive aid to Western European countries (close to $14 billion over five years), as well as close economic, trade, and military cooperation with the hope of preventing the spread of communism. It was a bold stroke for the United States, which historically had taken an isolationist approach to European affairs. As secretary of state (and later as secretary of defense under Truman), Marshall also played a pivotal role in the creation and implementation of NATO.

5. ROBERT F. KENNEDY—KENNEDY AND JOHNSON

When John Kennedy named his brother Robert as attorney general, his choice was met with skepticism. Critics maintained Robert "Bobby" Kennedy lacked the requisite experience for the position, and that his appointment was simply a product of nepotism. His more than three years in office, however, turned out to be among the most productive of any attorney general before or since. Not only was he one of the president's closest political advisers, he also had his brother's backing when it came to his key initiatives, including prosecuting organized crime and ending racial discrimination. During the Cuban missile crisis, Kennedy turned to Bobby for critical counsel and to facilitate back-channel communications with the Soviets through Ambassador Anatoly Dobrynin. Aside from the president himself, Bobby Kennedy was the most important contributor to a peaceful resolution of the stalemate. It was in the area of civil rights, however, where Bobby Kennedy made his greatest impact. He publicly spoke out for the need to end discrimination and zealously enforced the Supreme Court's desegregation ruling in *Brown v. Board of Education*, going so far as to send U.S. Marshals to the University of Mississippi to ensure that James Meredith, the first black student admitted to the university, was able to enroll for classes. Kennedy had a big hand in pushing President Kennedy to introduce the Civil Rights Act, which helped put an end to Jim Crow laws in the South. After his brother's assassination in 1963, Kennedy served as attorney general for another year before resigning his post to run for the U.S. Senate. Shortly after his tenure as attorney general, Congress passed a law prohibiting the president from appointing family members to the cabinet, the so-called Bobby Kennedy rule.

6. HERBERT HOOVER—HARDING AND COOLIDGE

He may have been an abysmal president, but Herbert Hoover rates as one of the most successful and accomplished cabinet members in history. His eight-year tenure at the Commerce Department was so successful, in fact, that it provided him a platform to win the presidency in 1928 without ever having held elected office—something few presidents have done. Hoover was a renowned businessman and engineer, and he used those skills to reorganize the Commerce Department into a service organization. His many accomplishments include standardizing thousands of consumer products, such as auto tires, window frames, nuts and bolts, paper, and so forth; opening up foreign markets to U.S. goods; mandating new standards for air-travel safety, including landing lights; reorganizing and enlarging the Census Bureau; and developing critical projects for irrigation and flood control. To that end, he facilitated the delicate negotiations between six western states to bring about the creation of the Hoover Dam. Hoover was also actively involved in conservation efforts and in children's safety, authoring the Child's Bill of Rights; it promoted immunization and vaccination against deadly diseases and formulated proper hygiene practices and nourishment for schoolchildren. As one of his last acts as the secretary of commerce, Hoover accepted President Coolidge's charge and mobilized the response to the horrific Mississippi levee flood of 1927, which left a million people along the river homeless. His ability to bring together state and local authorities, the Red Cross, army engineers, and other key agencies garnered him front-page headlines for months.

7. JAMES A. BAKER III—REAGAN AND G. H. W. BUSH

James Baker is the only person to serve as chief of staff to two presidents, as well a cabinet member for those same two presidents. As Ronald Reagan's secretary of the treasury, he played a pivotal role in passing Reagan's landmark Tax Reform Act of 1986, which resulted in the largest overhaul (and simplification) of the tax code in history. As secretary of state for George H. W. Bush, Baker was a key player in assembling the Desert Storm coalition following Saddam Hussein's invasion of Kuwait and helped build the strategies and policies for Germany's reunification after the Berlin Wall fell. Baker's close relationship with Soviet president Mikhail Gorbachev and foreign minister Eduard Shevardnadze helped navigate U.S. foreign policy during the collapse of the Soviet Union.

8. ELIHU ROOT—MCKINLEY AND T. ROOSEVELT

Elihu Root served as the secretary of war under Presidents McKinley and Theodore Roosevelt, and after leaving public life for a year he returned to serve as Roosevelt's secretary of state. A distinguished corporate lawyer in New York City, Root's appointment was a bit unusual in that he had no prior military experience or training. However, following the Spanish-American War (in which the United States "acquired" control of the former Spanish territories Puerto Rico, Guam, and the Philippines), President McKinley was looking for a sharp legal mind to reorganize the War Department, create a Philippines charter, and oversee the return of Cuba to the Cubans. Root tackled all three tasks and then some: he enlarged West Point, established the Army War College and the General Staff, created schools for the special branches of the service, and revised the procedures for promotions. Root left the administration in 1904 but returned a year later as Roosevelt's secretary of state. At the State Department his biggest accomplishment was to bring the vast consular service under the control of the Civil Service, thus taking it out of the domain of the "spoils system." He also helped formulate the so-called Open Door policy in the Far East and an important "gentlemen's agreement" regarding emigration with Japan. Henry Stimson, Franklin Roosevelt's secretary of war, paid Root the highest compliment when he remarked that "no such intelligent, constructive and vital force" had ever served as secretary of war before.

9. HENRY KISSINGER—NIXON AND FORD

Few cabinet members in history received as much public attention and notoriety as Henry Kissinger. As secretary of state under both Nixon and Ford, Kissinger was virtually the face of U.S. foreign policy for nearly a decade. A brilliant theoretician and scholar, Kissinger was instrumental in developing Nixon's policy of détente with the Soviet Union, as well as normalizing relations with China—the administration's two greatest accomplishments. He also won the Nobel Peace Prize in 1973 for helping bring about an end to the Vietnam War and negotiated an end to the Yom Kippur War between Israel, Syria, and Egypt. As Nixon became increasingly debilitated by the events and aftermath of the Watergate scandal, Kissinger's role in the administration grew; toward the end of Nixon's tenure, by some accounts, he was running the nation's foreign policy from the State Department. Kissinger also enjoyed the glamour and prestige of the office. For a while, he was a pop culture icon; he dated several Hollywood starlets, including Jill St. John and Candice Bergen, noting, "Power is the ultimate aphrodisiac." In recent years, with the release of the Nixon tapes, Kissinger has come under fire by some human rights groups for his alleged involvement in the coup of Chilean president Salvador Allende, as well as for his role in the bombing of Cambodia during the Vietnam War.

10. COLIN POWELL—G. W. BUSH

Rarely has a cabinet member been as universally admired and respected as Colin Powell. With his appointment as secretary of state by George W. Bush, Powell became the highest-ranking African American ever in the executive branch. Blazing a new path was nothing new for Colin Powell: in 1987, he became the first African American named as national security adviser and a few years later became the chairman of the Joint Chiefs of Staff. Many pundits believed Powell would have been elected president in 2000 had he run for office, though as a moderate he might not have survived the Republican primaries. Following the terrorist attacks of September 11, along with Vice President Cheney and Secretary of Defense Don Rumsfeld, Powell played a critical role in formulating the nation's strategy for the war on terror and the invasion of Afghanistan. He worked to rally world leaders to the cause, at times acting as the spokesperson for the administration and its efforts. He also played a pivotal role in gaining the United Nations' support for the invasion of Iraq and, as it turned out, provided faulty and incomplete evidence regarding Iraq's stockpile of weapons of mass destruction. Some believe Powell cautioned the more hawkish elements in the Bush White House to avoid war at all costs, but he ultimately went along with invasion. He left the administration late in 2004, his reputation mostly intact but slightly tarnished from the ongoing war in Iraq.

Great Speeches

One of the hallmarks of the presidency is speech making. In the republic's early years, prior to the advent of radio and television, speeches and their reprints in newspapers were the sole forum for communicating to the people. In recent years, formal speeches have taken on less importance, though two formal addresses—inaugurals and the State of the Union—give officeholders the chance to employ lofty rhetoric and impart a soaring vision.

1. GETTYSBURG ADDRESS, ABRAHAM LINCOLN, NOVEMBER 19, 1863

At 272 words, the Gettysburg Address is perhaps the most famous—and enduring—short speech in U.S. history. Delivered at one of the Civil War's bloodiest battlefields, Lincoln's oration before fifteen thousand onlookers took less than three minutes from start to finish. In the strictest sense, the speech was a consecration for the battlefield's new cemetery, but in the larger sense it was a rededication to preserving the Union and its ideals. The speech was printed in hundreds of newspapers the following day and was instantly recognized as a masterful piece of oration. The Gettysburg Address produced not one but two iconic phrases—"Four score and seven years ago" and "government of the people, by the people, for the people"—that rank among the most recognizable from presidential oratory. Ironically, perhaps unbelievably, Lincoln was not the primary speaker that day. Instead, former secretary of state Edward Everett, whom many considered the finest speech maker in the country, delivered the official, two-hour-long oration for the dedication. "It is the desire that, after the Oration, you, as Chief Executive of the nation, formally set apart these grounds to their sacred use by a few appropriate remarks," wrote the organizing committee when it invited Lincoln to Gettysburg. For all his speech's majesty and brilliance, Lincoln got one thing drastically wrong when he said, "The world will little note, nor long remember what we say here."

The full text of Lincoln's speech follows:

Four score and seven years ago our fathers brought forth on this continent a new nation, conceived in Liberty, and dedicated to the proposition that all men are created equal.

Now we are engaged in a great civil war, testing whether that nation, or any nation so conceived and so dedicated, can long endure. We are met on a great battle-field of that war. We have come to dedicate a portion of that field, as a final resting place for those who here gave their lives that that nation might live. It is altogether fitting and proper that we should do this.

But, in a larger sense, we can not dedicate—we can not consecrate—we can not hallow—this ground. The brave men, living and dead, who struggled here, have consecrated it, far above our poor power to add or detract. The world will little note, nor long remember what we say here, but it can never forget what they did here. It is for us the living, rather, to be dedicated here to the unfinished work which they who fought here have thus far so nobly advanced. It is rather for us to be here dedicated to the great task remaining before us—that from these honored dead we take increased devotion to that cause for which they gave the last full measure of devotion—that we here highly resolve that these dead shall not have died in vain—that this nation, under God, shall have a new birth of freedom—and that government of the people, by the people, for the people, shall not perish from the earth.

2. FAREWELL ADDRESS, GEORGE WASHINGTON, SEPTEMBER 19, 1796

George Washington's Farewell Address to the American people remains the single most influential document of its kind in American history. Though technically not a speech, since he delivered it as an open letter to the American people (it appeared in hundreds of newspapers), Washington's thoughts, observations, and admonitions helped established the context for political discourse in the country, and the ideas he set forth shaped public policy for generations thereafter. Washington wrote of the need for national unity over regional factionalism: "the name of American, which belongs to you in your national capacity, must always exalt the just pride of patriotism, more than any appellation derived from local discriminations." He also warned "in the most solemn manner" of the dangers of political parties, or "the baneful effects of the spirit of party, generally." Believing a permanent military establishment was a bad idea, Washington exhorted his fellow citizens to "avoid the necessity of those overgrown military establishments, which, under any form of government, are inauspicious to liberty, and which are to be regarded as particularly hostile to Republican Liberty." Above all else, the president stressed that the United States must avoid foreign entanglements: "Tis our true policy to steer clear of permanent alliances with any portion of the foreign world." To this last point, Washington's address was so influential that it wasn't until NATO's establishment in 1949 that the United States entered a foreign alliance.

3. "EVIL EMPIRE" SPEECH, RONALD REAGAN, MARCH 8, 1983

If Reagan's presidency could be summed up with one speech—or more accurately with a single paragraph in one speech—it would undoubtedly be his "evil empire" speech in the spring of 1983. It came at a time when the Cold War was at its coldest, and some in the body politic were suggesting that coexistence with Soviet-style communism was inevitable and tolerable. Reagan saw the struggle between freedom and communism in moral terms, as a battle between good and evil. He believed the Soviet Union was in the advanced stages of decline, and he wanted to hasten the process through his words and deeds. The president had originally planned to call the Soviet Union an "evil empire" in an address before the British Parliament a year earlier, but cautious diplomats at the State Department had removed the phrase at the last minute. Reagan wasn't going to be denied again, however, and when the nuclear freeze movement seemed to be gaining momentum in the spring of 1983, he used an address before the National Association of Evangelicals to turn the focus back on the Soviet Union. "So in your discussions of the nuclear freeze proposals," he told a surprised audience,

> I urge you to beware the temptation of pride—the temptation to blithely declare yourselves above it all and label both sides equally at fault, to ignore the facts of history and the aggressive impulses of an evil empire, to simply call the arms race a giant misunderstanding

and thereby remove yourself from the struggle between right and wrong and good and evil. (http://ronald reagan.com/sp_6.html)

Reagan's speech made headlines around the globe and put Soviet leaders on notice that there would be no letup in the arms race or a thaw in the Cold War.

4. STATE OF THE UNION ADDRESS, JAMES MONROE, DECEMBER 2, 1823

In his seventh State of the Union address, James Monroe used the opportunity to warn European nations that their interference in political events in the Western Hemisphere would no longer be tolerated; in effect, a hostile act toward any country in the Americas would be viewed as a hostile act toward the United States. "We owe it, therefore, to candor and to the amicable relations existing between the United States and those powers to declare that we should consider any attempt on their part to extend their system to any portion of this hemisphere as dangerous to our peace and safety," wrote Monroe. The impetus behind this Monroe Doctrine was the aggressive posture of France, Spain, and Russia toward recolonizing those South American republics that had successfully fought wars for independence a decade earlier. The Monroe Doctrine could just as easily be called the "Adams Doctrine," for it was Secretary of State John Quincy Adams who championed the concept, devised the language, and sold it to the president's cabinet. Though it thwarted the immediate recolonization plans of Russia, Spain, and France, the doctrine didn't have much impact until the late 1880s, when the U.S. Navy was finally large enough to enforce the policy. Teddy Roosevelt expanded the doctrine's meaning when he cited it in justifying U.S. involvement in the internal affairs of various South American countries. Since that time, the Monroe Doctrine has been one of the guiding principles behind U.S. foreign policy and was even invoked during the Cuban missile crisis as a basis for preventing the Soviet Union from housing nuclear missiles on the island.

5. INAUGURAL ADDRESS, JOHN F. KENNEDY, JANUARY 20, 1961

John F. Kennedy's inaugural address is best remembered for one of the most recognizable quotes in presidential history: "Ask not what your country can do for you—ask what you can do for your country." But like Reagan's evil empire speech, Kennedy's inaugural was mostly about putting the Soviet Union on notice that the United States was prepared for a long and protracted Cold War and that freedom would ultimately prevail. In fact, most of the speech focused on foreign policy, with its strongest language pointed directly at the Soviets: "Let every nation know, whether it wishes us well or ill, that we shall pay any price, bear any burden, meet any hardship, support any friend, oppose any foe, in order to assure the survival and the success of liberty. This much we pledge—and more." Kennedy also used the speech to remind the world that "that the torch has been passed to a new generation of Americans—born in this century, tempered by war, disciplined by a hard and bitter peace, proud of our ancient heritage. . . ." In both style and substance, Kennedy's address remains the standard by which all other inaugural speeches are measured.

6. "DAY OF INFAMY" SPEECH, FRANKLIN D. ROOSEVELT, DECEMBER 8, 1941

On December 8, 1941, Franklin Roosevelt went before Congress and asked for a formal declaration of war against Japan following its attack on Pearl Harbor. The nation was still in a state of shock when Roosevelt addressed Congress, and he used the moment to rally the American people with one of the most memorable opening lines in history: "Yesterday, December 7, 1941—a date which will live in infamy—the United States of America was suddenly and deliberately attacked by naval and air forces of the Empire of Japan." Much of the speech was a recitation of Japan's various acts of aggression, but Roosevelt also used it to steel the American resolve for what would undoubtedly be a long and difficult war: "Always will we remember the character of the onslaught against us. No matter how long it may take us to overcome this premeditated invasion, the American people in their righteous might will win through to absolute victory." Though he would not live to see the war's conclusion, President Roosevelt's speech set the bounds for the only acceptable conclusion—total victory.

7. *CHALLENGER* DISASTER SPEECH, RONALD REAGAN, JANUARY 28, 1986

The Great Communicator was at his finest when he delivered this speech from the Oval Office to a national television audience following the space shuttle *Challenger* disaster. On the night of the disaster, Reagan was supposed to deliver the State of the Union address, but he postponed it after the shuttle exploded seventy-three seconds after liftoff. What made the situation even more distressing was that millions of schoolchildren across the nation had witnessed it live on television in anticipation of seeing Christa McAuliffe become the first schoolteacher in space. Part of the president's role is to serve as "comforter in chief" during times of crisis and tragedy, and Reagan had that in mind when he spoke to the American people. "Today is a day for mourning and remembering," opened Reagan. "Nancy and I are pained to the core by the tragedy of the shuttle

Ronald Reagan speaks from the Oval Office following the
Challenger explosion. *Ronald Reagan Library*

Challenger. We know we share this pain with all of the people of our country. This is truly a national loss." He explained to America's schoolchildren that "sometimes painful things like this happen. It's all part of the process of exploration and discovery. It's all part of taking a chance and expanding man's horizons. The future doesn't belong to the fainthearted; it belongs to the brave." Reagan went on to reiterate his confidence in the space program and the National Aeronautics and Space Administration (NASA). He closed the speech with borrowed phrases from World War II aviator John Gillespie Magee's oft-quoted poem "High Flight": [They] "slipped the surly bonds of earth" to "touch the face of God."

8. RESIGNATION SPEECH, RICHARD NIXON, AUGUST 8, 1974

It was neither a particularly memorable nor moving speech, but Richard Nixon's resignation address stands out as a unique moment in American history, marking the only time a sitting president has relinquished power. Nixon had been battling for months to stay in office, but he finally gave up the fight after he lost the support of key Republican senators. Nixon looked worn down, agitated, and bitter during the address, though he never spoke truer words when he said, "I have never been a quitter. To leave office before my term is completed is abhorrent to every instinct in my body. But as President I must put the interests of America first. America needs a full-time President and a full-time Congress, particularly at this time with problems we face at home and abroad." Following his official resignation speech, Nixon gave an impromptu farewell address to the White House staff, during which he spoke about everything from his late mother to Teddy Roosevelt and about his regret at not having learned the names of the White House staff. He closed it with a remarkably ironic observation, which almost perfectly summarized his entire political career: "Always give your best, never get discouraged, never be petty; always remember, others may hate you, but those who hate you don't win unless you hate them, and then you destroy yourself." He should have heeded his own counsel.

9. TRUMAN DOCTRINE SPEECH, HARRY S. TRUMAN, MARCH 12, 1947

Just as the Monroe Doctrine served as the guiding principle for U.S. foreign policy in the nineteenth century, the Truman Doctrine established the framework for foreign policy in the twentieth century. President Truman set forth the doctrine before a joint session of Congress less than two years after World War II ended. He requested $400 million in aid for Greece and Turkey—at the time, an enormous amount of money—so that the two countries could fight Communist insurgents intent on overthrowing their democratic governments. While most of the particulars of the speech dealt with the threat confronting Greece, Truman laid out the thrust of his doctrine in three simple, declarative sentences:

> I believe that it must be the policy of the United States to support free peoples who are resisting attempted subjugation by armed minorities or by outside pressures. I believe that we must assist free peoples to work out their own destinies in their own way. I believe that our help should be primarily through economic and financial aid which is essential to economic stability and orderly political processes.

The Truman Doctrine represented a dramatic shift in America's foreign policy from passive détente to active containment of the Communist threat wherever it existed, and many historians view it as the beginning of the Cold War. The doctrine guided America's foreign policy for the next forty years and landed the United States in "hot" wars in Korea and Vietnam.

10. FIRST INAUGURAL ADDRESS, FRANKLIN D. ROOSEVELT, MARCH 4, 1933

Franklin Roosevelt took office in the midst of the worst economic crisis in our nation's history, the Great Depression. A third of the nation was unemployed, thousands of banks had closed, and many Americans were questioning whether capitalism still worked. Roosevelt had an ambitious legislative plan for his first hundred days in office and knew that he needed the public's support to move his agenda through Congress. He used the first minute of the speech to address the angst that gripped the country and asked for the public's support. In doing so, he delivered one of the most memorable lines in an inaugural address:

> So, first of all, let me assert my firm belief that the only thing we have to fear is fear itself—nameless, unreasoning, unjustified terror which paralyzes needed efforts to convert retreat into advance. In every dark hour of our national life a leadership of frankness and vigor has met with that understanding and support of the people themselves which is essential to victory. I am convinced that you will again give that support to leadership in these critical days.

Though the speech is mostly remembered for the line about fear, it is also one of the most substantive and detailed inaugural addresses. It is a departure from the typical inaugural fare.

Bold Decisions

A t some point during every administration, presidents are called on to make tough choices and bold decisions. Some presidents have been up to the challenge while others have shied from the responsibility.

1. LINCOLN PRESERVES THE UNION

Any discussion about bold decisions, courageous leadership, or pivotal moments in U.S. history has to begin with Abraham Lincoln—plain and simple. No president before or since has been confronted with such a dire reality upon taking office as Lincoln faced. Within weeks of his victory, the seven "cotton" states had seceded to form the Confederacy, and by the time of Lincoln's inauguration, rebel forces had seized federal forts and munitions within their states. Outgoing president James Buchanan chose to do nothing about southern aggression. His opinion wasn't all that uncommon in the days leading up to the Civil War: "The remedy for this state of things can only be supplied by Congress, since the Constitution has confided to that body alone the power to make war." Many Unionists, including some Republicans who were outspoken about abolishing slavery, were inclined to let the South secede as an alternative to war. Lincoln, however, was of a different mind-set, and he was fully prepared to take the country to war to preserve the Union. He stated in his inaugural speech: "I therefore consider that in view of the Constitution and the laws the Union is unbroken, and to the extent of my ability, I shall take care, as the Constitution itself expressly enjoins upon me, that the laws of the Union be faithfully executed in all the States." There was no doubt in Lincoln's mind that the first act of Southern aggression on his watch would mean war.

2. nixon VISITS CHINA

Richard Nixon's presidency will first and foremost be remembered for Watergate and rightfully so. He remains the only president to resign from office. But Nixon gets high marks for his handling of foreign policy, particularly for his historic visit to Communist China, which marked the beginning of normalized relations with that country. Nixon understood the Soviet Union and the People's Republic of China did not represent a Communist monolith, and he felt an opportunity existed for the United States to create a wedge between the two nations. In 1971, Nixon sent National Security Adviser Henry Kissinger on a secret mission to China to explore normalization, and the following year he stunned the world by announcing his intention to visit China. Nixon spent a week there, meeting with Chairman Mao Zedong, Premier Zhou Enlai, and scores of other officials as well as visiting cultural landmarks such as the Great Wall. At the end of his trip, the two countries issued the Shanghai Communiqué, which stated that both countries would work toward normalizing relations. Nixon's visit to China also affected relations with the Soviet Union. Not wanting China and the United States to form too close a friendship, the Soviets began a policy of détente with the United States that essentially led to a warming of relations between the two countries. What made Nixon's decision to normalize relations with China and pursue détente with the Soviet Union particularly impressive was that his political history had been that of a fierce anti-Communist cold warrior; he was best known for exposing Alger Hiss as a Communist spy in 1948 and for his famous "Kitchen Debate" with Soviet premier Nikita Khrushchev in 1959. His policy toward China and the Soviet Union flew in the face of his own history, and his political party's, but it didn't prevent him from charting a new course.

3. TRUMAN USES THE ATOMIC BOMB

Harry Truman's decision to drop the atomic bomb on the Japanese cities of Hiroshima and Nagasaki is unquestionably one of the most analyzed and debated acts in U.S. history. It is easy to apply modern ethics and morality in judging a decision made a half century ago, but it is also unfair. In mid-1945, President Truman was faced with the decision of either invading mainland Japan, which could have resulted in hundreds of thousands of American casualties and prolonged the war for months, or deploying the atomic bomb with the hope of achieving a swift victory. Just months earlier, the fighting at Okinawa—Japan's southernmost island—had proven to be brutal, relentless, and bloody and resulted in enormous casualties on both sides. Thus the prospect of a mainland invasion appealed to nobody. Truman ultimately decided that bringing the war to an immediate conclusion was paramount and that using the atomic bomb was justified and necessary. The bombs did bring about a swift victory—the Japanese surrendered a week after the second bomb's detonation—but also left untold suffering and destruction in their wake. "Nobody is more disturbed over the use of Atomic bombs than I am," Truman wrote Samuel Cavert, the general secretary of the Federal Council of Churches, in response to his plea to halt all bombing. "But I was greatly disturbed over the unwarranted attack by the

Japanese on Pearl Harbor and their murder of our prisoners of war. The only language they seem to understand is the one we have been using to bombard them."

4. REAGAN CONFRONTS THE EVIL EMPIRE

Ronald Reagan had three mandates, as he saw it, to his presidency: strengthen and grow the economy, promote moral values, and hasten the demise of the Soviet Union. His third goal, and its corresponding tactics, met with the most resistance and at times left him at odds with Congress and even some in his own party. Reagan's approach to the Soviet Union was radically different from that of previous administrations. Unlike his predecessors, most notably Jimmy Carter and Richard Nixon, Reagan saw the Cold War as an inevitable clash of civilizations with only one potential victor; in his mind, coexistence with Russia was not possible. Consequently, he called the Soviets for what he thought they were—"an evil empire"—and pushed for huge increases in defense spending and new weaponry systems with the goal of bankrupting the Soviets as they attempted to keep pace. His approach and actions drew rebukes from the Democrats in Congress, pacifist and disarmament organizations, the "elite" media, and even heads of state from around the globe, but it didn't deter Reagan from staying the course. In the end—even his detractors have come to concede—Reagan's approach to the Soviet Union did more to win the Cold War than perhaps any single policy in the preceding half century.

5. F. ROOSEVELT CREATES LEND-LEASE PROGRAM

Many historians cite the Lend-Lease program as a pivotal turning point in World War II. Franklin Roosevelt came up with Lend-Lease at the urging of British prime minister Winston Churchill, who, in the winter of 1940 told Roosevelt that Great Britain was on the verge of financial collapse and

could not afford to continue purchasing munitions and supplies from the United States. At the time, the United States
was not a combatant in the war, and the mood in Congress
was overwhelmingly isolationist. To complicate matters, existing laws prevented the U.S. government from lending
money to foreign countries with the purpose of underwriting
their purchase of U.S. armaments. To get around this road-
block, Roosevelt established the Lend-Lease program, which
essentially allowed him to give munitions and supplies away
to the Allies with the expectation that after the war the supplies would be returned. During a press conference,
Roosevelt explained it to the American people using the following analogy:

> Well, let me give you an illustration: Suppose my
> neighbor's home catches fire, and I have a length of
> garden hose 400 or 500 feet away. If he can take my
> garden hose and connect it up with his hydrant, I
> may help him to put out his fire. Now, what do I do?
> I don't say to him before that operation, "Neighbor,
> my garden hose cost me $15; you have to pay me
> $15 for it." What is the transaction that goes on? I
> don't want $15—I want my garden hose back after
> the fire is over.

Roosevelt managed to get the Lend-Lease program through
Congress in March 1941, and over the course of the war it
resulted in close to $50 billion in supplies provided to thirty-
five nations, with the bulk of it going to Great Britain and
Russia. Were it not for Roosevelt's determination and creative thinking, Great Britain may very well have sued for
peace with Germany and thus changed the war's outcome.

6. KENNEDY AND JOHNSON PUSH CIVIL RIGHTS

The decision by Presidents Kennedy and Johnson to pursue

civil rights legislation was highly controversial at the time, because a majority of Americans did not favor it and Democrats in the southern states were strongly opposed to it. President Kennedy first brought up the issue of civil rights at the Democratic National Convention, where he had it inserted into the party platform. During the first two years of his presidency, he was particularly moved by the African Americans' plight and their struggle to win basic freedoms in the Deep South. Further, he was appalled that Democratic governors such as George Wallace and Ross Barnett resorted to physically preventing the integration of their states' public schools. In a June 1963 speech, Kennedy made civil rights a legislative priority, telling a national television audience: "We face, therefore, a moral crisis as a country and as a people. It cannot be met by repressive police action. It cannot be left to increased demonstrations in the streets. It cannot be quieted by token moves or talk. It is a time to act, in the Congress. . . ." The Civil Rights Act was working its way through Congress when President Kennedy was assassinated. President Johnson made the bill's passage his biggest priority, and in short order he succeeded in doing what few thought was possible. Of course, it came with repercussions for the Democratic Party: the push for civil rights gave birth to the third-party candidacy of George Wallace in 1968 and all but ensured Hubert Humphrey's loss to the Republican candidate, Richard Nixon. It also began the process of moving the South, which for a hundred years had been a Democratic stronghold, into the Republican column. By 1980 this move had resulted in the total realignment of southern politics.

7. T. ROOSEVELT BUILDS THE PANAMA CANAL

Teddy Roosevelt earned a reputation as a man of action, and never was that more apparent than with the digging of the Panama Canal. Roosevelt believed that constructing the canal was of vital interest to global commerce and U.S.

hegemony in Latin America. The French had failed miserably some twenty years earlier to complete the canal and the government of Colombia (Panama was a part of Colombia then) refused to negotiate rights to the canal to the United States. That didn't deter Roosevelt one bit. His solution: help organize and support a Panamanian revolution, prop up a pro-U.S. regime, and have it sell the rights to the canal at a discount. "The canal was by far the most important action I took in foreign affairs during the time I was President," said Roosevelt. "When nobody could or would exercise efficient authority, I exercised it." While Roosevelt was single-handedly responsible for establishing the country of Panama and its canal, his brutish tactics gave him little pause for doubt. "There was much accusation about my having acted in an 'unconstitutional' manner," he once said in a moment of reflection. "I took the isthmus, started the canal, and then left Congress—not to debate the canal, but to debate me. . . . While the debate goes on, the canal does too; and they are welcome to debate me as long as they wish, provided that we can go on with the canal."

8. TRUMAN SUPPORTS THE MARSHALL PLAN

Following World War II, most of Europe lay in financial ruins. The economies of Great Britain, Germany, and France, in particular, were devastated, and the threat of global recession—similar to that following World War I—was real and imminent. Though the country's mood had moved toward isolationism, Harry Truman and others in his administration were convinced massive aid to Western Europe was needed to keep the world economy out of recession as well as to prevent the rise of communism inside the European democracies. Truman's secretary of state, George C. Marshall, came up with a plan to give $12.5 billion over four years (equivalent to $130 billion in today's dollars) to the countries of Western Europe in an unprecedented gesture

Secretary of State George C. Marshall, architect of Harry Truman's Marshall Plan. *George C. Marshall Foundation*

of "strategic" generosity. Initially, Congress balked at the plan, but it passed the enabling legislation after the democratically elected government of Czechoslovakia was overthrown by a Soviet-backed coup. The Marshall Plan had its intended effect: the European economy experienced record growth from 1948 to 1952, and the expansion of communism inside key democracies was halted.

9. G. H. W. BUSH LAUNCHES OPERATION DESERT SHIELD

President George H. W. Bush's decision to create an international coalition to defend Saudi Arabia and liberate Kuwait was both highly controversial and extraordinary and proved to be the right move. At the time of Iraq's invasion of Kuwait, few Americans could point to either country on the map. Almost immediately, President Bush worked through the United Nations and began assembling an international coalition. Thirty-four countries wound up sending troops to the Saudi border with the goals of protecting Saudi Arabia and of eventually expelling Iraq from Kuwait. Bush united the world community and even rallied the Democrats in Congress (most of whom opposed offensive action) to support a declaration of war (52–47). Were it not for Bush's decisive action, it's likely Saddam Hussein would still be camped out in Kuwait and sitting on a third of the world's oil reserves or, worse yet, would be in Saudi Arabia.

10. CLINTON PROPOSES TAX HIKE

This choice might seem odd for this list, but Bill Clinton deserves credit for taking on an unpopular issue—tax hikes—and doing so despite its potential cost to his party, namely, losing its control of Congress. Clinton had campaigned on balancing the budget and making the tax code "fairer." Shortly after taking office these promises became the centerpiece of his legislative agenda. Clinton proposed the largest tax hike in history, along with spending cuts, to help bring the budget back into alignment and to stimulate the economy. His budget raised taxes on the wealthy, corporations, Medicare recipients, Social Security recipients, and drivers (the gas tax was increased 4.3 cents per gallon). In the Democratic-controlled Senate, Vice President Al Gore broke a 50–50 tie vote, and in the House (also controlled by Democrats), the tax package passed by a single tie-breaking vote, 218–216. Republicans hammered Clinton on this issue (and his aborted attempt at universal health care) right through the midterm elections and capitalized on public outrage to sweep both houses of Congress for the first time in forty-two years. But contrary to the Republicans' dire predictions, the economy rebounded from the recession of 1991–92, and by 1994–95 the country was experiencing robust growth. Over time, the budget went from annual deficits to surpluses, and for a while there was talk about how to spend this newfound money.

Legislative Accomplishments and Notable Achievements

Many factors go into determining a president's legacy, including legislative accomplishments and other important domestic achievements. Most go unnoticed, but a few warrant special consideration.

1. LOUISIANA PURCHASE, THOMAS JEFFERSON, 1803

The most significant domestic accomplishment during Jefferson's two terms in office was the Louisiana Purchase—an acquisition of land from France that roughly doubled the size of the United States. The purchase contained parts (or all) of sixteen states and represents slightly more than 22 percent of the entire land mass of the modern United States, or approximately 530 million acres. It also put the United States on course to achieve its "manifest destiny" (a term that would be coined some forty years after the purchase) as a continental nation. Originally, Jefferson was interested in purchasing only the city of New Orleans, simply to ensure the United States would have access to the coastal port and a passageway to the Mississippi River. When the opportunity arose to purchase the entire territory, Jefferson had mixed feelings. On the one hand, he knew it would be a terrific acquisition for the United States, but he wasn't sure he had the constitutional power to authorize such a purchase. Jefferson believed in states' rights and took a strict approach to the Constitution when it came to federal power. Intellectually, he believed the president didn't have the authority to unilaterally strike such a deal and considered proposing a constitutional amendment to make the acquisition; however, politically he understood the process would take too long. Further, he had to act or Napoleon Bonaparte would likely change his mind. Jefferson's decision to make the deal turned out to be the right one and is probably the most significant non-legislative domestic act in U.S. history.

2. CIVIL RIGHTS ACT OF 1964, LYNDON JOHNSON

Many historians consider the Civil Rights Act of 1964 as the single most important piece of legislation passed in the twentieth century. Among other things, it outlawed once and for all Jim Crow segregation laws; banned discrimination in public facilities, the workplace, and the government; and encouraged the desegregation of schools. Also important, it made illegal any discrimination in accommodations used in interstate commerce, such as hotels, motels, restaurants, and the like. The legislation took shape in 1963, when President Kennedy gave a speech outlining the need for equal treatment of all Americans in society. Following President Kennedy's assassination, Lyndon Johnson took up the cause (partially to broaden his support base in the 1964 campaign), and he publicly worked for the bill's passage. LBJ used the bully pulpit, as well as his knowledge of parliamentary tactics, to get the bill through the House and past a Senate filibuster. The following year, Johnson signed into law the National Voting Rights Act of 1965, which outlawed discriminatory practices used to keep African Americans from voting, such as poll taxes and literacy tests, and gave the Department of Justice the power to oversee the voter registration process. The two pieces of legislation have done more to end discrimination than any other laws in U.S. history.

3. THE NEW DEAL, FRANKLIN D. ROOSEVELT, 1933–37

Franklin Roosevelt's New Deal program is by far the most successful—and ambitious—legislative agenda of any president in U.S. history. Roosevelt was elected, in part, because Americans had lost confidence in Herbert Hoover's ability to get the U.S. economy out of a depression. Roosevelt seized upon his mandate and passed scores of "recovery" acts designed to lift the nation out of its economic depression and to provide a social safety net for the elderly and unemployed. While the Supreme Court struck down some programs as unconstitutional, many survived, most notably Social Security, which today represents the largest entitlement program in the federal budget. In the 1930s, the notion of a government-sponsored retirement and unemployment insurance program was considered a radical idea; many opponents argued it would plunge the nation even further into recession and create a permanent class of dependent citizens. Today, Social Security is considered the "third rail" of American politics, meaning politicians are loath to tamper with it for fear of alienating older voters. In 1940, the total payment to beneficiaries was roughly $35 million; by 1990, that figure had grown to nearly $250 billion; and in 2004 payments neared $500 billion. As Americans live longer and the nation grows older, a new debate over funding has emerged; some advocate for growing the entitlement through more taxes while others maintain that it should be privatized, similar to a 401(k) investment plan.

4. EMANCIPATION PROCLAMATION AND THE THIRTEENTH AMENDMENT, ABRAHAM LINCOLN, 1863–65

On January 1, 1863, three years into the Civil War, Abraham

Lincoln issued the Emancipation Proclamation, which served to free slaves who lived in the Confederate states. As a legal document, the proclamation had limited reach since it was issued via executive order (and therefore was arguably un-constitutional) and pertained only to slaves on Confederate soil (and not to slaves in border states that remained loyal to the Union). As a moral statement and a symbolic act, however, it was one of the war's defining moments. It essentially transformed the battle into a crusade for freedom. Lincoln himself was dubious about the constitutionality of the proclamation, and as a result he pushed the lame-duck Thirty-eighth Congress into passing the Thirteenth Amendment, which banned slavery once and for all. Though Lincoln didn't live to see the amendment's ratification (that took place in December 1865), it was surely his most significant legislative achievement and lasting legacy. "I have been shaking hands since nine o'clock this morning, and my right arm is almost paralyzed," Lincoln told Secretary of State Seward moments before signing the Emancipation Proclamation. "If my name ever goes into history, it will be for this act, and my whole soul is in it. If my hand trembles when I sign the Proclamation, all who examine the document here-after will say, 'He hesitated.'"

5. CONSERVATION, THEODORE ROOSEVELT, 1901–9
Teddy Roosevelt's numerous legislative and other accomplishments included "trust busting," or breaking up large monopolies, and instituting a wave of oversight regulation, such as the Meat Inspection Act and the Pure Food and Drug Act. Arguably, however, his greatest impact came in the area of conservation. Prior to TR's presidency, conservation wasn't even part of the national consciousness; few gave little thought to preserving America's natural beauty. An avid outdoorsman all his life, Roosevelt did more to advance the

cause of conservation than any president before or since. Among other things, he created the U.S. Forestry Service; established five national parks and the first eighteen national monuments, including the Grand Canyon; and signed into law the Antiquities Act, which had the effect of giving himself and future presidents the ability to proclaim "historic landmarks, historic and prehistoric structures, and other objects of historic or scientific interest" as national monuments. Virtually every president since has used the act to protect large portions of land as national monuments.

6. PENDLETON ACT, CHESTER ARTHUR, 1883

The Pendleton Civil Service Reform Act might not appear in many history books as a significant legislative accomplishment, but it actually ended the patronage spoils system and ushered in the civil service era. Andrew Jackson created the spoils system after his 1828 victory, and over time it became increasingly inefficient and corrupt. President Garfield made civil service reform the centerpiece of his legislative agenda, but before he could act on it, he was assassinated (ironically by a madman who felt he deserved a spoils job for "helping" elect Garfield). Although Garfield's vice president, Chester Arthur, was opposed to civil service reform, he took up the cause following Garfield's assassination and signed the Pendleton Act into law in January 1883. The act set up the Civil Service Commission to administer government jobs based on merit, not political connections, and essentially created the federal bureaucracy. Today, the vast majority of federal government jobs are classified as civil service; only the highest positions are made by political appointment.

7. FEDERAL AID HIGHWAYS ACT, DWIGHT D. EISENHOWER, 1956

It's ironic that Eisenhower, the most fiscally conservative

president of the twentieth century and the last president to actually *cut* federal spending in real dollars, oversaw the largest public works projects of its era—the $41 billion investment to construct more than forty thousand miles of interstate highways. The idea of creating an interstate highway system had been around for decades, but previous administrations weren't committed to funding it. Eisenhower believed an elaborate interstate highway system was critical to promoting commerce and national defense. He had seen firsthand how quickly troops could be transported across the German autobahns during World War II and felt having a similar system in the United States was important. Eisenhower actually signed the highway bill from his hospital room while recovering from a heart attack. Today, the interstate highways represent only 1 percent of the nation's roads, but they carry 20 percent of the auto traffic.

8. TAX REFORM ACT OF 1986, RONALD REAGAN

When Ronald Reagan took office in 1981, he had three primary goals: strengthen national defense, promote strong moral values, and grow the economy. Reagan was a supply-sider, meaning he believed lowering taxes was the best way to stimulate the economy and *increase* government revenues. In 1981, Reagan signed into law the Kemp-Roth Tax Cut, which cut marginal tax rates and indexed them for inflation. He considered it a moderate success, and in his second term he set out to overhaul the tax code. Working with Democratic leaders Dick Gephardt in the House and Bill Bradley in the Senate, Reagan came up with a plan to dramatically simplify the tax code into two brackets—28 percent and 15 percent—and eliminate many long-standing loopholes and deductions. To date, it was by far the largest tax overhaul in history and is considered Reagan's greatest legislative achievement. Both the economy and government revenues boomed in the following years, and many credit it with creating the strongest economic expansion in history. For those interested, the 1986 Tax Reform Act was immortalized in Jeffrey Birnbaum and Alan Murray's terrific book, *Showdown at Gucci Gulch.*

q. POLK ACQUISITIONS, JAMES K. POLK, 1845–49

The only president to set a one-term limit on his presidency, James K. Polk's primary objective was to resolve the land disputed with England and with Mexico. During his four years in office, the United States acquired more land than during any previous administration (including Jefferson's). He signed the Oregon Treaty with Great Britain, which ended three decades of joint control of the Northwest territories and established the forty-ninth parallel as the northernmost boundary for the United States. The agreement eventually led to the creation of five states: Washington, Oregon, Idaho, Montana, and Wyoming. Polk was also president when Texas was formally annexed; in fact, its annexation was the central promise of his campaign. Polk's most valuable land grab, however, resulted from the Mexican-American War's settlement. With the Treaty of Guadalupe Hidalgo, Mexico ceded to the United States territories for three states—California, Utah, and Nevada—as well as parts of Arizona, New Mexico, Colorado, and Wyoming. The United States paid $15 million for the land. Thus during Polk's tenure, the United States finally fulfilled its "manifest destiny."

10. SHERMAN ANTITRUST ACT, BENJAMIN HARRISON, 1840

Though Senator John Sherman of Ohio gets most of the credit (deservedly so) for passing the first law designed to curb industrial monopolies, it was moderate Republican Benjamin Harrison who signed it into law. Harrison knew that public outrage over monopolistic practices had reached a boiling point and that it was in the country's—and thus his—best interest to sign the bill. The law was rarely used until Teddy Roosevelt assumed office, and then it became a primary tool in his trust-busting crusade. Over the years, the Sherman Antitrust Act has been strengthened by supple- mental laws, including the Clayton Antitrust Act of 1914, the Hart-Scott-Rodino Antitrust Improvement Act of 1976, and most recently the Criminal Antitrust Penalty Enhance- ment and Reform Act, which President Bush signed into law in 2004.

Memorable Quotes

Most memorable presidential quotes and sayings come from scripted remarks and speeches. It's the unscripted lines, however, that sometimes reveal the most about the person and his presidency.

1. GEORGE W. BUSH, GROUND ZERO, SEPTEMBER 14, 2001

"I can hear you! I can hear you. The rest of the world hears you. And the people who knocked these buildings down will hear all of us soon."

It's arguably the most memorable moment from George W. Bush's two terms in office and one of the most poignant extemporaneous remarks in our country's history. It's easy to forget that in the immediate aftermath of the September 11 terrorist attacks, President Bush's public remarks seemed unsteady and, at times, understated. Because he had less than a year of on-the-job experience, some doubted whether President Bush was up to the challenge of rallying the nation and leading during difficult times. As he stood on the rubble at Ground Zero with his arm slung around a gritty New York fireman, President Bush seemed to find his "voice" and delivered these memorable remarks after someone shouted, "We can't hear you!" The moment was captured on live television and seemed to steady both the president and the nation and to mark a turning point in the war on terror.

2. RONALD REAGAN, OPERATING ROOM, MARCH 30, 1981
"Honey, I forgot to duck."

Known for his scripted remarks and rehearsed speeches, Ronald Reagan was also an all-time great ad-libber, and his skill was on display the day John Hinckley, Jr., shot him in Washington, D.C. While fighting for his life at George Washington University Hospital, the sixty-nine-year-old president somehow managed to get off two memorable zingers: he said the first one to wife Nancy when she first saw him at the hospital and quipped the second—"I hope you're a Republican"—to the emergency room doctor as he was wheeled into the operating room. The remarks were classic Reagan: self-deprecating, humorous, timely, and sometimes borrowed from his favorite stories. He actually borrowed the "forgot to duck" line from boxer Jack Dempsey, who after losing the heavyweight championship to Gene Tunney, responded to his wife's incredulity with "Honey, I forgot to duck." Both of Reagan's lines were repeated in the media the following day and helped put the nation at ease, knowing that the president was stable and would soon be on the road to a full a recovery.

3. BILL CLINTON, PRESS CONFERENCE, JANUARY 26, 1998
"I want to say one thing to the American people. I want you to listen to me. I'm going to say this again. I did not have sexual relations with that woman, Miss Lewinsky. I never told anybody to lie. Not a single time. Never."

Although he accomplished many notable achievements

during his two terms in office, including balancing the budget and presiding over the biggest economic expansion in U.S. history, the most memorable and often-replayed quote from his presidency was his terse denial of having had a sexual affair with his young intern. He delivered the line several days after the scandal broke and only when it became obvious that the media's feeding frenzy wasn't about to dissipate. What stood out at the time about the statement was the forcefulness of the denial (and the fingering waving and righteous indignation that went along with it), as well as the reference to Monica Lewinsky as "that woman" (some women's groups took exception to that). Of course, it later turned out that, in fact, he did have a sexual affair with Monica Lewinsky, although the charge of suborning perjury—that is, asking someone to lie—was never proven. President Clinton has never revealed if the line was totally scripted or something he simply came up with on the spot.

4. RICHARD NIXON, PRESS CONFERENCE, NOVEMBER 11, 1973
"People have got to know whether or not their president is a crook. Well, I'm not a crook."

Perhaps the most memorable line ever uttered at a presidential press conference, the "I'm not a crook" retort has become the signature phrase associated with Richard Nixon. While not directly commenting on the Watergate cover-up when he spoke the words—he was actually responding to charges that he had raised milk support prices in exchange for campaign contributions—over the years his remark has come to represent his denial of wrongdoing in the Watergate scandal. Of course, it turns out he was a crook, of sorts, and less than nine months after making the remark, he resigned from office. Nixon's other memorable quote—"You won't have Dick Nixon to kick around anymore"—which he made at a press conference following his defeat in the 1962 California gubernatorial election, also turned out to be untrue. The press had another twelve years to kick him around.

5. ABRAHAM LINCOLN, SPEECH IN CLINTON, ILLINOIS, 1858

"You can fool all of the people some of the time, and some of the people all of the time, but you can not fool all of the people all of the time."

Over the years, Abraham Lincoln has been credited with scores of quotes and aphorisms—some he spoke, and some he didn't. The above quote is one of his most famous, though historians disagree as to whether he actually uttered it. It's attributed to a speech he delivered in Clinton, Illinois, during his 1858 Senate campaign against Stephen Douglas. The text of the speech, printed in the local paper the following day, does not contain the quote, but years later two people present at the speech claim he made the remarks extemporaneously. Apocryphal or not, the quote certainly *seems* in keeping with Lincoln's other aphorisms and remains one of the most often repeated.

6. THEODORE ROOSEVELT, LETTER TO A FRIEND, 1900

"Speak softly and carry a big stick."

Arguably no other quote so completely captured a president's philosophical essence as Teddy Roosevelt's "speak softly and carry a big stick." What's most interesting about the line is that while Roosevelt was governor of New York, he wrote it in a letter to a friend and, according to Roosevelt, was quoting a West African proverb that he had heard on one of his trips. The actual full line in Roosevelt's letter is "Speak softly and carry a big stick; you will go far," but over the years the latter part has been dropped. Roosevelt used the quote not to illustrate some lofty principle for America's foreign policy, but rather to describe how he had won a brass-knuckles political battle with the New York Republican Party bosses over his refusal to reappoint a corrupt insurance commissioner. Even so, the statement found its way into the press, captured the mood of the country, and made Roosevelt an overnight political star. Today, of course, the quote is most associated with Roosevelt's approach to foreign policy—with America flexing its growing might around the globe—and in some ways serves as the demarcation point for the nation's emergence as a global superpower.

7. HARRY S. TRUMAN
"If you can't stand the heat, get out of the kitchen."

It's unclear if Harry Truman originated the line or was simply quoting another, but there's no doubt that he said it on several occasions both before and during his presidency. According to an Idaho newspaper, he used the admonition as early as 1942 when discussing the difficult work of investigating war contracts, although the line was slightly different: "If you don't like the heat, get out of the kitchen." He used the more well-known version on several occasions during his presidency, most notably when speaking about the criticism that administration officials sometimes have to endure. Truman was revered for his plainspokeness; he wasn't shy about speaking his mind or telling the blunt truth. This quality served him well on his "Give 'Em Hell" barnstorming tour during the 1948 election, when he pulled an "upset" win over Governor Thomas Dewey. Truman is also remembered for another plain-spoken phrase on a placard that sat on his desk in the Oval Office: "The bucks stop here." He frequently made references to it in his speeches and remarks.

8. JIMMY CARTER, *PLAYBOY* MAGAZINE INTERVIEW, 1976
"I've looked on a lot of women with lust. I've committed adultery in my heart many times."

Jimmy Carter made this remark during the 1976 presidential campaign when interviewer Robert Scheer asked if the candidate was concerned about coming off as too religious and self-righteous. In his eagerness to appear humble and contrite for his flaws—something voters seemed to want following Watergate—Carter dropped this bombshell, which made headlines around the globe and immediately tightened his lead over Gerald Ford. "Do not underestimate what a crisis that interview and the 'lust in my heart' caused Carter," Carter historian Douglas Brinkley told Ray Suarez on PBS years later. "It almost derailed the entire Carter campaign. They were in havoc over it." Carter managed to win a narrow victory over Ford, but the quote remains one of Carter's most memorable sound bites.

9. BILL CLINTON, GRAND JURY TESTIMONY, AUGUST 17, 1998
"It depends on what the meaning of the word *is* is."

Although Clinton's "I did not have sexual relations" sound bite is the more memorable quote, his parsing of the definition of the word *is* perhaps speaks more about Clinton the politician than any other utterance of his presidency. Clinton earned the nickname "Slick Willie" in part because it became such a chore to get the truth out of him, so say his critics. One of the skills he mastered was parsing the literal definitions of words so as to create "linguistic loopholes" that shielded him from telling outright lies. Clinton used this technique many times throughout the Lewinsky and other scandals, but none were so obvious as his grand jury testimony. Clinton's rationale that he had not lied under oath when denying an affair with Monica Lewinsky was simply that the word *is* could have two meanings:

> If "is" means is and never has been, that is not—that is one thing. If it means there is none, that was a completely true statement . . . Now, if someone had asked me on that day, are you having any kind of sexual relations with Ms. Lewinsky, that is, asked me a question in the present tense, I would have said no. And it would have been completely true.

That explanation sums up Bill Clinton the politician.

10. GEORGE H. W. BUSH, COMMENT AT THE REPUBLICAN NATIONAL CONVENTION, 1988

"That's Jebby's kids from Florida, the little brown ones."

Like his son, President George H. W. Bush is known to sometimes mangle the English language, but on this occasion he was perfectly clear. He made the comment (unknowingly within range of an open microphone) to Ronald Reagan as he was pointing out his grandchildren. Hispanic groups were up in arms over the comment, labeling it "insensitive" and "racist." Bush countered that he was simply being affectionate. Ironically, one of the "little brown ones" was George P. Bush, who later played a prominent role in President George W. Bush's election and reelection and is considered by many to be the next political star in the Bush dynasty.

Generals Who Became President

For the first hundred years of the country's existence, being a general in the army—and a military hero at that—was practically a prerequisite for becoming president. In the past hundred or so years, however, things have changed: only one general—Dwight D. Eisenhower—has occupied the highest office in the land.

1. GEORGE WASHINGTON

In addition to being the "father" of his country, George Washington was also the first commander in chief of the military and established the precedent of military figures ascending to the presidency. While not regarded as a brilliant military tactician—during the Revolutionary War he actually lost more battles than he won—Washington's greatest impact as a military leader may have been his general approach to war: he believed that civilian leadership should always maintain final authority over the military and that the army should be disbanded during times of peace. Washington feared a permanent standing army could accrue too much power and ultimately threaten the civilian government. During the Revolutionary War, he made a point of including political leaders in decision making and ceding to their wishes on overall strategy.

Washington began his military career at the onset of the French and Indian War, during which, as a twenty-two-year-old major, he led the first battle of the war. Washington quickly distinguished himself, and within a few years he was appointed commander in chief of the Virginia forces. After being passed over for a commission in the British Army, which was considered more prestigious than a state commission, Washington returned to his plantation. After sixteen years the Second Continental Congress coaxed him out of retirement. He reluctantly took command of the colonial army and spent the next five years battling the British for independence. Washington was a genius general strategist. His primary goal was to keep his army together (he feared if they disbanded, they wouldn't return), to attack the better-trained and equipped British Army while they were in transit, and to suppress the British loyalists, particularly in the south. His greatest victory came at the siege of Yorktown, where he captured General Cornwallis's forces and effectively ended the war. In perhaps his most noble gesture as a military figure, Washington voluntarily resigned his position following the war, disbanded the army, and returned to private life, ensuring that civilian authority would take precedence over military power.

2. ULYSSES S. GRANT

Most historians consider Grant's legacy as a general far superior to his legacy as president. He is arguably the greatest field general in U.S. history and in the same company of such legends as George S. Patton, Douglas MacArthur, and Grant's Civil War adversary Robert E. Lee. While Grant was a failure at just about everything else in life (some would even include politics), his genius on the battlefield helped preserve the Union, and for that he rates as one of the greatest American military leaders in history.

Prior to the Civil War, Grant's military and civilian career had been mostly a series of undistinguished ventures and outright failures. He served uneventfully under Winfield Scott and Zachary Taylor during the Mexican-American War and resigned from the military several years later. He then tried his hand at several business ventures, including real estate and farming, with little success. When the Civil War began in 1860, Grant was a clerk in his father's leather store. He tried to regain his commission, but the army was not interested in him. Grant finally secured a volunteer regiment, and within months he had begun to distinguish himself on the battlefield. He caught the attention of Lincoln and the military brass after he captured Fort Henry and Fort Donelson in early 1862 and further displayed his battlefield brilliance with a string of victories that included Shiloh, Vicksburg, and Chattanooga. It wasn't until after his victory at Vicksburg, where he effectively split the Confederacy in half, that Grant was finally given an appointment to the regular U.S. Army. It would be another year—March 1864—before Lincoln made Grant general in chief of the entire Union Army, an amazing feat for someone who had been turned down for a commission only four years earlier. Lincoln gave Grant total autonomy for running the war, and Grant used the Union's strengths—greater resources, more men, better morale—to slowly grind the Confederacy to defeat. He personally accepted Robert E. Lee's surrender at the Appomattox Court House in April 1865, bringing the war to a conclusion.

A quote from Lincoln summed up Grant best:

Grant is the first general I have had. You know how it's been with all the rest. As soon as I put a man in command of the army, they all wanted me to be the general. Now it isn't so with Grant. He hasn't told me what his plans are. I don't know and I don't want to know. I am glad to find a man who can go ahead without me. He doesn't ask impossibilities of me, and he's the first general I've had that didn't.

3. DWIGHT D. EISENHOWER

Like Zachary Taylor, Dwight Eisenhower was a career military officer who held only one elected position his entire life—that of president of the United States. Most historians rate Eisenhower one of the greatest military figures in U.S. history, even though he never saw field combat. He graduated from West Point in 1915 and spent the next quarter century slowly working through the army's ranks in mostly administrative positions. During the 1930s, he spent four years in the Philippines as Gen. Douglas MacArthur's chief of staff. But it wasn't until the onset of World War II that Eisenhower's career took off. Eisenhower impressed Army chief of staff Gen. George C. Marshall with his logic, organizational skill, and strategic thinking. Marshall increasingly relied on Eisenhower to organize the European theater of operations, and in 1942 he appointed Ike commanding general of the European theater, leapfrogging him ahead of scores of higher-ranking generals. Eisenhower was later named supreme Allied commander and charged with creating and implementing the plan to liberate Europe, Operation Overlord. In this role Eisenhower made his greatest impact: he oversaw the D-Day invasion at Normandy, France, which marked the beginning of the end of World War II. It's easy to forget that the invasion's outcome was in doubt, so much so that Eisenhower actually wrote two different sets of remarks for the press—one for its victory and one in case of its failure. Fortunately, he didn't have to use the latter:

Our landings in the Cherbourg-Havre area have failed

and I have withdrawn the troops. My decision to attack at this time and place was based on the best information available. The troops, the air and the Navy did all that bravery and devotion could do. If any blame or fault attaches to the attempt it is mine alone.

Following the war, Eisenhower was made army chief of staff (succeeding his mentor George Marshall) and in 1950 was appointed the supreme commander of NATO.

4. WILLIAM HENRY HARRISON

While Harrison is best remembered for being both the second-oldest president to take office (only Reagan was older) and the shortest tenured (his administration was all of thirty days), he also came from one of the most prominent families in history. His father was a delegate at the Continental Congress, signed the Declaration of Independence, and served as the governor of Virginia, while both his brother and father-in-law were members of Congress. Harrison left college at age eighteen to join the army, was as an aide-de-camp to Gen. "Mad Anthony" Wayne, and participated in the decisive victory in the Northwest Indian War at the Battle of Fallen Timbers, which resulted in the creation of the Ohio Territory. Harrison resigned from the army in 1798 to serve as the governor of the Indiana Territory, where his primary responsibilities were to prevent Indian attacks against the settlers and to expand the territory. His most famous victory came at the Battle of Tippecanoe, during which he repulsed an attack by the great Shawnee leader Tecumseh and his brother Tenskwatawa, and thus earned the nickname "Old Tippecanoe." The following year, Harrison was given command of the Army of the Northwest during the War of 1812 and won key battles in Ohio and Indiana before finally crushing the British at the Battle of the Thames and effectively ending the war. Harrison parlayed his military fame into a long career in Ohio politics, and after losing to Martin Van Buren in 1836, he finally won the presidency four years later.

5. **ANDREW JACKSON**

After George Washington, Jackson was the second war hero to win the presidency and is generally regarded as one of the great military leaders in U.S. history. He won accolades and fame for his victories during the Creek War (1813–14), the War of 1812 (1812–15), and the First Seminole War (1817–18). Like most generals of the day, Jackson had no formal military training; in fact, he was a well-respected lawyer and politician in the Tennessee Territory when he was given command of its militia in 1801. Jackson spent much of his time defending against Creek Nation attacks and won a decisive victory at the Battle of Horseshoe Bend, which resulted in the Creeks ceding 23 million acres of land (half of Alabama and part of Georgia). Jackson kept his militia intact during the War of 1812 and advanced to the rank of major general as he rolled up the victories. Jackson won the final battle of the war at New Orleans (it actually took place two weeks after a peace treaty had been signed), where his 6,000 men routed 12,000 British troops and the British suffered 2,000 casualties to Jackson's 58. The victory made him a national icon and earned him the nickname "Old Hickory" for being as tough as hickory in the battlefield. At President Monroe's request, Jackson led a campaign in Georgia against the Seminole Indians, who were being assisted by the British and Spanish in their attacks against settlers. Jackson exceeded his orders and took his men into Florida, where he deposed the Spanish governor. Secretary of State John Adams used the victory to convince Spain to cede Florida to the United States, and Jackson became its

first territorial governor. While some in the Monroe administration wanted Jackson censured for his actions, most Americans viewed him as a hero, and his ensuing fame propelled
him to the White House. Although Jackson lost narrowly to
John Quincy Adams in 1824, he crushed him in a rematch
four years later.

6. ZACHARY TAYLOR

Zachary Taylor was the first president who had never held
elected office prior to winning the White House. Taylor was
a professional solider and served more than forty years in
the military. He first saw action in the War of 1812. As a
captain he staved off a key attack at the Battle of Fort
Harrison, which was the first land victory for the United
States in the war. In the following decades, he saw prominent action in the Black Hawk War (1832) and the Second
Seminole War (1835–42) and was eventually promoted to
commanding general of all U.S. forces in Florida. Taylor
rose to national prominence during the Mexican-American
War after turning back a Mexican ambush, even though his
troops were outnumbered four to one. He followed that success with others at Monterrey and Buena Vista, which essentially assured a U.S. victory. Fearful that Taylor might
make a strong presidential candidate, President Polk kept
Taylor from advancing into Mexico and instead allowed Gen.
Winfield Scott to capture Mexico City. Even so, the Whig
Party nominated Taylor, and he easily won the election despite not campaigning at all.

7. FRANKLIN PIERCE

Franklin Pierce was a lifelong lawyer and politician who
served briefly in the volunteer services during the Mexican-
American War. His lasting military legacy was being made a
brigadier general of the volunteer forces that served as

reinforcements for Gen. Winfield Scott's march on Mexico City. Pierce's forces joined Scott's at the Battle of Contreras, where Pierce was seriously injured after falling from his horse. He rebounded from his injury to lead the volunteer forces in several key battles that culminated with the victory at Mexico City. Though he had no military training whatsoever, Pierce showed skilled in commanding his troops, and he parlayed his successes to a "dark-horse"nomination for the presidency in 1852. Ironically, his opponent was General Scott, under whom he fought during the Mexican-American War, but Pierce easily won the White House.

8. ANDREW JOHNSON

President Lincoln appointed Andrew Johnson the military governor of Tennessee after the Union captured the state in 1862. Johnson was the only Southern senator who remained loyal to the Union at the onset of the Civil War. Johnson ruled Tennessee with a firm hand and in doing so caught the eye of Republicans in Congress who were looking for a moderate Southerner to join Lincoln on the ticket and help with Reconstruction. Of course, Johnson changed his tune about Reconstruction almost immediately upon taking office after Lincoln's assassination. He was eventually impeached for firing his secretary of war and nearly convicted and removed from office, but he was saved by a single vote in the Senate.

9. RUTHERFORD B. HAYES

At the outbreak of the Civil War, the forty-year-old Hayes joined the Ohio Volunteer Infantry as a major, even though he had no prior military experience. He was nearly killed in the Battle of South Mountain and shortly thereafter was promoted to colonel. He led a brigade at the Battle of Cloyd's Mountain and was made a brigadier general of the volunteers during the Shenandoah Valley Campaign of 1864. Shortly before the war's end, he was given a brevet-ted to major general of the volunteers, the highest rank of any volunteer during the war. At around that time he was nominated to serve in Congress.

10. JAMES A. GARFIELD

Garfield was another career lawyer and politician who joined the military during the Civil War, though he enlisted rather than serve as a volunteer. His primary assignment was to drive Confederate forces out of eastern Kentucky, and he won acclaim for his victory at Prestonsburg. He served as a brigade commander at the Battle of Shiloh and the siege of Corinth, playing a key role in Union victories. In 1863 he was promoted to the chief of staff for the commander of the Army of the Cumberland William Rosencrans. Following the Union's defeat at the Battle of Chickamauga, Rosencrans was relieved of his command and Garfield was promoted to major general. Garfield left the military shortly thereafter and won a seat in the House of Representatives, where he quickly rose through the ranks to become speaker of the House.

Assassinations and Attempts

Becoming president comes with risks. Four presidents have been assassinated, and several more nearly assassinated. In the early years of the republic, the president received little protection, but over time it has increased dramatically. Today, hundreds of Secret Service agents work around the clock to "cocoon" the president, the vice president, and their families from danger.

1. ABRAHAM LINCOLN, 1865

Historians often cite Abraham Lincoln's assassination as one of the pivotal moments in American history. One can only wonder how Reconstruction and the post–Civil War era would have turned out had Lincoln served a full second term. John Wilkes Booth's original intent was to kidnap Lincoln and ransom him for the return of Confederate prisoners, but he decided to assassinate him instead after attending a speech in which Lincoln advocated giving African Americans the right to vote. Booth and his coconspirators planned to kill Lincoln, Vice President Andrew Johnson, and Secretary of State William Seward, and their hope was that the ensuing chaos would somehow give rise to the Confederacy (even though the war was already over). After military tribunals, four of Booth's primary co-conspirators were hanged, including Mary Surratt, who became the first woman the U.S. government sentenced to death. Three others were given life sentences, which President Johnson commuted several years later. Some conspiracy theorists believed Vice President Johnson was behind the assassination plot. Mary Todd Lincoln wrote to her friend Sally Orne:

> That, that miserable inebriate Johnson, had cognizance of my husband's death—Why, was that card of Booth's, found in his box, some acquaintance certainly existed—I have been deeply impressed, with the harrowing thought, that he, had an understanding with the conspirators & they knew their man . . . As sure, as you & I live, Johnson, had some hand, in all this.

Only three days prior to his death, Lincoln had a dream, which he shared with his wife and several close friends, that he would be assassinated.

2. JOHN F. KENNEDY, 1963

President John F. Kennedy's assassination has been one of the most studied, debated, and written about events in U.S. history. Few incidents have been as dissected, analyzed, and hypothesized, and even so it still remains shrouded in mystery and controversy. More than four decades later, the American public remains divided on the culprit: some believe assassin Lee Harvey Oswald acted alone, but others contend there were multiple shooters (as part of a larger conspiracy). One impact of the Kennedy assassination was the adoption in 1965 of the Twenty-fifth Amendment, which deals with the issue of presidential incapacity and vice presidential succession. Prior to this development, when the vice president ascended to the presidency resulting from the president's death or illness, the office of vice president remained vacant, in some cases for upward of three years. The Twenty-fifth Amendment gives the president the power to nominate a new vice president. It also provides a provision for the president to temporarily transfer power to his vice president in the event that he is incapable of discharging his duties.

3. WILLIAM MCKINLEY, 1901
Twenty-eight-year-old revolutionary Leon Czolgosz assassinated President William McKinley less than a year after McKinley won a second term in office. Czolgosz was a radical anarchist who believed all forms of government were illegitimate, and he sought attention for the anarchist movement by killing the president. He shot McKinley twice from point-blank range while the president was greeting onlookers at the Pan-American Exposition in Buffalo. Doctors were able to locate and extract the first bullet, but they struggled to find the second (and in the process may have caused more harm to the president). McKinley lingered for a week but eventually succumbed to infection. His assassin was tried, convicted, and executed within two months of the shooting. Ironically, the first X-ray machine was on display at the Pan-Am Exposition, but nobody thought to use the device on McKinley to locate the second bullet.

4. JAMES A. GARFIELD, 1881
Fifteen years after Lincoln's murder, Charles Guiteau shot James Garfield as he was about to board a train on his way to a college reunion. The mentally ill Guiteau assassinated Garfield because he believed the president had slighted him in not appointing him ambassador to France, and he thought Vice President Chester Arthur would rectify the situation. Guiteau had nominally been a part of the Garfield-Arthur campaign (he often sat around campaign headquarters

reading newspapers), and he believed he had befriended Arthur. Guiteau shot Garfield twice, and one bullet passed through his shoulder and the other lodged somewhere in his chest. Doctors struggled to find the second bullet, and in the process they almost certainly worsened his condition. The physicians moved Garfield to the New Jersey shore, where they hoped the fresh air and quiet would help his recovery. After two months Garfield was felled by a massive heart attack brought on by severe infection. Guiteau's lawyers pleaded not guilty by reason of insanity, one of the first times the insanity defense was ever used. He was found guilty and hanged the following year.

5. RONALD REAGAN, 1981

As Ronald Reagan was walking to his limousine outside the Hilton Hotel in Washington, D.C., John Hinckley, Jr., shot him at close range. The mentally disturbed Hinckley fired six shots, wounding Reagan; his press secretary, James Brady; a secret service agent; and a Washington, D.C., police officer. Hinckley's motive for the shooting was to impress the actress Jodie Foster; he had been stalking her for years and was desperate to gain her attention. Reagan nearly died while at George Washington University Hospital and took several months to fully recover. Many close to Reagan claim the wound took a large toll physically on the seventy-year-old Reagan and may have exacerbated his physical and mental decline. In an interesting side note, Neil Bush, son of then–vice president George H. W. Bush, and Scott Hinckley, John Hinckley's older brother, were social acquaintances in Denver. They were supposed to have dinner together the evening that Reagan was shot.

6. ANDREW JACKSON, 1835

Andrew Jackson was the first president to have an assassination attempt on his life. A deranged man named Richard Lawrence fired two shots from a close distance at Jackson while he was leaving a funeral in the U.S. Capitol Building. Lawrence, an unemployed house painter, believed Jackson was conspiring to keep him out of work and ambushed the president as he exited the funeral. The first shot discharged the percussion cap only, and the bullet remained lodged in the pistol, at which point the startled Jackson instinctively began throttling his would-be assassin with his cane. Lawrence took out a second derringer gun, but it misfired as well, at which point onlookers took him down. Lawrence was found to be acting alone, though Jackson maintained his political enemies had encouraged Lawrence to attack. In an interesting postscript, some hundred years later the Smithsonian Institution purchased both derringers to find the cause of the misfires and successfully discharged bullets from both guns on the first try. It's estimated that the odds of both derringers malfunctioning in 1835 were 125,000 to 1.

7. THEODORE ROOSEVELT, 1912

Teddy Roosevelt may be the only president—or in this case ex-president, as he was shot while campaigning in 1912 for a third term on the Bull Moose ticket—to have his life spared by his own myopia and long-windedness. Roosevelt was campaigning in Milwaukee and was about to deliver a speech when an unemployed saloon keeper named John Shrank shot the former president in the chest. According to newspaper accounts, Shrank actually aimed for Roosevelt's head, but an alert bystander deflected Shrank's arm enough to divert the bullet. Luckily for Roosevelt, the bullet pierced his coat pocket, which contained his fifty-page speech (double folded) and a metal glasses case. Doctors believe the speech and glasses case slowed the bullet enough so that it only caused a superficial flesh wound. Amazingly, Roosevelt refused immediate medical attention and delivered most of the speech as planned before being taken to the hospital. He began the oratory by holding the speech's bloodied manuscript in his hand and saying, "It takes more than that to kill a Bull Moose."

8. GERALD FORD, 1975

President Gerald Ford was the target of two assassination attempts, both coming within three weeks of each other in September 1975. First, Lynette "Squeaky" Fromme, a follower of convicted killer Charles Manson's, pointed a loaded .45 pistol at Ford outside an event in Sacramento. Fortunately, alert Secret Service agents were able to wrestle the gun away before any shots were fired. Fromme was sentenced to life in prison, where she remains today. The second occurred later in the month, when Sara Jane Moore, a wife and mother of four who turned radical revolutionary, tried to shoot Ford outside the St. Francis Hotel in San Francisco. An alert bystander, Oliver Sipple, tackled Moore as she pulled the trigger, causing the bullet to miss the president by five feet. Like Fromme, Moore is also serving a life sentence, though she is up for parole in 2007.

9. HARRY S. TRUMAN, 1950

In the fall of 1950, two Puerto Rican nationalists from New York City traveled to Washington and attempted to ambush President Truman at the Blair House, where he resided while the White House was under renovation (1948–52). Griselio Torresola, an expert gunman, and Oscar Collazo wanted to kill Truman and bring attention to the cause of Puerto Rican independence. Their plan was to surround both entrances to Blair House and shoot their way inside. Within seconds of opening fire, White House police returned fire, and

Torresola died instantly from a shot to the head. Though the two assassins never made it inside the building, three police officers were wounded, and one died the following day. Collazo was sentenced to death, but Truman commuted his sentence to life in prison a week before his scheduled execution. In 1979, Jimmy Carter commuted his life sentence and sent him back to Puerto Rico, where he died in 1994 at the age of eighty. Following the incident, Congress passed legislation authorizing Secret Service protection for the president, the vice president, the president-elect, and vice president-elect, and their immediate families.

10. FRANKLIN D. ROOSEVELT, 1933

Just weeks before he was to be sworn into office, president-elect Franklin Roosevelt was nearly assassinated when a gunman opened fire outside his open-top car following a speech he had delivered in Miami. The gunman was a deranged immigrant named Giuseppe Zangara. Though Roosevelt was unharmed, five bystanders were injured, including Chicago mayor Anton Cermak, who was shot in the stomach. Zangara was quickly tried and convicted for attempted murder and sentenced to life in prison. Three weeks after the shooting, however, Mayor Cermak died, and Zangara was hastily retried for murder and sentenced to death. He was electrocuted five weeks after his attempt on Roosevelt's life.

Illness

Just like everyone else, presidents are susceptible to illness and disease. Four have died in office, and many others have concealed ailments from the public. Today, the president's health is as much a part of the public record as anything else.

1. WILLIAM HENRY HARRISON

Not only was William Henry Harrison the first president to die in office he also holds the distinction of serving the fewest days in office, a mere thirty days. Harrison's bad luck began on inauguration day, when, despite blistering cold weather, he decided to give his inaugural speech without an overcoat (mostly to prove that at sixty-eight years old, he was still virile and energetic). He then caught a cold, which quickly developed into pneumonia and then pleurisy. Doctors tried an assortment of treatments, but his condition only worsened. His last words were, "Sir, I wish you to understand the true principles of the government. I wish them carried out. I ask nothing more."

2. ZACHARY TAYLOR

The cause of Zachary Taylor's death may never be known. The twelfth president fell ill after attending a Fourth of July celebration that included laying the cornerstone for the Washington Monument. It was a scorching hot day in the nation's capital, and after returning to the White House he reportedly consumed large quantities of fruit, water, and milk and quickly took ill with violent stomach pains. He suffered from vomiting, diarrhea, and fever for almost a week before finally succumbing to his ailment. At first it was believed Taylor was done in by either cholera or typhoid fever, and some even thought food poisoning. Over the years a growing number of historians have suggested he was probably felled by complications from a heat stroke. As evidence, they point to the oppressive heat and humidity that day and the slurred speech and drowsiness he reportedly exhibited throughout the monument ceremony. His official cause of death was listed as multiple organ failure, which could have been brought on by a heat stroke. For years, conspiracy buffs contended Taylor was the victim of arsenic poisoning, but that theory was disproved in 1991 after an examination of his exhumed body indicated nothing unusual.

3. WARREN G. HARDING

Like Zachary Taylor, Warren Harding's official cause of death remains a mystery. In the summer of 1923, Harding embarked on a barnstorming tour of the western states, mostly to avoid the growing Teapot Dome scandal back in Washington. On his way back from Alaska, he took ill and came down with food poisoning while in Vancouver. When he later arrived in San Francisco, Harding was in a considerably weakened state (thought to be the aftereffects of food poisoning as well as pneumonia) and was confined to his hotel room. He died suddenly from what the White House described as "a stroke of apoplexy." Doctors were prohibited from performing an autopsy on the order of Harding's wife, which led some to speculate that foul play may have been involved—either a poisoning or maybe even suicide. The consensus today seems to be that, given his history of coronary disease, Harding most likely suffered a series of heart attacks, which led to his death.

4. GROVER CLEVELAND

Shortly after winning office for a second term (the only president to hold nonconsecutive terms), Grover Cleveland had a cancerous lesion removed from his mouth. Cleveland hid his condition from the press because he thought news of the cancer would rattle the already skittish financial markets; moreover, he had campaigned on repealing the controversial Sherman Silver Purchase Act—a law Vice President Adlai Stevenson favored—and feared the specter of a Stevenson presidency would plunge the economy into recession. The operation was performed on a private yacht, with the cover story being that the president was on a vacation cruise. Two physicians and a dentist removed a large portion of Cleveland's jaw and later replaced it with a vulcanized rubber prosthesis. The surgery only affected the inside of his mouth, and a month later Cleveland spoke in public without any trace of the procedure. Only weeks after the operation, the Philadelphia *Inquirer* reported that he had had a cancerous growth removed from his mouth, but the White House dismissed the story as a fabrication, stating that he merely had two infected teeth removed. The truth didn't come out until 1917, when one of the surgeons wrote an article about the operation.

5. WOODROW WILSON

In the fall of 1919 Woodrow Wilson suffered a massive stroke toward the end of his presidency and was an invalid for his remaining eighteen months in office. It occurred while on a grueling cross-country tour to sell his League of Nations plan to the American people. Save for his wife, physicians, and a few close advisers, including the secretary of state, Wilson's condition was kept secret. Even his own cabinet and the vice president had little knowledge of his condition's severity; the press and public were simply told that Wilson had suffered from a nervous breakdown. Except for a handful of occasions, Wilson remained sequestered in the White House's living quarters while his wife, Edith, essentially ran the administration, delegating assignments and acting as his surrogate at events. Wilson died shortly after leaving office, and it wasn't until years later that his true condition became public knowledge. Wilson's situation was one of the examples sited by proponents of the Twenty-fifth Amendment, specifically providing for presidential incapacity, during the ratification process.

6. FRANKLIN D. ROOSEVELT

In the history of the presidency, perhaps the best-kept medical secret was Franklin Roosevelt's disability stemming from polio. It's hard to imagine today, but Roosevelt's crippling disease was hidden from the public, even though the media was well aware that he could not walk under his own power. Roosevelt was rarely photographed while in his wheelchair, and it was seldom mentioned in press accounts of the day. A far more serious condition—advanced heart disease—was also kept from the public; even Roosevelt himself wasn't aware of his rapidly declining health as he sought an unprecedented fourth term. His physician and close advisers, however, knew that Roosevelt was in the late stages of heart disease and that he probably wouldn't live through a fourth term. In fact, some believe that's why Roosevelt's advisers convinced him to add Harry Truman to the ticket; they felt he was capable of stepping into the office should something happen to the sitting president. The stress of World

A rare photo of FDR in a wheelchair (with his dog, Fala, and the granddaughter of a friend). *Margaret Suckley, Franklin D. Roosevelt Presidential Library and Museum*

War II only worsened FDR's physical condition, which some historians feel had a deleterious impact on the Yalta Conference negotiations between the United States, Britain, and Russia. Roosevelt was the last president to die of natural causes while in office.

7. CHESTER ARTHUR

Chester A. Arthur succeeded Garfield after he was assassinated, and for his nearly three years in office, Arthur suffered from a rare kidney condition known as Bright's disease. Though it's a curable disease today, in the late nineteenth century there was no known treatment, and it often left victims in excruciating pain and a weakened state. Arthur wasn't diagnosed until a year in office, and he kept it secret from the press throughout his presidency. He nearly succumbed to complications from the disease while on a trip to Florida in 1883 and was noticeably weak and ill for the remainder of his presidency. Sensing that he was too ill to run for a second term, Arthur didn't really attempt to win the Republican nomination in 1884. He succumbed to the disease less than two years after leaving office, leaving him with the second-shortest postpresidential career after Franklin Pierce. Arthur's condition wasn't revealed to the public until 1911.

8. DWIGHT D. EISENHOWER

Dwight Eisenhower suffered a serious heat attack, a stroke, and an intestinal blockage, which required surgery, during his eight years in office. In breaking with past presidents, Eisenhower was unusually forthcoming with details of his maladies. His openness was especially bold given that the Cold War was in full bloom. Ike suffered his heart attack while visiting his in-laws in Denver in the fall of 1955. He remained hospitalized in an army medical center there for seven weeks while recuperating. Less than a year after the heart attack, Eisenhower suffered from a serious intestinal blockage and could have died were it not for surgical intervention. In the fall of 1957, Ike sustained a mild stroke, which left him struggling to speak at times. Of the three ailments, the stroke was the most debilitating, impacting his speech and stamina and, according to some, slightly impairing his mental acuity. Eisenhower was concerned enough about his deteriorating health that he made private arrangements—in the form of a letter—with Vice President Nixon to transfer authority should the president become too impaired to carry out his duties.

9. Lyndon Johnson

Lyndon Johnson is the only president in history to reveal a twelve-inch surgical scar during a live television interview. It happened just days after undergoing surgery to remove his gall bladder in the fall of 1965, and his gesture simultaneously amused and disgusted the American people. LBJ did it mostly to show the American public he was recuperating well and that the surgery wouldn't slow his ambitious legislative agenda. Johnson underwent a second procedure in 1967 to remove some cancerous cells from his ankle, though that operation was kept secret from the press and public. Johnson felt if word got out that he had skin cancer, it would create unnecessary panic and hysteria. His condition wasn't revealed until ten years later, when the *New York Times* broke the news. Since then, Presidents Reagan and Clinton, as well as Vice Presidents Gore and Cheney, have all had cancerous basal cells removed while in office.

10. John F. Kennedy

Throughout most of his life, John F. Kennedy suffered from an assortment of maladies. By one count, he was hospitalized more than three dozen times during his life and received last rites by a Catholic priest on three occasions. Since his early teenage years, he suffered from severe back pain. Twice in 1954 he underwent major back surgery, which left him wearing a back brace the remainder of his life. In 1947, he was diagnosed with Addison's disease, a condition brought on when the adrenal glands stop functioning. During the 1960 presidential campaign, Kennedy flatly denied he had Addison's disease, even though he was being treated for it with a cocktail of pills and medications, including steroids and cortisone. While he projected an image of youth and vitality, Kennedy spent most of his presidency in some form of pain, and at times he was heavily medicated.

Biggest Blunders

L ike all politicians, presidents are prone to making poor decisions. Sometimes these decisions are a result of blind ideology, sometimes it's a result of poor information, and sometimes the culprit is simply bad judgment. But these decisions have one thing in common, disastrous results for the United States.

The case can be made that the worst blunder in presidential history was James Buchanan's failure to avert civil war, but it would be unfair to saddle the blame on Buchanan alone. His lack of leadership on the issue certainly exacerbated the problem and virtually guaranteed war. Because of his inaction he ranks near the bottom of all the presidents, but it's doubtful that any one person could have prevented the war.

1. HERBERT HOOVER'S RESPONSE TO THE STOCK MARKET CRASH, 1929–32

While the underlying conditions for the Great Depression preceded Hoover's administration and it wasn't the first depression to hit the United States, his policy decisions certainly aggravated and deepened the financial crisis. It began shortly after the stock market crash in the fall of 1929, though the conditions for a depression were in place well before that. At first President Hoover's reaction to the stock market crash and ensuing financial downturn was to let the markets resolve the problem without government intervention; in other words, he took the laissez-faire approach. When the situation failed to improve, in the summer of 1930 the Republicans in Congress and Hoover passed the Smoot-Hawley Tariff Act, which imposed a 60 percent tariff (quadrupling previous tariff rates) on more than three thousand imported goods. Not surprising, most U.S. trade partners adopted similar protectionist policies, bringing global commerce to a screeching halt. At the time Smoot-Hawley was signed into law, unemployment was at 9 percent; the following year it jumped to 15 percent, and by 1932 a quarter of all Americans were out of work. To make matters worse, Hoover was a strict adherent to balanced budgets and refused to infuse the economy with new spending projects. In fact, he raised taxes sharply in 1932 to narrow a budget gap, plunging the economy further into depression. It wasn't until 1954 that the stock market reached its pre-crash levels.

2. GEORGE W. BUSH'S INVASION OF IRAQ, 2003

It's hard not to consider the invasion of Iraq anything but a colossal failure and a historic blunder. President Bush made the case for invading Iraq based on intelligence that Iraq had weapons of mass destruction, but none were found. He then declared an end to major operations just months after the invasion (in a dramatic photo opportunity [photo op] on a U.S. aircraft carrier, no less), only to watch insurgents retake large parts of the country. What was thought to be a quick victory has lasted longer than World War II and has been five times more expensive. By 2007, innocent civilians were killed by the dozens every day, as the country sank into civil war. Voters repudiated Bush's policies by voting the Republicans out of power in the 2006 midterm elections, and his approval rating now stands at an all-time low. It's too early to determine what the precise impact the invasion of Iraq will have on the war on terror, but few believe it has been positive.

3. Lyndon Johnson's Tonkin Gulf Resolution, 1964

With forty years as hindsight, there's little doubt Lyndon Johnson greatly exaggerated the Tonkin Gulf incident in order to receive congressional approval to escalate the war in Vietnam; without it, it's unlikely the full-blown Vietnam War could have taken place. The incident began on August 2, 1964, when the destroyer U.S.S. *Maddox* was attacked by three Vietnamese gunboats while in international waters off Vietnam's coast. Though the ship sustained no damage, the Johnson administration alleged that the attack was unprovoked (in fact the *Maddox* was on a reconnaissance mission and was looking to provoke North Vietnamese retaliation). Two days later, an alleged second attack took place against the *Maddox,* prompting Lyndon Johnson to give a nationally televised speech in which he informed Americans that he had authorized air strikes against North Vietnam. (It turned out no such second attack ever occurred. As LBJ himself said a year later, "For all I know, our Navy was shooting at whales out there.") On August 7, based on Johnson's speech and Defense Secretary Robert McNamara's insistence that a second attack had occurred, the Senate easily passed a resolution giving the president the power to "take all necessary measures to repel any armed attack against the forces of the United States and to prevent further aggression." The Gulf of Tonkin Resolution became the legal basis for the Vietnam War, and both Johnson and Nixon repeatedly cited it for various actions in the years to come. In 2005, a report from a National Security Agency (NSA) historian concluded that the August 4 incident was fabricated.

Later that year McNamara admitted the same, noting the intelligence fabrications were decisive in escalating the war.

4. ANDREW JOHNSON'S APPROACH TO RECONSTRUCTION, 1865

Abraham Lincoln selected Tennessee senator Andrew Johnson as his running mate in 1864 because the Southern legislator had been an outspoken critic of the Confederacy; at one point he even spoke publicly about hanging Confederate president Jefferson Davis. But on taking office after Lincoln's assassination, Johnson retreated from his hard line. To the dismay of Republicans in Congress who supported civil rights for the freed slaves and drastic reforms for the readmitted states, Johnson's vision for Reconstruction was much more lenient on the South. Within a month of taking office, he pardoned most Confederate leaders, restored property to the rebels, and allowed the Confederate states to write their own constitutions and select members to Congress. In 1866, Congress passed the Freedmen's Bureau Bill, which provided land to the freed slaves and schools for their children and established a military court system in the old Confederacy to protect the newly freed slaves from abuses. To the country's shock and dismay, Johnson vetoed the bill. The following month he also vetoed the Civil Rights Act, which would have made ex-slaves citizens and allowed them to own property. Congress overrode Johnson's veto—the first time in history Congress overrode a presidential veto—and soon thereafter impeached him for illegally firing Secretary of War Edwin Stanton. Though he survived the impeachment by a single vote, his presidency was effectively over.

5. GEORGE H. W. BUSH'S END TO THE FIRST GULF WAR, 1991

While President George H. W. Bush gets high marks for building the coalition that led to Saddam Hussein's ouster from

Kuwait, Bush must also take some of the blame for deciding not to go to Baghdad and topple Hussein's regime once and for all. Bush brilliantly rallied the world against Hussein, working through the United Nations to impose sanctions and even convincing Democrats in Congress to authorize the use of force; the resolution passed by a razor-thin margin. When the air strikes began on January 17, 1991, planners generally believed it would takes months to "soften up" the Iraqis' stranglehold on Kuwait (they had the fourth-largest army in the world at the time) before coalition ground forces could proceed. A little more than a month later, the ground war began, and allied forces took only a hundred hours to liberate Kuwait. Coalition forces reached 150 miles south of Baghdad before President Bush ordered a cease-fire and halted all military operations. At the time, there was debate within the administration as to whether Hussein's regime should be toppled. President Bush decided against it, stating that it would have fractured the coalition and forced a long-term commitment of U.S. troops for the purpose of nation building. A decade later, his son would confront that exact reality but with disastrous results.

6. JOHN F. KENNEDY'S BAY OF PIGS, 1961
Only months into his presidency, John F. Kennedy suffered one of the most embarrassing military debacles in U.S. history with the failed invasion of Cuba at the Bay of Pigs. The plan was actually formulated during the Eisenhower administration after Fidel Castro overthrew the pro-U.S. government and gained control of the island country. The Cuban exiles were trained in Miami by the CIA and equipped by the government, and on April 17 U.S. vessels transported them to the Bay of Pigs, where they were hoping to be greeted as liberators. President Kennedy declined to provide air support, however, and Castro's army easily defeated

the exiles, killing almost a hundred and capturing the rest in a matter of days. The incident embarrassed Kennedy, who fired CIA director Allen Dulles, and made Castro even more popular with the Cuban people.

7. FRANKLIN D. ROOSEVELT'S COURT-PACKING SCHEME, 1937

Shortly after winning a second term in a landslide, Franklin Roosevelt committed his biggest political blunder when he announced a plan to "reorganize" the federal judiciary. Frustrated that the Supreme Court had declared unconstitutional several New Deal programs—including the National Industrial Recovery Act, the Railroad Retirement Act, and the Agricultural Adjustment Act—Roosevelt wanted to shift the balance of power to more progressive justices by "packing" the court with six new members. Officially, his plan called for a voluntary retirement age of seventy years with the proviso that any justice who remained on the court beyond seventy years and six months of age would be "paired" with a new justice. Roosevelt assumed the heavily Democratic Congress would follow along, but he had miscalculated the level of opposition he would face. Both Democrats and Republicans sharply criticized his plan. The Senate Judiciary Committee, controlled by Democrats, issued a scathing report on the plan, stating that FDR's proposal was "needless, futile, and an utterly dangerous abandonment of constitutional principles." The Senate easily defeated the Judiciary Reorganization Bill, and Roosevelt wasted much political capital with conservative Democrats in the process.

8. JIMMY CARTER'S "MALAISE" SPEECH, 1979

On July 15, 1979, Jimmy Carter gave what he described as the most important speech of his presidency to a prime-time television audience, an address that would forever be known as his "malaise speech," even though he never used

the word in his text. The late 1970s were a difficult time for
the country, with high unemployment, out-of-control interest rates and inflation, and gasoline rationing. Carter decided to take matters into hand with a speech that he hoped
would rally the American people, but instead it had the opposite effect. He put forward a six-point energy plan and
then told the American people that the biggest threat to the
country was their lack of confidence:

> The threat is nearly invisible in ordinary ways. It is a
> crisis of confidence. It is a crisis that strikes at the
> very heart and soul and spirit of our national will. We
> can see this crisis in the growing doubt about the
> meaning of our own lives and in the loss of unity and
> purpose for our Nation. The erosion of our confidence
> in the future is threatening to destroy the social and
> the political fabric of America.

The speech did little to rally the American public, and only
a few weeks later Carter fired five cabinet members, including his secretary of energy. A year later, Carter's gloomy
pessimism gave way to Reagan's cheery optimism.

q. BILL CLINTON'S UNIVERSAL HEALTH CARE, 1993

During the 1992 campaign, one of President Clinton's key
campaign promises was delivering universal health coverage for all Americans. Upon winning office, he put First Lady
Hillary Clinton in charge of a task force to create a plan for
universal coverage. In the fall of 1993 the group submitted
to Congress a thousand-page report that became known as
"Hillary-care," but the complicated set of proposals con-
fused most Americans and even some in Congress. Democrats in Congress attempted to make it work; however, they
ultimately buried the legislation after Republicans had

rallied the country against it. Newt Gingrich used "Hillary-care" as one of the campaign themes for the successful midterm elections, which saw the Republicans capture the House and Senate for the first time in forty-two years.

10. WOODROW WILSON'S LEAGUE OF NATIONS, 1919

Woodrow Wilson suffered one of the most famous defeats in presidential history when the Republican-controlled Senate rejected the Versailles Treaty and its provision for a League of Nations, which Wilson had created. It was a devastating blow to Wilson's presidency, as well as to the league itself, which stood little chance of survival without U.S. backing. The Senate rejected both the treaty and the league for many reasons; foremost among them was Wilson's refusal to include the Senate in the peace-making process or to modify a few of the treaty's more controversial provisions. Wilson's intransigence, coupled with the Senate's misgivings about the league usurping its ability to declare war, doomed the treaty. Though the League of Nations was still created, the United States did not participate, and it was ineffective in preventing wars in the 1920s and did nothing to thwart Adolf Hitler's rise to power. Ironically, even though Wilson failed to gain Senate approval for the Treaty of Versailles, he still won the Nobel Peace Prize for "creating" the League of Nations.

Feuds and Rivalries

Like all politicians, presidents are prone to feuds and rivalries. In fact, some of the most interesting political feuds have been between former presidents and even between presidents and their vice presidents.

1. THEODORE ROOSEVELT AND WILLIAM TAFT

Few presidents were as politically and personally close as William Howard Taft and Theodore Roosevelt, but their relationship soured into a bitter political feud that wound up splitting the Republican Party and handing the White House to Democrat Woodrow Wilson. Taft was Roosevelt's hand-picked successor, and he only accepted the Republican nomination in 1908 at Roosevelt's insistence. At the time, he was Roosevelt's secretary of war (and acting secretary of state), and his true ambition was to be the chief justice of the Supreme Court. Assuming Taft would build on his progressive legacy, Roosevelt became disillusioned when Taft ignored his campaign promise to reduce protective tariffs (Roosevelt was adamantly against tariffs) or failed to speak out against corporate monopolies. The final straw came when Taft fired Gifford Pinchot—a popular conservationist, head of the Forestry Division, and Roosevelt's close friend—because Pinchot refused to allow corporate developers access to public wilderness lands in Alaska and Colorado. Enraged, Roosevelt ultimately emerged from retirement and opposed Taft for the Republican nomination in 1912. When he came up a few votes short, Roosevelt decided to run a third-party candidacy and finished second ahead of Taft but still well behind Wilson. The two men reconciled, however, several years before Roosevelt's death.

2. JAMES A. GARFIELD AND CHESTER ARTHUR

Without question, the oddest presidential ticket in history was the pairing of James Garfield and Chester Arthur. Garfield and Arthur were from opposite ends of the Republican Party—Arthur was from the "Stalwart" wing, and Garfield was part of the liberal faction called the "Half-Breeds." Garfield was a dark-horse candidate for the Republican nomination in 1880 and finally won on the thirty-sixth ballot, but only after he cut a deal with his nemesis, New York senator Roscoe Conkling, to put a Stalwart on the ticket. The former tax collector for the port of New York, Arthur hardly qualified to serve as vice president, and he cared little for Garfield or his policies. As vice president, Arthur spent most of his time working *against* Garfield to defeat his nominees in the Senate, and things got so bad that Garfield banned Arthur from the White House. In a strange irony, it was an Arthur supporter—a madman named Charles Guiteau—who fatally shot Garfield and screamed at the top of his lungs, "I am a Stalwart of the Stalwarts!"

3. ANDREW JOHNSON AND ULYSSES S. GRANT

Ulysses S. Grant was the commander in chief of the armed forces when Andrew Johnson was sworn in as president following Lincoln's assassination. From the beginning, the relationship between Johnson and Grant was strained. Neither man liked the other, but each knew his political

fortunes, to some extent, rested with the other. The relationship soured, however, as Johnson began implementing
lenient policies regarding the Confederacy's reintegration,
and it only worsened after his veto of the Freedman Act
(which would have given freed slaves land). But it wasn't
until the Edward Stanton firing that they publicly feuded.
Johnson fired Secretary of War Stanton, seemingly in viola-
tion of the Tenure in Office Act, because Stanton disagreed
with his Reconstruction plan. Johnson replaced him with
Grant in the hopes that appointing the country's most popular
man would quell any outrage from the radical Republicans
in Congress who supported Stanton. Congress thought otherwise and ordered Stanton's reinstatement as secretary of
war. When Johnson asked Grant not to vacate his office,
Grant sided with Congress—not the president—and resigned,
stating that Stanton's removal was illegal and inappropri-
ate. Congress subsequently impeached Johnson, who narrowly avoided conviction by one vote. By refusing to side
with Johnson, Grant became a hero to the Republicans in
Congress and easily captured their presidential nomination
and ultimately the presidency.

4. ANDREW JACKSON AND JOHN C. CALHOUN

One of the strangest political feuds was between Andrew
Jackson and his vice president, John C. Calhoun. Never
close allies, Calhoun only accepted the vice presidency because he thought Jackson's frail health would give out during the term, making him president. The relationship turned
downright hostile after Jackson signed the Tariff of 1828,
which Calhoun opposed because he thought it unfairly im-
pacted the South. In response, Calhoun developed the "nullification" doctrine, which essentially held that states have
the right to nullify (or disregard) any federal law they deem
to be unconstitutional. Jackson wholeheartedly disagreed

with this view and excluded Calhoun from all cabinet meetings and deliberations. The relationship became so strained that Calhoun ultimately resigned his office—one of only two people to resign the vice presidency voluntarily—and returned to the Senate, where he helped lead South Carolina toward secession from the union.

5. JOHN QUINCY ADAMS AND ANDREW JACKSON

An intense dislike (some would say hatred) developed between the two men following the election of 1824, when the House of Representatives chose Adams as president even though Jackson received the most votes. Jackson and his supporters believed that the House selected Adams because he cut a deal with Speaker of the House Henry Clay in return for making Clay the secretary of state. The charges were never proven, but it rallied Jackson and his supporters, who easily defeated Adams in the following election. The rift between the two presidents actually caused a splinter in the one national party of the Democratic Republicans and essentially led to the emergence of the two modern-day parties: Jackson's faction became known as "Democrats," while Adams's followers eventually became knows as "Whigs" and later as "Republicans." After losing the White House, Adams returned to the House of Representatives, where he often played protagonist to Jackson and his policies.

6. HARRY S. TRUMAN AND DWIGHT D. EISENHOWER

Unlike some of the other rivalries on this list, the feud between Harry Truman and Dwight Eisenhower was strictly personal. It began when Truman tried to recruit Eisenhower to run for office as a Democrat, and the former supreme Allied commander politely turned him down. Though Eisenhower then ran against Democrat Adlai Stevenson in 1952, Ike's campaign mostly served as a referendum against the Truman administration. Eisenhower, like other Republican office seekers, made the issues of corruption and communism the primary focus and pointed out that the Truman administration was weak on both. What really infuriated Truman, however, was Eisenhower's indifference to the attacks against Ike's mentor (and Truman's secretary of state) George Marshall, who right-wing Republicans, such as Senator Joe McCarthy, had labeled a "traitor" for supposedly being soft on communism. Truman believed Ike owed his career to Marshall and found it unconscionable that Ike allowed right-wingers to portray Marshall as a traitor. Things got so testy that on inauguration day, Eisenhower bucked tradition and refused to meet Truman inside the White House prior to their limo ride to the Capitol.

7. JOHN F. KENNEDY AND RICHARD NIXON

Television pundit and author Chris Matthews contends the rivalry between Kennedy and Nixon actually shaped postwar America. While it's difficult to define the exact impact of their rivalry, it's less difficult to pinpoint its origins—the 1960 election. Prior to the 1960 campaign, the two were actually somewhat friendly. In fact, they had been traveling companions in the late 1940s during a series of national debates and once had Senate offices across from each other while Kennedy served in that chamber and Nixon was vice president. The 1960 campaign, however, erased any good feelings and left Nixon feeling particularly bitter given the rampant speculation that Kennedy had "stolen" the election with the help of Chicago mayor Richard Daley. Matthews and other Nixon biographers posit Nixon became somewhat obsessed with the Kennedy family, and the Watergate break-in was motivated, in part, by Nixon's desire to "get dirt" on Senator Ted Kennedy (for fear that he would challenge him in 1972). Of course, the Chappaquiddick accident ended

Teddy's presidential ambitions while Watergate ended Nixon's presidency.

8. JOHN F. KENNEDY AND LYNDON JOHNSON

While the feud with Nixon may have been more real to Nixon than to Kennedy, Kennedy's rivalry with LBJ was certainly a two-way street. They served together in the Senate—LBJ was the powerful majority leader; Kennedy, the mostly absentee backbencher—and shared presidential ambitions. While Kennedy decided the best route to the nomination was by winning primaries, LBJ decided to skip the process altogether, hoping for a divided convention where he could emerge as the compromise candidate. Kennedy won the nomination outright, however, and to assuage Johnson's wing of the party, he offered the vice presidency to LBJ with the belief that he would turn it down. When Johnson accepted, Kennedy dispatched his brother Bobby to talk him out of accepting and in the process worsened the already strained relationship. Once he took office, Johnson had a limited role, and Kennedy kept him out of the loop on the most pressing matters. For someone who had been a power broker his entire life, it was a bitter pill for Johnson to swallow. After JFK's death, the rivalry picked up with Bobby Kennedy—Kennedy wasn't welcome in LBJ's White House, and for his part Kennedy was an outspoken critic of LBJ's war in Vietnam.

9. THOMAS JEFFERSON AND JOHN ADAMS

The second and third presidents had a stormy relationship throughout their lives. At times close friends and at times bitter enemies, they went years without talking to one another until a mutual friend reunited them. Adams and Jefferson actually ran against each other in 1796. Adams won, and through an oddity in the electoral system that has since been amended, Jefferson became his vice president. Jefferson again opposed Adams in 1800 and this time easily defeated him, sending Adams into retirement. Before leaving office, however, Adams made some last-minute judicial appointments (dubbed the "midnight appointments"), several of whom Jefferson considered to be arch enemies. Jefferson felt Adams betrayed him and refused to speak to him for almost a decade. They resumed their correspondences after Jefferson left office and remained pen pals until their deaths, which took place on the same day, July 4, 1826, fifty years after the adoption of the Declaration of Independence. Adams's last words were, "Jefferson survives me."

10. BILL CLINTON AND AL GORE

For most of their two terms in office, Vice President Gore was Bill Clinton's closest policy adviser (perhaps with the exception of Clinton's wife, Hillary) and most trusted confidant. Clinton's affair with Monica Lewinsky, however, changed everything. It is rumored that during the final months of Clinton's presidency the two weren't on speaking terms, and neither were their spouses. When seeking the presidency for the 2000 election, Gore tried to distance himself from Clinton's moral shortcomings, going so far as calling his affair "inexcusable and shameful." Clinton, for his part, ignored his sexual foibles and blamed Gore's failure to win the White House on the veep's unwillingness to campaign on Clinton's record.

Scandal

Virtually every administration has been confronted with scandals of some kind. Staff and other officials have brought most of them about, but in a few instances the instigator was the commander in chief himself.

1. WATERGATE, NIXON ADMINISTRATION, 1972–74

Watergate remains the only scandal to result in the resignation of a president—Richard M. Nixon. The name "Watergate" usually refers to the actual break-in at the Democratic National Committee offices and its subsequent cover-up, but the Watergate scandal actually encompassed a broader range of criminal activity in the Nixon White House, including other break-ins, illegal campaign contributions, and scores of political "dirty tricks." However, while the initial break-in occurred in June 1972 (a full six months before the presidential election), it didn't have any impact on Nixon's re-election; he trounced Senator George McGovern in one of the biggest landslides in history. The Watergate crimes may not have been completely revealed were it not for the work of reporters, particularly Bob Woodward and Carl Bernstein of the *Washington Post*, whose persistent reporting helped reveal the full nature of the criminal activity and subsequent cover-up. Their reporting eventually led to a Senate investigation and impeachment hearings. Nixon would certainly have been convicted had he not resigned on August 9, 1974. Dozens of officials and campaign workers were implicated, and several aides close to the president—including White House chief of staff H. R. "Bob" Haldeman, senior adviser John Ehrlichman, and Attorney General John Mitchell—were ultimately convicted for hindering the investigation. Richard Nixon was an unindicted co-conspirator in these trials and could have faced a criminal prosecution had President Gerald Ford not pardoned him in September 1974. In Watergate's aftermath, the Democrats picked up over forty seats in the House of Representatives, and pardoning Nixon may have cost Gerald Ford the 1976 election. The scandal also led to dozens of "good government" reforms, including campaign finance reforms, and helped spawn a generation of investigative journalists.

2. CRÉDIT MOBILIER AND THE WHISKEY RING, GRANT ADMINISTRATION, 1872 AND 1875

With the exception perhaps of Richard Nixon, Ulysses S. Grant presided over the most corrupt administration in U.S. history, for his time in office was marked by the two biggest financial scandals involving administration officials. The bigger of the two was the "Whiskey Ring," a complex tax-avoidance scheme that involved hundreds of lawmakers, whiskey distillers and distributors, and government officials. Working in secret and without the president's and attorney general's knowledge, Secretary of the Treasury Benjamin Bristow uncovered the tax-avoidance ring and forced Grant to appoint a special prosecutor to oversee the criminal prosecutions. In the end, more than three hundred people were indicted—including President Grant's private secretary, Gen. Orville Babcock, and the chief clerk in the Treasury Department—and a hundred were convicted. It

remains the broadest sweeping government criminal conspiracy of its kind.

The Crédit Mobilier scandal centered on a shell corporation created by Union Pacific Railroad called Crédit Mobilier
of America. The purpose of the company was to obtain lu-
crative government contracts, including five hundred miles
of the Transcontinental Railroad, through bribing high-ranking government officials with shares of stock. The *New York
Sun* newspaper, which opposed Grant's reelection, broke
the story after receiving incriminating letters from an involved party. Thirteen members of Congress were investigated, and two were censured. Those implicated (though
never indicted or formally reprimanded) included Grant's
vice president, Schuyler Colfax, as well as future president
James Garfield and several prominent senators.

3. SPIRO AGNEW'S RESIGNATION, NIXON ADMINISTRATION, 1973

Richard Nixon wasn't the only crook in his administration.
His vice president, Spiro T. Agnew, remains the only vice
president to be forced from office. Agnew resigned after
pleading nolo contendere (no contest) to charges of tax
evasion and money laundering stemming from his term as
governor of Maryland. As part of a negotiated plea deal, he
received three years' probation and was fined $10,000. He
was later disbarred by the state of Maryland and ordered to
pay $300,000 in restitution to the state. Agnew's resigna-
tion came as the Watergate scandal began to engulf the Nixon
administration, and for a short while it seemed to divert attention from Nixon. After leaving office, Agnew wrote his
memoir, which he titled *Go Quietly ... Or Else* (a threat Al
Haig made to him, or so he claimed). In the book, Agnew
implied officials inside the Nixon White House had leaked
details of the bribery charges against him to draw attention

away from the Watergate investigation. Agnew never spoke to Nixon after leaving office.

4. IRAN-CONTRA SCANDAL, REAGAN ADMINISTRATION, 1985–87

The Iran-Contra scandal was a two-headed scandal that rocked the Reagan administration and essentially turned President Reagan into a lame-duck president. The first part involved arms sold to Iran in exchange for U.S. hostages held by pro-Iranian groups in Lebanon. The approximately $12 million in profits from the illegal arm sales were then used to fund right-wing Nicaraguan insurgents, known as Contras, who were trying to topple the democratically elected Socialist government. The administration had to use non-government funds to support the Contras because the U.S. Congress had passed a law banning any assistance to the rebels. The operation's two primary organizers, Marine Lt. Col. Oliver North and National Security Adviser John Poindexter, were later convicted on several charges, but both had their convictions overturned on appeal. Defense Secretary Caspar Weinberger was indicted for lying to the independent counsel, but President George H. W. Bush pardoned him in his administration's final days. Questions arose as to how much then–vice president Bush knew about the arms sales and money transfers, and some thought the scandal would hurt his chances in the 1988 election; however, Bush sidestepped potential pitfalls by steadfastly denying any knowledge of the actions.

5. TEAPOT DOME SCANDAL, HARDING ADMINISTRATION, 1922

The Teapot Dome scandal resulted in the first presidential cabinet member to go to prison for actions taken while in office. At the center of the scandal was President Harding's secretary of the interior, Albert Fall, who in 1922 awarded Mammoth Oil and Pan American Petroleum leases to oil reserves on federal property, including a field in Wyoming known as Teapot Dome, in exchange for interest-free loans and other gifts. While the no-bid leases were structured in accordance with the General Leasing Act of 1920, the gifts and bribes were clearly illegal, and Fall raised suspicions when he suddenly adopted a lavish lifestyle after taking office. The *Wall Street Journal* broke the story, which prompted a two-year Senate investigation. Fall proved to be a skillful politician and nearly covered his tracks except for one check that he had received for $100,000 in 1921. The evidence ultimately led to his bribery conviction and that of several oil executives. While President Harding died before the Senate investigation uncovered Fall's criminal behavior, the scandal posthumously tainted him and his administration. Along with Nixon and Grant, he's mostly remembered as presiding over one of the most corrupt administrations in history.

6. LEWINSKY AFFAIR, CLINTON ADMINISTRATION, 1995–98

President Clinton's affair with intern Monica Lewinsky remains the "signature" scandal for an administration rife with scandals. The affair would never have come to light were it not for the Paula Jones sexual harassment lawsuit, which stemmed from an incident while Clinton was governor of Arkansas. Clinton repeatedly denied the affair until he was forced to admit it while testifying to Independent Counsel Ken Starr. The admission, along with charges of perjury and suborning perjury, served as the basis for Clinton's impeachment, for which the U.S. Senate easily acquitted him. Clinton remains only the second president to be impeached; Andrew Johnson was also acquitted, though by a single vote. During his eight years in office, President Clinton's administration faced nearly a dozen scandals, including "Travelgate," Whitewater, the Lincoln bedroom fund-raisers, the

Rose Law Firm's missing files, the Buddhist temple fund-raisers, and so on. Even Clinton's last day in office was marred by "Pardon-gate" for his controversial pardon of fugitive financier Marc Rich.

7. THE XYZ AFFAIR, ADAMS ADMINISTRATION, 1797

As presidential scandals go, the XYZ Affair rates among the tamest of the lot, though it was the first incident of its kind to hit the young country. It concerned a diplomatic stalemate between the United States and France after France seized three hundred U.S. ships in protest over the Anglo-American alliance (or so they believed) that resulted from the Jay Treaty of 1795. President Adams sent three emissaries to France to negotiate the ships' return, but the French government refused to enter into talks without first receiving a $250,000 bribe and a $10 million loan. Insulted by the demands, the U.S. contingent withdrew from the talks and returned to the United States, and President Adams released to the public the terms of the negotiation, setting off a wave of anti-French sentiment. An undeclared war ensued for the next two years, with U.S. and French merchant ships doing battle in the Caribbean and off the coast of the United States. The hostilities ended in 1800 with the Treaty of Mortefontaine.

8. EATON AFFAIR, JACKSON ADMINISTRATION, 1831

The Eaton Affair was the first major sex scandal for the young republic and toppled an entire administration *except* for the president. It centered around a young Washington socialite, Peggy Eaton, and her affair with Secretary of War John Eaton, whom she married shortly after her first husband passed away (while on an overseas assignment arranged by John Eaton, no less). Jackson's cabinet members, save Secretary of State Martin Van Buren, demanded that Eaton be removed from office for the illicit affair, and when the president refused to fire his good friend, the cabinet—including Vice President James Calhoun—resigned in protest. The scandal and ensuing resignations had little impact on Jackson politically, however, and he rewarded Van Buren's loyalty by making him vice president. Van Buren would go on to succeed Jackson as president.

9. CIA LEAK, G. W. BUSH ADMINISTRATION, 2003

The CIA leak scandal resulted from journalist Robert Novak "outing" CIA operative Valerie Plame Wilson as an agent in his newspaper column as part of a Republican retaliation plan against her husband, Joe Wilson, who had been critical of the White House for exaggerating evidence of Sudan's weapons programs. Novak pegged her as the reason her husband, Joe Wilson, went on a fact-finding mission to Niger and checked on Iraq's reported plans for obtaining uranium ore. Novak cited "two government officials" as his source for Plame's identity and cover. The uproar over his column led to the naming of a special prosecutor to investigate the leak and to determine if any crimes had been committed in revealing her classified identity. The special prosecutor identified several high-ranking White House officials as the leakers, including then–deputy chief of staff Karl Rove and Vice President Cheney's former chief of staff, Lewis "Scooter" Libby. Libby was indicted for obstruction of justice, perjury, and providing false statements in the case.

10. SHERMAN ADAMS'S RESIGNATION, EISENHOWER ADMINISTRATION, 1958

Arguably the lamest scandal to broadside a White House, Eisenhower's chief of staff and closest political adviser was forced from his post after it was revealed he had accepted a fur coat and an oriental rug from an old friend who happened to be under investigation by the Federal Trade Commission. While the value of the gifts was only a few thousand dollars and Adams steadfastly denied he had done his friend any favors, the weight of the accusations ultimately forced his departure. In accepting his resignation, President Eisenhower wrote to him, "I deeply deplore the circumstances that have decided you to resign as the Assistant to the President. Your selfless and tireless devotion to the work of the White House and to me personally has been universally recognized."

Embarrassing Moments

Every politician suffers through an embarrassing moment or two during his or her political career. For presidents, however, those moments usually become front-page news and, in some cases, can define their presidency.

1. G. H. W. BUSH VOMITS ON JAPANESE PRIME MINISTER

Few who saw it happen on video can forget the image of George H. W. Bush vomiting on Japanese prime minister Kiichi Miyazawa's lap at a state dinner in January 1992. The picture was transmitted around the world, and for a brief while, there was concern that it was symptomatic of a serious health issue for President Bush. (Months earlier he had been diagnosed with Graves' disease, a thyroid condition.) The incident turned out to be a simple case of the flu, something President Bush claimed he had never had before, and he made light of it in a subsequent press conference. The Japanese actually coined a verb after the incident, *bushu-suru,* which means to "commit an instance of embarrassing public vomiting." The "Bushu-suru" film is one of the most popular videos on YouTube.

2. QUAYLE MISSPELLS POTATO(E)

From the moment Senator Dan Quayle stepped on the

national stage at the 1988 Republican National Convention, the national press branded him a political lightweight for his lack of requisite experience and his "deer-in-the-headlights" expression. Fairly or unfairly, he was tagged as a minor "dim-wit," and the caricature stuck with him throughout his term in office. Playing to stereotype, Quayle made one of the biggest gaffes in political history when he mistakenly changed a student's correct spelling of the word *potato* to *potatoe* at a spelling bee contest in New Jersey. The incident was caught on camera, and within twenty-four hours Quayle was the butt of jokes all over the world. To this day, it's one of the few things anyone remembers about former Vice President Quayle.

3. REAGAN OUTLAWS THE SOVIET UNION
Having been around cameras and the media most of his life, President Ronald Reagan should have been the last person to horse around in front of an open microphone. But on August 11, 1984, while preparing to deliver his weekly radio address, he said in a microphone check, "My fellow Americans, I am pleased to tell you I just signed legislation which outlaws Russia forever. The bombing begins in five minutes." The statement didn't make it on the air, but someone leaked the audio. Soviet leaders were not amused. Reagan's supporters delighted at the comment while his detractors pointed to it as evidence that Reagan was unstable and irresponsible. Some pundits contend Reagan purposefully made the comments, knowing full well they would send a message to the Soviet Union while allowing him to laugh it off as a mistake.

4. G. W. BUSH CALLS *NEW YORK TIMES* REPORTER "A MAJOR LEAGUE A-HOLE"
During the 2000 election while at a Labor Day campaign

event in Naperville, Illinois, candidate George W. Bush leaned into running mate Dick Cheney and said, "There's Adam Clymer, major league asshole from the *New York Times*." Cheney responded, "Yeah, he is, big time." Only problem was that he said it in front of an open microphone, and the audio was picked up by the various news organizations covering the event. The Gore campaign pounced on the gaffe, pointing out Bush had already broken his promise to "change the tone" in Washington; the remark dominated the news cycle for several days. For his part, Bush never apologized directly for the remark and stated only that he regretted his private conversation had become public. The following year he made light of it at the White House Correspondents' Dinner, and he referred to Clymer as a "major league ass . . . et."

5. CARTER IS ATTACKED BY A KILLER RABBIT

Teddy Roosevelt hunted wild game in Africa and survived an assassin's bullet. Dwight Eisenhower served with distinction in both world wars. John F. Kennedy and George H. W. Bush barely escaped death during World War II. And Jimmy Carter was once attacked by a rabbit. As improbable as it sounds, while fishing in a swamp in Plains, Georgia, Carter had to use a paddle to ward off a "menacing, hissing" swamp rabbit that attempted to board his presidential boat. Carter recited the harrowing tale to a couple of his staffers, one of whom then inadvertently leaked it to an Associated Press reporter. The story quickly made front-page news, and for several days Carter was asked mostly about his close call with the "killer" rabbit. The incident seemed to affirm the feeling that the Carter administration was simply snakebit (or in this case, bunny-bit). Bunny-gate was captured on film by the Secret Service, and the following year the Reagan administration leaked the photos to the press.

Jimmy Carter tries to stop a "menacing, hissing" rabbit from boarding his boat in Plains, Georgia. *Jimmy Carter Library*

6. FORD STUMBLES (AND STUMBLES AND STUMBLES)

Though he was unquestionably the most athletic president of the twentieth century and certainly the only one to start on consecutive undefeated college football teams (while at the University of Michigan), Gerald Ford somehow developed the reputation for being clumsy and oafish. A combination of accidents that were caught on film—Ford hitting a golf ball into spectators at the Bob Hope Desert Classic golf tournament, hitting his tennis partner in doubles with the ball, tripping down stairs—that contributed to his clumsy image. His biggest stumble (physically, not politically) occurred as he was exiting Air Force One upon arrival in Austria for a state visit. Ford slipped and fell down the plane's staircase in full view of photographers and news crews, and the image made headlines around the world. Ford's image

as a klutz was cemented when comedians on the NBC television show, *Saturday Night Live*, began ruthlessly parody-
ing his missteps and stumbles in their skits.

7. CARTER SOLICITS DAUGHTER AMY FOR ADVICE

It's hard to believe now because Ronald Regan won the 1980
election in a landslide, but two weeks before election day
and headed into the only debate of the campaign, President
Carter held a slight edge over Ronald Reagan in the polls.
Thus Reagan, not Carter, desperately needed the debate to
change the campaign's dynamics. The 1980 debate is considered one of the most memorable in history for three reasons: first, Regan showed the nation he could remain calm
under intense pressure, using the line "there you go again"
to dismiss Carter's laundry list of attacks. Next, he also asked
a rhetorical (and devastating) question in his closing statement—"Are you better off today than you were four years
ago?"—that put the Carter era in perfect perspective. But
perhaps the most remarkable part was Carter' revelation
regarding consulting his thirteen-year-old daughter, Amy,
about nuclear proliferation. "I had a discussion with my
daughter, Amy, the other day, before I came here, to ask her
what the most important issue was. She said she thought
nuclear weaponry." Carter was trying to make the point that,
even to a thirteen-year-old girl, it was obvious that nuclear
proliferation was a critical issue of the day; however, it appeared as though Carter was taking counsel from the teenager. The debate quickly became known as the "Amy Carter
debate," and in the following days Carter's slight lead van-
ished. Reagan won by a landslide. President Reagan made
light of it years later, telling Jim Lehrer of PBS in an interview that

> you could almost feel an attitude from the audience
> on it, that the President was going to make a major

policy based on what a child told him? And I'm sure
he didn't have that in mind, but that's the way it came
out. And I was prepared to say to the people, I promise them I wouldn't ask my kids what I should do.

8. CLINTON CAUGHT ON AUDIOTAPE

A few weeks prior to the New Hampshire primary, one of
Clinton's (many) purported lovers, Gennifer Flowers, released six audiotaped conversations between herself and
then-governor Clinton (who was on the campaign trail) that
detailed how she should respond to the press about an alleged affair. Clinton coached her through several explana-
tions she could give the press—including to just blame it on
Republicans—and in general tried to soothe her fears about
what might lie ahead. At a point in one of their conversations, Flowers mentioned that Mario Cuomo, then-governor
of New York and still an undeclared presidential aspirant,
seemed like someone with Mafia connections:

> Flowers: Well, I don't particularly care for Cuomo's,
> uh, demeanor.
> Clinton: Boy, he is so aggressive.
> Flowers: Well, he seems like he could get real
> mean. . . . I wouldn't be surprised if he didn't have
> some Mafioso major connections.
> Clinton: Well, he acts like one.

At first Clinton denied it was his voice on the tape, but he
backpedaled when voice experts confirmed it was the candidate. He then sent a letter to Cuomo apologizing for his
remarks. As with all the other bombshells that broadsided
Clinton's 1992 campaign, he took this one in stride and eventually overcame it.

9. G. W. BUSH CHOKES ON A PRETZEL

Not to be outdone by his father, who had famously vomited on the Japanese prime minister, President George W. Bush sported a half-dollar-size bruise on his face and a swollen lip after choking on a pretzel and passing out. The incident happened while he was watching a football game alone in the residential quarters of the White House. Doctors said the pretzel didn't go down the president's throat correctly and stimulated a nerve in the throat that caused him to pass out. According to the president, "I hit the deck and woke up and there was Barney and Spot [his dogs] showing a lot of concern." Doctors ruled out anything more serious, and late-night comedians had a field day with the incident. David Letterman quipped, "Our president is in town, George W. Bush. It's a fund-raiser. They're being very creative, you've got to give them credit. For $10,000 you can give George Bush the Heimlich Maneuver." And Jay Leno remarked, "Over the weekend, the president passed out after choking on a pretzel. Better than the old days, when he used to choke on vowels. Remember that?" Even First Lady Laura Bush couldn't resist a funny jab. "Now you'll be glad to know the president will practice safe snacks," she joked with Jay Leno on the *Tonight Show*.

10. CHENEY SHOOTS HIS HUNTING PARTNER

One of the oddest moments in recent times occurred in 2006, when Vice President Dick Cheney accidentally shot his hunting partner, Harry Whittington, in the face while the two were quail hunting on a friend's estate. Fortunately, Whittington only suffered superficial injuries and, though he suffered a heart attack after birdshot migrated to his heart, he wound up making a full recovery. This didn't stop late-night comedians—or just about everyone else for that matter—from ridiculing Cheney. The vice president was the butt of jokes for a solid two weeks following the incident. Even President Bush got in on the act. As Cheney recounted, Bush told him, "Dang, Dick, you shot the only trial lawyer who supports me!"

Closest Elections

The closest presidential elections in history have been measured by either of two ways—the popular vote and electoral votes. Because the winner is determined by electoral votes, the popular vote's winner doesn't always become president. In three cases, the candidate receiving the most popular votes has not won the presidency, with the most recent being Al Gore in 2000. A tight electoral count usually means the popular vote was fairly close, though the opposite isn't always true.

1. ELECTION OF 1800: JEFFERSON, BURR, ADAMS

The election of 1800 was certainly the strangest election in U.S. history and led directly to the passage of the Twelfth Amendment, which changed the presidential election process. The race was between John Adams, the incumbent, and Thomas Jefferson, the challenger. Though Jefferson's running mate was Aaron Burr, and Adams's was Charles Cotesworth Pinckney, somehow Jefferson and Burr wound up tied with seventy-three electoral votes. This tie occurred because the Constitution provided electors with two votes each, but they could not indicate which vote was for the president and which was for the vice president (in effect, they were only voting for president). The framers created

113

this system because they wanted the vice president to be the second-most-qualified person, or in effect the loser of the presidential election; however, they hadn't anticipated the evolution of political parties or that candidates might run as a ticket. (Congress subsequently passed the Twelfth Amendment, which created separate ballots for the election of the president and vice president.) Because Jefferson and Burr finished in a dead heat, the election was thrown to the House of Representatives. On the thirty-sixth ballot Jefferson finally topped Burr, thanks, in part, to some fancy backroom-deal making by Alexander Hamilton. Burr blamed Hamilton for his defeat and four years later—while serving as vice president—shot and killed Hamilton during a duel.

2. ELECTION OF 1824: ADAMS, JACKSON, CLAY, CRAWFORD

Since the Twelfth Amendment's adoption in 1804, this election is the only one where the House of Representatives determined the outcome. This situation occurred because none of the candidates—John Quincy Adams, Andrew Jackson, Henry Clay, and William Crawford—received a majority of the electoral votes. Andrew Jackson easily won the popular vote with 41 percent (Adams was second with 30 percent). Jackson failed to garner the 131 electoral votes needed for a majority, however; he had 99 to Adams's 84, and the other candidates split the remainder. It's important to keep in mind that six states, including New York and South Carolina, didn't have a popular vote; in those states, the state legislature chose the electors. When the House of Representatives convened, Adams won easily on the first ballot, mostly because Henry Clay, who detested Jackson, threw his support to Adams. ("I cannot believe that killing 2,500 Englishmen at New Orleans qualifies for the various, difficult, and complicated duties of the Chief Magistracy," Clay said of Jackson.) Jackson was stunned and angered by the turn of events, particularly since Adams then appointed Clay secretary of state. Jackson and his supporters used the result as motivation for the election of 1828 and easily defeated Adams in the rematch.

3. **ELECTION OF 1876: HAYES, TILDEN**

As close and contentious as the 2000 election was, the election of 1876 remains the closest and most contentious election in U.S. history. Though he lost the popular vote by 4 percent, Rutherford B. Hayes managed a one-vote electoral advantage (185–184) for the narrowest margin since the adoption of the Twelfth Amendment. And on top of it, Congress had to create a special electoral commission to determine the winner because the results from three states— Florida, Louisiana, and South Carolina—were contested (think of the 2000 election times three). The Republicans claimed that in those states, intimidation and threats were used to keep Republican voters at home and that the Democrats had used a Republican symbol—a picture of Abe Lincoln—next to their candidates to deceive illiterate voters. Though Samuel Tilden carried all three states, their respective state electoral commissions (which were still dominated by Republicans during Reconstruction) discarded thousands of ballots, and in each instance the outcome swung to Hayes. In Florida, for example, Tilden initially had a ninety-four-vote lead until the recount, when the state electoral commission gave Hayes a thousand-vote margin, but then the Florida Supreme Court got involved and declared Tilden the winner. (Sound familiar?) In all three states, the Democrats cried foul and sent to Congress their own slate of Tilden electors. Faced with an unprecedented constitutional crisis—neither the Constitution nor the Twelfth Amendment addressed this situation—Congress created a temporary fifteen-member electoral commission to sort the mess out and determine a winner. The commission consisted of eight Republicans and seven Democrats, and not surprisingly they voted along party lines to award Hayes the twenty contested votes. Both houses of Congress still had to certify the results, and some Democrats considered filibustering to prevent the results' certification. Hayes's supporters and Democrats struck an informal agreement known as the "Compromise of 1877" whereby the Democrats would drop the filibuster and acknowledge Hayes's presidency if the Republican promised to remove federal troops from the South and end Reconstruction (which he did). The deal led to a century of Democrats' supremacy in the South and African American disenfranchisement. It also led to the Electoral Count Act of 1887, which mandates that the state executive in charge of certifying results is the final determinant for the outcome, unless both houses of Congress decide otherwise. This law would figure prominently during the 2000 election recount.

4. ELECTION OF 1884: CLEVELAND, BLAINE

The race between Grover Cleveland and James Blaine was noteworthy for the near dead heat in the popular vote— Cleveland edged Blaine by approximately 14,000 votes out of 10 million votes cast, the second-closest margin ever— and the nastiness of the personal attacks. Blaine's Republican campaign slogan became "Ma, Ma, Where's My Pa?" after it was revealed that Cleveland had fathered a child out of wedlock; meanwhile, the Democrats made Blaine's rumored corruption their central theme. As one newspaper of the day put it, the choice was between a candidate who lacked ethics in his professional life and a candidate who lacked ethics in his private life. Cleveland defeated Blaine by thirty-seven electoral votes, with the margin of difference coming in the former's home state of New York.

5. ELECTION OF 1888: HARRISON, CLEVELAND

Four years later, Grover Cleveland was involved in another memorable election. This time, he won the popular vote by almost 100,000 votes, or a full percentage point, but he lost the electoral count by a fairly wide margin, 233–168. Tariffs were the big issue of the day, with Benjamin Harrison in favor of them and Cleveland opposed. In the end, Harrison picked up two states—New York and Indiana—that Cleveland had carried during the previous election, which made the difference.

6. ELECTION OF 1916: WILSON, HUGHES

Woodrow Wilson campaigned on the slogan "He Kept Us out of War," and staved off a strong challenge by Associate Justice of the Supreme Court Charles Evans Hughes by twenty-three electoral votes (277–254). Election night was a seesaw affair, with returns not final until well into the evening. Thus Wilson believed he had lost when he went to sleep while Hughes thought he had won. One story tells of a reporter calling Hughes's home to get a reaction to the loss, and his butler answered, "The president is sleeping." The reporter responded, "When he wakes up, tell him he isn't the president anymore." It turned out Wilson had won California, a state he was expected to lose, by a mere four thousand votes, and that had put him over the top.

7. ELECTION OF 1960: KENNEDY, NIXON

John F. Kennedy defeated Richard Nixon by three-tenths of a percentage point, or less than 100,000 votes out of 68 million cast; however, his electoral margin was a bit wider, 303–219. To this day, some observers contend Kennedy's margin of victory was provided by two sources: Lyndon Johnson's operation in Texas, which was known for skillfully rigging elections; and Mayor Daley's political machine in Chicago, which delivered an extraordinary 450,000-vote margin in Cook County. (Many believe the Chicago margin was fraudulent; as one Chicago newspaper put it, "Once an election has been stolen in Cook County, it stays stolen."). Though Nixon refused to press for a recount or make noise about the alleged fraud in Texas and Illinois, he privately simmered over the outcome for years. In some respects it may have fueled his paranoid behavior when he later served as president.

8. ELECTION OF 1976: CARTER, FORD
Jimmy Carter's victory was the last time a Democrat garnered 50 percent of the vote (Clinton failed both times to reach 50 percent), and it was only the second time since 1944. On the one hand, former one-term governor Carter ran as an outsider and a reformer; on the other hand, after having been appointed vice president to replace Agnew and later becoming president after Nixon resigned, former congressman Gerald Ford sought his first national victory. Carter maintained a huge edge following the Democratic convention, but his lead slowly evaporated as the campaign progressed. Ford stumbled during the second debate, however, when he denied there was any Soviet domination in Eastern Europe and then refused to retract his statement for almost a week following the gaffe. In the end, Carter managed a narrow 2 percent victory in the popular vote and a 297–240 edge in electoral votes.

9. ELECTION OF 2000: BUSH, GORE
The 2000 election was easily the most contentious of the twentieth century and was probably second only to the election of 1876 for sheer confusion and rancor. It was the third time in history that the winner of the popular vote lost the electoral vote, and for the first time, the Supreme Court got

directly involved in a presidential election. Most expected a close election between George W. Bush and Al Gore, but few could have predicted the strange turn of events that unfolded on election night. First, Al Gore was declared the winner of Florida (based mostly on faulty exit poll data provided to the network broadcasts), and later that call was retracted and George W. Bush was declared the winner of Florida. Just minutes before Al Gore was about to give his concession speech, Florida was moved back into the "too-close-to-call" column because Bush's lead had shrunk to a couple of hundred votes. Over the next six weeks, the nation became engrossed with the Florida recount, with its "dimpled chads," court decisions and injunctions, protests, endless parade of screeching political commentators on cable TV, and oddball conspiracy theories about how both sides were trying to steal the election. At times during the thirty-six-day recount, it more resembled a circus than an election. It took the unprecedented step of the Supreme Court ruling five to four that the recount was unconstitutional for the election to be decided finally for Bush. Gore conceded the following day.

10. ELECTION OF 2004: BUSH, KERRY

George W. Bush topped John F. Kerry in the popular vote quite handily, 50–48 percent (or 3 million votes) but squeaked by in the electoral vote, 286–251. The difference was Ohio's twenty electoral votes, which George Bush captured by a slim 100,000-vote margin. Bush also picked up New Mexico and New Hampshire (which he had lost in 2000) while not losing any states from 2000. Bush managed to top the 50 percent mark—the first president to accomplish that margin since his father had in 1988. Both sides were prepared for a drawn-out affair similar to that of the 2000 decision, with tens of thousands of lawyers positioned in key states where the vote was close, but Kerry wound up conceding the following day, when it became apparent that Ohio was outside the recount margin.

Presidential Losers

History remembers only the winners; rarely does it stop to consider the losers. Some presidential aspirants, however, stand out from the rest.

1. WILLIAM JENNINGS BRYAN, 1896, 1900, 1908

Nobody in American history sought the presidency as vigorously—or as often—as William Jennings Bryan, the only "loser" who was a major-party nominee three times. At age thirty-six, he was also the youngest major-party candidate to seek the presidency when William McKinley first defeated him in 1896. Though a Democrat his entire life, Bryan's policies—most notably his rejection of the gold standard and his support of agrarian interests—were more populist than Democratic mainstream; consequently, he had a difficult time putting together the traditional Democratic coalition. The election of 1896 would be the closest that Bryan got to the White House, as he lost by "only" a hundred electoral votes to McKinley. During that election, he practically invented the modern campaign as he crisscrossed the country, delivering five hundred speeches in a hundred days. Prior to that venture, most presidential nominees didn't travel to campaign; rather, they delivered speeches from their "front porches" and had surrogates traverse the country. When

Bryan faced McKinley again in 1900, the popular incumbent defeated him fairly handily. Bryan wisely sat out the 1904 election, when Teddy Roosevelt routed little-known New York judge Alton Parker, and received his last nomination in 1908. This time he suffered his worse defeat to Roosevelt's anointed successor, William Howard Taft. This loss marked the end of Bryan's presidential aspirations, though he would later serve as secretary of state for Woodrow Wilson.

2. THOMAS DEWEY, 1944, 1948

Three times Thomas Dewey sought the presidency, and three times he failed—twice in the general election and once in the nominating process. As the Mafia-busting district attorney of New York, he sought the 1940 Republican nomination, even though he had lost the New York gubernatorial election two years earlier. He actually led after the first ballot but was eventually overtaken by little-known industrialist Wendell Wilkie. Dewey was elected the governor of New York in 1942, and two years later he was the Republican challenger against President Franklin Roosevelt. Dewey stood little chance against the popular Roosevelt, though he did manage to receive the most votes of any Republican candidate since 1928. Dewey again received the Republican nomination in 1948 and was considered the front-runner against the vulnerable Harry Truman, who was slumping in the polls and struggling to keep the Democratic coalition together (the Dixiecrats would end up running their own candidate, Strom Thurmond). As the presumptive front-runner, Dewey decided to play it safe and mostly avoided the major issues; instead, he spoke in generalities and platitudes about "moving the country forward." Truman, meanwhile, took to the campaign trail with his vigorous "Give 'Em Hell" whistle-stop tour, crisscrossing the country and galvanizing the Democratic base with attacks against the "do-nothing" Republican Congress. As late as election night, most pundits expected Dewey to defeat Truman, and based on faulty exit polling, one newspaper—the conservative *Chicago Tribune*—even created early editions with the headline "Dewey Defeats Truman." Dewey flirted with the idea of running again in 1952 but opted instead to play kingmaker for Dwight Eisenhower, helping him win the nomination and the presidency. Four years later, Eisenhower privately floated the idea of dumping Vice President Nixon in favor of Dewey, but party leaders talked him out of it.

3. AL SMITH, 1928

New York governor Al Smith was the first Roman Catholic to run for president on a major ticket, though Herbert Hoover trounced him in a landslide. Nonetheless, Smith's nomination was important for several reasons. First, it helped politicians overcome fears about having a Roman Catholic head a national ticket. Until that time, great skepticism about the viability of a Catholic candidate abounded, for the thinking was that as president, a Catholic would take orders from the pope rather than follow the Constitution. Smith's candidacy certainly helped pave the way for John F. Kennedy three decades later. Next, his candidacy also opened the door for Franklin Roosevelt to become the governor of New York, which positioned him to take advantage of Hoover's poor showing during the Great Depression four years later. Had Smith decided not to run in 1928 and had instead waited until 1932, he probably would have defeated Hoover. Finally, by bringing millions of Catholics to the voting booths for the first time, Smith managed to win many of the big cities, forging a forerunner of the new Democratic coalition. The reality is that in 1928, with the economy doing well and the Republicans in favor, no Democrat was going to defeat

Hoover; however, Smith's candidacy marked the beginning of a new Democratic coalition.

4. SAMUEL TILDEN, 1876

Perhaps with the exception of Al Gore, nobody came closer to attaining the White House in defeat than New York governor Samuel Tilden. He handily beat Republican nominee Rutherford B. Hayes in the popular vote (51–48) and held a nineteen-vote electoral lead with three contested states—Florida, South Carolina, and Louisiana—leaning in his favor. Republicans cried foul in the contested states, however, and convinced Congress to void the results and award the electoral votes to Hayes on account of fraud and intimidation at the ballot box. Hayes wound up winning by a single electoral vote, and to this day many believe his victory was the result of a "compromise" deal with the Southern states to discontinue Reconstruction in return for a Hayes victory. Bitter from the experience, Tilden left politics and refused the Democratic nomination in 1880 and 1884.

5. AL GORE, 2000

Like Samuel Tilden, Al Gore won the popular vote and seemingly had a chance to win the electoral vote, which was mired by a contested election in Florida. Unlike Tilden, however, Gore was a sitting vice president during a time of prosperity and peace and should have been considered a heavy favorite to win the presidency. Some pundits contend Gore was hurt by President Clinton's moral failings and Gore's decision not to campaign on the Clinton record. For his part, President Clinton did little campaigning on Gore's behalf, and what should have been a romp turned out to be a dead-heat election. Had Gore carried his home state of Tennessee or Clinton's native Arkansas, he would have won the presidency. As it turned out, several factors—including Green

Party candidate Ralph Nader's vote tally in Florida and New Hampshire, and the confusing "butterfly ballot" in Palm Beach that resulted in three thousand votes for Pat Buchanan—conspired to turn the election against Gore. Gore decided to forgo the 2004 election and insists that he is finished with electoral politics.

6. STEPHEN DOUGLAS, 1860

Though Stephen Douglas is best known for his successful 1858 Senate contest against Abraham Lincoln, which produced the famous Lincoln-Douglas debates, he also squared off against Lincoln two years later for the presidency. It was a four-way race between the Republicans; the Northern Democrats, who nominated Douglas; the Southern Democrats, who nominated John Breckinridge; and remnants of the Whig Party (called the "Constitutional Union Party"), which nominated John C. Bell. Douglas positioned himself as a "compromise" candidate between the Northern abolitionists and the Southern secessionists, arguing that slavery should be a popular sovereignty issue best decided by the people. Breaking with tradition, he traveled and campaigned on his own behalf (instead of relying on surrogates) in an effort to keep the nation together. Though he finished second with a respectable 29 percent of the popular vote, he finished last in electoral votes with only twelve after winning only one state, Missouri. Following his defeat, Douglas became an outspoken critic of Southern secession and urged the Southern leaders to cede to Lincoln's victory. At Lincoln's request, he gave several passionate speeches about the need for unionism in key border states before he died of typhoid fever in June 1861.

7. JAMES BLAINE, 1884

James Blaine was one of the most accomplished and

qualified politicians not to win the presidency. He lost by a razor-thin margin to Grover Cleveland in 1884, mostly because a Protestant clergyman made a slur against Catholics (he said the Democrats stood for "rum, Romanism, and rebellion") while campaigning for Blaine. The remark set off a firestorm of criticism and probably caused Blaine to lose New York State, which had a large population of Roman Catholics. Blaine had an unassailable record of public service, including stints as the speaker of the House, a U.S. senator, and secretary of state on two separate occasions. He was considered a brilliant orator and the premier statesmen of the day, and he came close to receiving the Republican nomination for president in 1876 and 1880. Many historians consider Blaine among the most influential public figures of the nineteenth century.

8. BARRY GOLDWATER, 1964

Although Barry Goldwater suffered one of the worst shellackings in presidential history, his candidacy marked an important realignment in presidential politics that is still felt today. As a candidate, Goldwater was prone to making blunt (and sometimes outrageous) statements, including his famous line at the Republican nominating convention: "Extremism in the defense of liberty is no vice. And let me remind you also that moderation in the pursuit of justice is no virtue." President Johnson used statements like this one and others to paint Goldwater as a dangerous extremist, an image Goldwater couldn't overcome. He lost the popular vote by 22 percent (only George McGovern in 1972 was beat more soundly) and managed just fifty-two electoral votes. The states he won, however, included the stronghold of the old Confederacy—Louisiana, Alabama, South Carolina, Mississippi, and Georgia—marking the first time the South had gone for a Republican candidate since Reconstruction.

Goldwater's strong showing in the South marked the beginning of the Republicans' domination in the region and formed the basis for Nixon's "southern strategy" in 1968 and 1972. Goldwater's campaign is also notable for helping give rise to a future Republican star, Ronald Reagan, who stumped for Goldwater on several occasions. Reagan caught the attention of national leaders with his thirty-minute televised speech on Goldwater's behalf just days before the election.

9. ADLAI E. STEVENSON, 1952, 1956
The highly intellectual governor of Illinois came from a strong political pedigree: his grandfather had served as Grover Cleveland's vice president, and his father had been a secretary of state for Illinois. Even so, it wasn't enough to help him defeat popular war hero Dwight Eisenhower in 1952 or 1956. Stevenson was drubbed both times with near identical tallies; his only support came from the old Confederacy. He toyed with the idea of pursuing the nomination in 1960 but became convinced that Kennedy was the best candidate. He stumped for Kennedy during the general election and was rewarded with the position of ambassador to the United Nations, where he delivered one of the most memorable performances in UN history when he confronted the Soviet ambassador Valerian Zorin about his country's missiles in Cuba. It was the defining moment of Stevenson's political career.

10. CHARLES COTESWORTH PINCKNEY, 1804, 1808
Charles Pinckney was the Federalist standard bearer for the 1804 and 1808 elections, and he was trounced both times. Although he never held elected office and his only public service to the United States was serving as George Washington's minister to France, nonetheless, he was the Federalist candidate for vice president in 1800. Then he was

their challenger to Thomas Jefferson in 1804, when Jefferson captured 72 percent of the popular vote and all but fourteen electoral votes (out of 178). The Federalists nominated him again in 1808, and this time James Madison crushed him. The Federalist Party disbanded several years later.

Debates

Some of the most memorable moments of presidential elections have occurred during the debates. The debates are one of the few times in a campaign when the candidates are unscripted and left to their own devices.

1. BUSH-GORE, FIRST DEBATE, OCTOBER 3, 2000

It was roundly expected that Al Gore, an expert political debater, would have little difficulty dispatching George W. Bush in their three confrontations, and for the most part, at least on substance, he did. It was his off-camera antics—rolling his eyes when George Bush spoke and audibly sighing every time his opponent made a point—that cost him dearly. The spin following the first debate was that Gore scored on substance but lost badly on style and that Bush was the more likable person. The debate is perhaps best remembered for the parody that appeared later that week on NBC's television show *Saturday Night Live,* where Daryl Hammond captured Gore's over-the-top theatrics so perfectly that the Gore campaign staff actually had the vice president watch the spoof and learn from his mistakes. The parody must have made an impact on the veep, because in the second debate he seemed so stiff and emotionless that some thought he might have been sedated. The final debate produced a memorably awkward moment when Gore seemingly invaded Bush's personal space as the governor was answering a question and produced startled laughter from Bush. Pundits took it as another sign of Gore's inability to "find his voice" in the campaign.

2. NIXON-KENNEDY, FIRST PRESIDENTIAL DEBATE, SEPTEMBER 26, 1960

This first televised debate in presidential history is still regarded as the benchmark in measuring the impact that debates can have on elections as well as the importance of candidates' style and appearance. From the moment both candidates received their respective party's nomination, the 1960 election was virtually a dead heat. It was believed that Nixon, the more seasoned politician and experienced debater, would have an advantage down the homestretch because most pundits considered him the heavy favorite in the debates. In the weeks leading up to the first showdown, however, Nixon was hospitalized with a knee injury and the flu, and on debate night he looked fatigued and gaunt. Making matters worse, his "five o'clock shadow" was on full display because he refused to wear any makeup. Kennedy, meanwhile, looked tan and relaxed following a three-day campaign stint in California, and he had been coached on how to play to the television camera. For the vast majority of Americans who watched the debate on television, Kennedy was the clear-cut winner, mostly because he looked so much better than Nixon under the hot television lights. For the much smaller audience who had listened on radio, the majority considered Nixon the winner. With Kennedy winning the election by less than a tenth of a percentage point, the first debate may have been the deciding factor in the outcome.

3. BUSH-CLINTON-PEROT, SECOND DEBATE, OCTOBER 15, 1992

The second of three debates featuring President Bush, Governor Bill Clinton, and third-party candidate Ross Perot is best remembered not for anything that was said, but rather a simple action. The debate was a "town hall"–style format, which clearly suited Governor Clinton's "I-feel-your-pain" style, and it became obvious early in the debate that it was going to be a good night for Clinton. Toward the end of the debate, as Clinton was answering a question, the cameras caught President Bush glancing at his watch. For many viewers, this gesture confirmed their feeling that Bush was a bit detached from the country's problems and seemingly too aloof to care about the voters' concerns. Bush's move couldn't have contrasted more starkly with Bill Clinton's performance that evening, for Clinton's empathy practically enveloped the audience. President Bush reminisced with PBS reporter Jim Lehrer years later about the incident: "They made a huge thing out of that. . . . Now, was I glad when the damn thing [the debate] was over? Yeah, and maybe that's why I was looking at it, only 10 more minutes of this crap."

4. REAGAN-MONDALE, SECOND DEBATE, OCTOBER 21, 1984

For much of the 1984 election, President Reagan held a commanding lead over former vice president Walter Mondale, mostly because the economy was in strong shape and many Americans agreed with Reagan's tough stance with the Soviet Union. The only time the race seemed to tighten at all was following the first debate, where the seventy-three-year-old Reagan seemed a little tired and unsteady at times. Mondale was able to close the gap slightly, building on his strong performance, and for a few days it looked as if there might be a race after all. Heading into the second debate, Reagan's campaign wanted to assure the country that he wasn't too old to remain commander in chief. When panelist Henry Trewhitt hit him with the question about being too old to lead during a crisis, Reagan countered, "Not at all. And, Mr Trewhitt, I want you to know also I will not make age an issue of this campaign. I am not going to exploit for political purposes my opponent's youth and inexperience." Reagan's comment caused everyone to laugh, including Walter Mondale. Reagan had masterfully diffused the issue and would go on to win in a landslide. In an interesting note, another Reagan zinger in his lone debate with Jimmy Carter four years earlier—"Are you better off now than you were four years ago?"—helped warm voters to Reagan, who was still relatively unknown at the time.

5. FORD-CARTER, SECOND DEBATE, OCTOBER 6, 1976

Most memorable debate moments are a product of scripted one-liners or a revealing extemporaneous remark. One such moment, however, resulted from President Ford's factual gaffe in his second encounter with Jimmy Carter. In this instance, he seemed to imply the Soviet Union was not a dominant presence in Eastern Europe. It resulted in one of the weirdest exchanges in debate history:

> Ford: "There is no Soviet domination of Eastern Europe, and there never will be under a Ford Administration."
>
> Max Frankel, *New York Times:* "I'm sorry, could I just follow—did I understand you to say, sir, that the Russians are not using Eastern Europe as their own sphere of influence in occupying most of the countries there?"
>
> Ford: "I don't believe, uh—Mr. Frankel that, uh—the Yugoslavians consider themselves dominated by the Soviet Union. I don't believe that the Romanians

consider themselves dominated by the Soviet Union.
I don't believe that the Poles consider themselves dominated by the Soviet Union."

Of course, those countries were dominated by the Soviet
Union, and Ford's answer made front-page news around
world. According to one poll, almost overnight Carter turned
a narrow deficit into a six-point lead. For the remainder of
the campaign, Ford refused to admit he had misspoken,
though years later he confessed this misstatement had probably cost him the election. It turned out to be a tough debate season all around for the Republicans. Vice presidential candidate Bob Dole, in responding to a question about
Watergate during his debate with Walter Mondale, charac-
terized the four wars of the twentieth century—World War I,
World War II, the Korean War, and Vietnam—as "Democrat
wars" and said Walter Mondale would no more want to talk
about that than Dole would want to discuss Watergate. The
statement would haunt Dole for the rest of his career.

6. BUSH-DUKAKIS, SECOND DEBATE, OCTOBER 13, 1988

Massachusetts governor Michael Dukakis was hit with one
of the most difficult (some would say unfair) questions ever
asked of a presidential candidate during a debate, and his
answer may have cost him the election. CNN newsperson
Bernard Shaw opened the debate by asking the question, "If
Kitty Dukakis were raped and murdered, would you favor
an irrevocable death penalty for the killer?" According to
Dukakis's campaign manager Susan Estrich, Dukakis had
been prepared to answer that type of question by empathiz-
ing with crime victims and even revealing that his dad had
been a victim of a violent crime. Instead, however, Dukakis
launched into a clinical recitation of his position on capital
punishment: "No, I don't, Bernard. And I think you know

that I've opposed the death penalty during all of my life. I don't see any evidence that it's a deterrent, and I think there are better and more effective ways to deal with violent crime." He did not reveal any emotion or how he would handle that situation. Dukakis's answer seemed to confirm for some voters that he lacked the warmth and empathy to be a leader, and following the debate the election was never close again.

7. QUAYLE-BENTSEN, VICE PRESIDENTIAL DEBATE, OCTOBER 5, 1988

The sole vice presidential debate of the 1988 election produced perhaps the most famous line in presidential debate history, one that has been repeated many times and has become part of the political lexicon. Leading up to the debate, George H. W. Bush's running mate, little-known senator Dan Quayle, had been addressing his lack of experience on the campaign trail by making comparisons to another two-term senator, President John Kennedy. The Dukakis-Bentsen campaign found the comparison "a reach" for Senator Quayle and prepared candidate Lloyd Bentsen with a retort if it came up during the debate. Sure enough, in response to a question from NBC's Tom Brokaw about his qualifications for stepping into the highest office in the case of a tragedy, Quayle responded that he had as much experience in Congress as Jack Kennedy had when he sought the presidency. Bentsen then replied, "Senator, I served with Jack Kennedy, I knew Jack Kennedy, Jack Kennedy was a friend of mine. Senator, you are no Jack Kennedy." A sheepish Quayle was caught partially smiling to Bentsen's remark, and the moment seemed to confirm for voters Quayle's status as a "not ready for prime-time player." In the end, it had little impact on the campaign as Bush won handily, but it did permanently brand Quayle as a political lightweight.

8. REPUBLICAN PRIMARY DEBATE IN NEW HAMPSHIRE

One of the most pivotal moments in Ronald Reagan's political career actually occurred *before* the 1980 New Hampshire primary debate, where he changed the election's trajectory with a simple utterance. Following on the heals of an upset loss to George H. W. Bush in the Iowa caucus, Reagan's campaign was in something of a free fall heading into the New Hampshire primary, where anything but a victory would have likely knocked him out of the race. Reagan and Bush were invited by the *Telegraph* of Nashua—the state's second-largest newspaper—to a one-on-one debate without the other five candidates, but before it could take place the Federal Communications Commission (FCC) intervened and said it would be considered an illegal contribution to the Bush and Reagan campaigns if the others were excluded. Wanting the other candidates on the stage with him, Reagan agreed to pay for the additional costs to include all seven candidates. Along with the other candidates and the audience, Reagan was shocked to find only two chairs and microphones set up on stage when he arrived on debate night. Reagan took a microphone and began to explain to the audience what was happening, when the editor of the newspaper told the soundman, "Turn Mr. Reagan's microphone off." As Reagan would tell it years later,

> Well, I didn't like that—we were paying the freight for the debate and he was acting as if his newspaper was still sponsoring it. I turned to him, with the microphone still on, and said the first thing that came to my mind: "I am paying for this microphone, Mr. Green." Well, for some reason, my words hit the audience, whose emotions were already worked up, like a sledgehammer. The crowd roared and just went wild. I may have

won the debate, the primary—and the nomination—
right there.

Ironically, he got the editor's name wrong—it was John
Breen—and he lifted the line, not surprisingly, from a movie.

9. VICE PRESIDENTIAL DEBATE, OCTOBER 13, 1992

While the 1992 vice presidential debate had little (or no)
impact on the election's outcome, it did produce one of the
more memorable—and parodied—opening lines in debate
history. The Reform Party candidate, Adm. James Stockdale,
opened with the line, "Who am I, and why am I here?" Most
Americans were probably wondering themselves. With his
deadpan delivery and "deer–in-the-headlights" look, it wasn't
altogether certain whether the question was rhetorical, and
he elicited laughter from the auditorium audience. Stockdale
hadn't been much of a campaigner in Perot's on-again, off-
again presidential bid in 1992, and he admitted years later
he had never "had a single conversation about politics with
Ross Perot in my life," much less prepared for the debate.
Ironically, while it was Stockdale's uneven debate performance that brought him to national prominence, he gained
millions of admirers as Americans learned of his heroism
and bravery in Vietnam, where he was brutally tortured for
seven years as a prisoner of war.

10. LINCOLN-DOUGLAS, DEBATES OF 1858

Abraham Lincoln and Stephen Douglas participated in a
series of debates during the campaign for U.S. senator from
Illinois. While the debates were not part of a presidential
campaign, many of the issues and topics presaged the 1860
presidential campaign, and the series is widely regarded as
the greatest in U.S. history. The debates typically lasted three
to four hours and attracted upward of ten thousand people

at each of the seven stops. The two candidates differed dramatically on the big issue of the day, slavery: Lincoln was against the expansion of slavery into new territories while Douglas believed that states had the right to vote on the issue for themselves—a point of view that became known as "popular sovereignty." The Lincoln-Douglas debates have served as a template for debate series, and political candidates who want to engage their opponents in serious discussion often cite them.

Third-Party Candidates

Since 1856, most presidential elections have been two-party contests between Republicans and Democrats. Occasionally, a third-party candidate has had an impact on an election's outcome—most recently Ralph Nader in 2000—but none of these candidates has seriously threatened to win the presidency.

1. THEODORE ROOSEVELT, 1912

Teddy Roosevelt remains by far the most successful third-party candidate in history. Though he finished fourteen percentage points behind Woodrow Wilson (41–27 percent) and won only eighty-eight electoral votes, he swamped incumbent president William Howard Taft, who received eight electoral votes and 23 percent of the popular vote. In doing so, Roosevelt handed the White House to Woodrow Wilson. Ironically, Taft was Roosevelt's handpicked successor; Roosevelt expected his protégé to continue his legacy of conservation, trust busting, and an expansionist foreign policy. Roosevelt came out of retirement to challenge him in the Republican primaries when it became clear that Taft had a different agenda and priorities. Roosevelt nearly overtook Taft for the Republican nomination in 1912, and going against the counsel of party elders, he decided to form the Bull Moose

Progressive Party to stage his third-party candidacy in the general election. It was the last time a third-party candidate finished second in a presidential election.

2. MILLARD FILLMORE, 1856
Along with Teddy Roosevelt, Millard Fillmore is the only former president to seek office as a third-party candidate. Fillmore never won national office on his own; as vice president, he succeeded to the presidency when Zachary Taylor passed away shortly into his term. The Whig Party decided not to nominate Fillmore in 1852, choosing instead to go with acclaimed Gen. Winfield Scott. In 1856, Fillmore received the nomination for the American Party, or the "Know-Nothing Party," which was agnostic on slavery and stood mostly for anti-immigration policies in the big cities. In the election, the Democrat, James Buchanan, easily defeated his Republican opponent, Charles Fremont, who was the first Republican candidate for president in history. If Freemont's 33 percent and Filmore's 21 percent had been combined, they would have easily defeated the Democrat. The Republicans were convinced that bringing the Know-Nothings into the Republican fold in 1860 would be critical to victory.

3. STROM THURMOND, 1948
Strom Thurmond carried four states and won thirty-nine electoral votes as the standard-bearer for the Dixiecrats, a splinter group from the Democratic Party whose sole agenda was a virulent opposition to desegregation. The first-term governor of South Carolina jumped into the race after Minneapolis mayor Hubert Humphrey successfully lobbied the Democratic National Convention to include a plank supporting racial integration in its platform. Thurmond, who campaigned on the slogan "Segregation forever," won South

Carolina, Mississippi, Louisiana, and Alabama—four states that normally would have gone to the Democratic candidate, President Harry S. Truman. Most experts thought New York governor Thomas Dewey held the advantage going into election day, in part, because Thurmond was expected to do well in the South (which he did). Contrary to the *Chicago Tribune*'s famous headline "Dewey Defeats Truman," however, Truman won both the popular and electoral votes fairly easily, even without Thurmond's thirty-nine electoral votes. Thurmond would later switch to the Republican Party and serve in the Senate for more than fifty years, the longest tenure in history.

4. ROBERT LA FOLLETTE, 1924

A liberal Republican senator from Wisconsin, Robert "Fighting Bob" La Follette left the Republicans to form the Progressive Party in order to run for president against incumbent Calvin Coolidge and Democratic challenger John Davis in 1924. His base of support consisted of union members, farmers, civil libertarians, and the remnants of Teddy Roosevelt's Bull Moose Party. La Follette scored an impressive 17 percent of the popular vote and won his home state of Wisconsin. He clearly siphoned votes from the Democratic challenger, as Davis was routed by Coolidge, 54–28 percent in one of the worst showings ever by a major-party candidate. La Follette passed away the following year, but his Progressive Party survived in Wisconsin, where it won several congressional seats. Both of his sons—Robert Jr. and Phillip—held elected office, with Robert Jr. serving in the Senate for two decades and Phillip serving two terms as governor of Wisconsin. In 1957, a Senate committee headed by John F. Kennedy chose La Follette as one of the five greatest senators in U.S. history.

5. **GEORGE WALLACE, 1968**

The four-time Alabama governor, George Wallace, sought the presidency four times: three times he ran as a Democrat, and once in 1968 he was as an Independent, nearly acting as a spoiler for Richard Nixon. An avowed segregationist and political maverick— who famously said, "Segregation now, segregation tomorrow, segregation forever," Wallace's goal was to block Nixon and Humphrey from receiving an outright majority of electoral votes. He wanted the election thrown to the House of Representatives, where he believed he could serve as a power broker behind the scenes. Wallace nearly pulled it off, garnering 14 percent of the popular vote and forty-six electoral votes with wins in Georgia, Louisiana, Arkansas, Mississippi, and Alabama— states that probably would have gone for Nixon over Humphrey. Based on his strong showing, Wallace again ran in 1972 (but in the Democratic primaries) and was beginning to gain support in the North and industrial Midwest when a would-be assassin shot him. The attack left Wallace paralyzed, but it didn't stop him from winning four primaries and finishing third in the delegate count. Wallace again ran in 1976 but dropped out quickly after losing to Jimmy Carter in several southern primaries.

6. **ROSS PEROT, 1992, 1996**

Ross Perot holds the distinction of having the two most successful back-to-back third-party candidacies in history. The Texas billionaire was actually even in the polls with President George. H. W. Bush and Bill Clinton during the early months of the 1992 campaign before he temporarily pulled out and then rejoined the campaign in the fall. Perot's folksy appeal, commonsense approach, and performance in the three debates helped propel him to a 19 percent finish, one of the highest of any third-party candidate in history (though he didn't win any electoral votes). His campaign four years later wasn't quite as successful—he won about 9 percent of the vote—as Bill Clinton easily defeated Senator Bob Dole. Perot figured less prominently in that election and was not invited to participate in the major debates. Perot's Reform Party fielded Pat Buchanan as its candidate in 2000, and aside from winning a few key votes in Florida (mostly because of ballot confusion), it had no impact on the campaign. The party folded shortly thereafter.

7. RALPH NADER, 2000, 2004

In 2000, public watchdog and environmental crusader Ralph Nader had the most impact of any third-party campaign in history, when he siphoned critical votes from Al Gore in Florida and New Hampshire and may well have cost the vice president the election. Nader's campaign focused on a few main issues: reforming campaign finance, rolling back "corporate welfare," and taxing the wealthy. Though he received only 2.5 percent of the popular vote nationwide and won no electoral votes, his 90,000 votes in Florida far exceeded Bush's 527-vote margin, as did his 22,000 votes in New Hampshire. In both instances, Nader likely took crucial votes away from Al Gore (though some Nader supporters contend his voters wouldn't have voted at all if Nader hadn't been on the ballot). In 2004, Democratic nominee John Kerry tried to talk Nader out of another run but failed to keep him on the sidelines. The Green Party, fearing a repeat of the 2000 election, decided not to give Nader its nomination; instead, he ran as an Independent, capturing less than .05 percent of the vote (and didn't impact any states).

8. JOHN ANDERSON, 1980

Former Republican congressman John Anderson ran in the

1980 Republican primary as the liberal alternative to Ronald Reagan and the Republican establishment, and after failing to win any states, he bolted the party for an independent run at the White House. He became the Independent Party candidate in the general election and made reelection nearly impossible for Jimmy Carter as he siphoned off liberal support in key northeastern states. His 7 percent of the popular vote came mostly from Carter and contributed, in part, to Reagan's landslide victory of forty-four states. Anderson considered running again in 1984, but he opted instead to endorse Democratic candidate Walter Mondale, who won only his home state of Minnesota.

9. EUGENE V. DEBS, 1912, 1920

Eugene Debs holds the distinction of garnering the most votes for a Socialist candidate in U.S. history, getting close to a million votes both in 1912 and 1920. His 6 percent showing in 1912 remains the highest percentage total for a Socialist candidate and placed him a distant fourth behind Wilson, Roosevelt, and Taft in the contest. Debs ran again in 1920—this time, from an Atlanta prison, where he was serving a ten-year sentence for violating the Espionage Act of 1917 by obstructing the draft (the offending act: an antiwar speech in Canton, Ohio). Debs received close to a million votes, or 3 percent of the popular tally, even though he was incarcerated and unable to campaign. The following year, President Harding commuted his sentence, and Debs died a few years later.

10. JAMES BAIRD WEAVER, 1892

As a founder of the Populist Party, in 1892 Weaver—a former one-term congressman from Iowa—won 9 percent of the vote and picked up twenty-two electoral votes from Colorado, Kansas, Idaho, and Nevada. Weaver had bolted the

Republican Party a decade earlier because he believed that "monied interests" had too much influence. His Populist platform included establishing civil rights for African Americans, relaxing the gold standard, and instituting a graduated income tax. Though he undoubtedly took votes from the Democrats, Grover Cleveland still won the election fairly handily, knocking off incumbent Benjamin Harrison. Weaver's Populist party disappeared following the 1896 election.

Primary Upsets

Presidential primaries are a fairly modern creation. Until the 1960 campaign, primaries played mostly a minor role in the nominating process, with backroom deal making still the party bosses' favored method of selecting candidates. In the last several decades, however, the primary process has reigned supreme. Two in particular, the Iowa caucus and New Hampshire primary, have been far and away the most important in the process. Along the way, there have been some unusual moments and unexpected upsets.

1. HARRY TRUMAN, 1952

Heading into the 1952 election Harry Truman was genuinely undecided about whether he should seek a third term (second elected) or support another candidate. Just a year earlier, the Twenty-second Amendment was ratified, limiting the president to two elected terms or one elected term if he served in the office more than two years following the death of a president—in this case, FDR. Truman, however, was "grandfathered" around the limitation, meaning the amendment didn't apply to him. Truman actually began courting Dwight Eisenhower in the early 1950s to consider running as a Democrat, but Eisenhower, it turned out, was a Republican. Truman also tried to persuade Supreme Court chief justice Fred Vinson to run, but Vinson had no desire to leave the bench. Alben Barkley, Truman's vice president, was considered too old to run, and so Truman's name was on the ballot for the New Hampshire primary against Tennessee senator Estes Kefauver (whom Truman took to derisively calling "Senator Cowfever"). Kefauver defeated Truman decisively, 55–44 percent, and then Truman declared his intention not to seek another term. Kefauver went on to win twelve of the fifteen primaries that year, but he fell a few hundred delegates short at the nominating convention. He was passed over for Adlai E. Stevenson, who, in turn, was trounced by Dwight Eisenhower.

2. Lyndon Johnson, 1968
On March 31, 1968, Johnson famously declared, "I shall not seek and I will not accept the nomination of my party for another term as your president" following a stunning performance by little-known antiwar senator Eugene McCarthy in the New Hampshire primary. Although Johnson actually defeated McCarthy 49–42 percent, the margin was a clear sign of weakness for the president and a repudiation of his handling of the Vietnam War. McCarthy wound up winning only 23 percent of the delegates to the 1968 convention (far short of the number needed to secure the nomination), and party leaders never showed him serious consideration as a viable nominee. McCarthy's strong showing in New Hampshire, however, convinced Robert Kennedy to announce his candidacy. Kennedy seemed to be on his way to winning the nomination when he was assassinated in California.

3. John F. Kennedy, 1960
John F. Kennedy scored his biggest victory in the 1960 primary season in West Virginia, a mostly Protestant state that

was thought to be tough sledding for the Catholic Kennedy. The primary took place only a month before the nominating convention, and Kennedy needed a victory to prove he could overcome any anti-Catholic bias, as well as build the momentum for his nomination. Kennedy's opponent was Minnesota senator Hubert Humphrey, a highly popular pro-union figure in West Virginia and a Protestant. Kennedy wisely turned the race into a referendum on anti-Catholic bias and managed to score a big victory, garnering 60 percent of the vote. Humphrey dropped out of the race that very evening, and Kennedy became a virtual lock for the nomination. It's been rumored for years, however, that Kennedy's victory had less to do with political tactics and messaging and more to do with his father, Joseph Kennedy, and his "street money" for gaining the support of party leaders, union bosses, and church officials.

4. JIMMY CARTER, 1976

According to a Gallup Poll, Jimmy Carter had only 4 percent of registered Democrats' support as late as January 4, 1976—just weeks before the primary season was to begin. The one-term Georgia governor had begun his quixotic campaign with the "peanut brigade" in tow a full year earlier, but he was making little headway until he stunned the field with back-to-back victories in the Iowa caucus and New Hampshire primary. He won mostly on the strength of his grassroots political organization, as well as on his more than fifty appearances in both states leading up to the primaries. Some even joked Carter should have filed taxes in Iowa because he had spent so much time there. That a little-known southern governor could win in the Midwest and Northeast made him the front-runner almost overnight, and after defeating George Wallace in Florida a few weeks later, Carter quickly became the only national candidate. Carter's

early momentum led to victories in Illinois, Wisconsin, Pennsylvania, and Ohio and all but ensured his nomination.

5. GEORGE H. W. BUSH, 1988

One of the strangest upsets in primary history occurred in
1988, when George Herbert Walker Bush, the sitting vice
president, finished third in the Iowa caucuses to Senator
Robert Dole and televangelist Pat Robertson. Without prior
experience seeking elected office, Robertson had run on an
ultraconservative platform, which included eliminating the
Department of Education and banning pornography; garnered 25 percent of the vote to Bush's 19 percent; and for a
brief moment was a serious contender for the Republican
nomination. Bush rebounded in New Hampshire, however,
with the help of the state's governor, John Sununu (who
would go on to be his White House chief of staff), and eventually won the nomination and the presidency. Bush's victory ended Robertson's brief political career.

6. RONALD REAGAN, 1976

Ronald Reagan came within a whisker of taking the Republican nomination away from President Gerald Ford in 1976.
Reagan, who at the time was out of office after serving two
terms as California's governor, was a favorite with the Republican Party's conservative wing. Further, he had begun
criticizing Ford's policies in the fall of 1975, in particular,
the Panama Canal Treaty and the Helsinki Accords, which
Ford supported. Backers convinced Reagan to enter the New
Hampshire primary, and he nearly upset Ford. He lost the
next four primaries before finally defeating Ford in North
Carolina, and then he ran up an impressive string of victories that included most of the southern and midwestern states
(as well as his home state of California). When they arrived
in Kansas for the Republican convention, neither candidate

had enough delegates to secure the nomination outright. At that time, Reagan made the decision to announce liberal Pennsylvania senator Richard Schweiker as his running mate, a move that seemed to backfire (it annoyed conservatives and didn't assuage moderates). Ford captured the nomination on the first ballot but went on to lose the general election to Jimmy Carter.

7. BILL CLINTON, 1992

It's difficult to recall an election where a candidate was blindsided with as many crises as Bill Clinton was in the New Hampshire primary and yet somehow managed to survive. Clinton didn't actually win the New Hampshire primary—he finished second to former senator Paul Tsongas—but he was still dubbed the "Comeback Kid" for enduring an assortment of scandals, including the Gennifer Flowers affair (which played out tabloid-style across the country) and the Vietnam War–era draft-dodging controversy. Few thought Clinton could survive one of those scandals, let alone both, but it showed his resiliency and ability to absorb a punch (or two). He turned his campaign around when he and his wife, Hillary, appeared on *60 Minutes* following the Super Bowl, and he admitted to being less than perfect. Clinton used the momentum from a strong second-place finish to sweep the southern primaries and easily win the Democratic nomination. It was the first time a Democratic candidate had won the nomination without winning the New Hampshire primary.

8. PAT BUCHANAN, 1992, 1996

Television commentator Pat Buchanan scored one of the biggest upsets in New Hampshire primary history when he defeated Senate majority leader Robert Dole in the 1996 Republican primary. Buchanan, who four years earlier had unexpectedly won 37 percent of the New Hampshire vote from President George Bush, was expected to be an after-thought in the 1996 primary, but his skillful debating style and populist rhetoric resulted in a narrow victory over a fragmented field. Buchanan gave one of the more memorable speeches in New Hampshire history, which earned him the nickname "Pitchfork Pat": "We shocked them in Alaska. Stunned them in Louisiana. Stunned them in Iowa. They are in a terminal panic. They hear the shouts of peasants from over the hill. All the knights and barons will be riding into the castle pulling up the drawbridge in a minute. All the peasants are coming with pitchforks. . . ." Buchanan turned out be a better wordsmith than candidate, as he would go on to lose every primary afterward and eventually played a minor role at the Republican National Convention in San Diego. Buchanan disproved, at least on the Republican side, the theory that the New Hampshire winner always goes on to win the nomination.

q. JOHN McCAIN, 2000

In 2000 Senator John McCain nearly derailed the George W. Bush juggernaut before it got off the ground with a big upset victory in New Hampshire. McCain took a calculated gamble, decided to skip the Iowa caucus (conceding the state to Bush), and instead focused all his energy on winning New Hampshire. He virtually camped out in the state for months and built an impressive grassroots organization that helped deliver a twenty-point victory over the heavily favored and better-funded Bush. To some experts, it looked as if his victory was enough to deliver a knockout punch to Bush's campaign, but the Texas governor rebounded the following week with a hard-fought (some would say dirty) victory in South Carolina that halted McCain's momentum and reaffirmed Bush's front-runner status. Though McCain won a few more primaries along the way and stayed in the race until the convention, Bush's nomination was never in doubt after South Carolina.

10. HOWARD DEAN, 2004

Howard Dean's quixotic bid for the White House in 2004 may be best remembered for the "Dean Scream" or the "I Have a Scream" speech the media repeatedly aired following his devastating loss in the Iowa caucus to Senator John Kerry. For months heading into the caucus, Dean had held a commanding lead in the polls and seemed to have all the momentum, including a late endorsement from former vice president Al Gore. When Dean finished third behind John Edwards in Iowa and delivered his unusual concession speech, which concluded with a seemingly uncontrollable scream, his momentum stopped cold. Combined with his second-place finish in New Hampshire the following week, it all but ended his campaign. To quote Dean's Iowa concession speech:

> Not only are we going to New Hampshire, [Senator] Tom Harkin, we're going to South Carolina and Oklahoma and Arizona and North Dakota and New Mexico, and we're going to California and Texas and New York . . . And we're going to South Dakota and Oregon and Washington and Michigan. And then we're going to Washington, D.C., to take back the White House! Byaaah!!!

Campaign Slogans

Just about every successful presidential campaign has had a catchy campaign slogan or phrase. Some conveyed serious ideas while others were little more than simple plays on words.

1. "TIPPECANOE AND TYLER TOO," WILLIAM HENRY HARRISON, 1840

William Henry Harrison earned the nickname "Old Tippecanoe" after defeating Native Americans at the Battle of Tippecanoe in 1811. The victory put an end to Indian leader Tecumseh's dream of creating a unified Indian nation and was a springboard to later successes in the War of 1812. Nearly three decades after earning fame on the battlefield, Harrison received the nomination of the Whig Party, which was on its last legs. Along with former senator John Tyler, he ran against incumbent president Martin Van Buren. His simple slogan of "Tippecanoe and Tyler Too" reminded voters of Harrison's past heroics and bravery, and the ticket easily won office. Of course, that was the high-water mark of Harrison's career, for his presidency lasted a mere thirty days. He passed away from a severe case of pneumonia, which he had caught on inauguration day.

2. "FIFTY-FOUR–FORTY OR FIGHT," JAMES K. POLK, 1844

The slogan "Fifty-four–Forty or Fight" arose out of the Oregon Territory border dispute between the United States and Great Britain. Since 1818, the two nations had shared control of the territory, which extended north to the fifty-fourth parallel (the southern border of Alaska). In the election of 1844, the Democrats nominated James K. Polk, who believed the United States had a "clear and unquestionable" claim to the entire Oregon Territory. Senator William Allen of Ohio actually coined the phrase "Fifty-four–Forty or Fight" during a speech on the Senate floor, but it quickly became the rallying cry for the Democratic ticket. In the end, expansionist fever won out as Polk narrowly defeated Henry Clay, who opposed expansion both in Oregon and Texas. After two years of negotiations, in which Polk repeatedly threatened war, the two nations finally settled on a boundary at the forty-ninth parallel, the current boundary.

3. "HE KEPT US OUT OF WAR," WOODROW WILSON, 1916

During the 1916 election incumbent Woodrow Wilson narrowly defeated Republican Charles Evans Hughes on the strength of his record that he had "kept us out of war." The phrase became his campaign slogan in the general election, even though he privately believed that U.S. involvement in World War I was probably inevitable. At the time, the United States was overwhelmingly isolationist, and most Americans adamantly opposed getting involved. Wilson did show restraint in the spring of 1915 after the Germans sank the *Lusitania*, a luxury liner that carried 128 Americans (all of whom died). He resisted the temptation to declare war, knowing full well most Americans didn't support the position, and got assurances from the Germans that they would not target passenger ships. Wilson eventually declared war on Germany in 1917 after German U-boats began sinking merchant ships in the Atlantic Ocean and after discovering the Germans secretly tried to convince Mexico to attack the United States with the promise of receiving its lost territories.

4. "KEEP COOL WITH COOLIDGE," CALVIN COOLIDGE, 1924

Calvin Coolidge became president after Warren Harding suddenly passed away in 1921. During his first term the country prospered as the Roaring Twenties were in full swing. Coolidge was a quiet, taciturn man not prone to great displays of exuberance or even eloquence. During the 1924 campaign his party developed the slogan "Keep Cool with Coolidge" to remind the voters that Coolidge was a leader who would keep the good times rolling. The slogan caught on as Coolidge trounced the opposition, but perhaps Coolidge was simply too cool to notice that on the horizon was an impending financial disaster—the stock market crash.

5. "A FULL DINNER PAIL," WILLIAM MCKINLEY, 1900

It might not have been the catchiest campaign slogan in American history, but William McKinley's reelection slogan, "A Full Dinner Pail," came to represent the prosperity that Americans were enjoying. McKinley had pulled the country out of a deep recession, and while big business was booming, the Republicans wanted to position McKinley as a friend of working Americans. The slogan was meant to convey how well ordinary Americans were doing (hence their bountiful food at dinnertime) and to prevent populist opponent William Jennings Bryan from positioning the president as out of touch with ordinary Americans. The strategy worked, for McKinley crushed Bryan.

6. "I LIKE IKE," DWIGHT D. EISENHOWER, 1952

Dwight Eisenhower's 1952 slogan may have not have conveyed any big campaign ideas, but what it lacked in intellectual heft it made up for in rhetorical simplicity. The popular Eisenhower's well-known nickname was "Ike," and his handlers used it effectively to "brand" the career military leader as likable, approachable, and trustworthy. The campaign enlisted Roy Disney, Walt Disney's brother, to create an animated cartoon commercial—the earliest television commercials in presidential history—starring Uncle Sam leading a parade of ordinary Americans to the musical refrain of "I Like Ike." The slogan appeared on everything from buttons to napkins, bumper stickers, and more. Turns out voters did, indeed, like Ike as he easily defeated Adlai E. Stevenson. For his rematch against Stevenson in 1956, Eisenhower's campaign created the slogan "I Still Like Ike," though it took a backseat to the more serious slogan of "Peace and Prosperity."

7. "NIXON'S THE ONE," RICHARD NIXON, 1968

Richard Nixon's 1968 "comeback" campaign pulled a page from Eisenhower's playbook when it chose the simple refrain "Nixon's the One" as its slogan and then made it the tag line for its advertising. The campaign even mailed out millions of 45 records containing excerpts from Nixon's acceptance speech at the Republican National Convention and emblazoned "Nixon's the One" on the covers. Turns out that Nixon was the one, though just barely, as he narrowly defeated Hubert Humphrey.

8. "MORNING IN AMERICA," RONALD REAGAN, 1984

It might not have been Ronald Reagan's official campaign slogan in 1984, but it quickly became the theme that drove his reelection rout over Walter Mondale. The phrase "Morning in America" was actually the opening line of one of his television commercials, which was formally titled "Prouder, Stronger, Better." Mostly depicting ordinary Americans heading to their jobs, the commercial's cheery optimism reflected Reagan's belief that America had recaptured its greatness and that its best days were ahead. The press picked up on the theme and quickly dubbed his reelection campaign "Morning in America." It's considered one of the most effective political advertisements in history and undoubtedly contributed to Reagan's forty-nine-state landslide victory.

9. "A RETURN TO NORMALCY," WARREN G. HARDING, 1920

Harding's handlers came up with this campaign slogan to contrast Harding with outgoing president Woodrow Wilson, who had led the United States into war and failed to convince the Senate to ratify the Versailles Treaty and the League of Nations. Harding promised stability, peace, and prosperity and little else. After eight years of progressive policies, the nation was apparently ready for a "return to normalcy," for Harding easily defeated James Cox and his running mate, Franklin Roosevelt.

10. "HE'S MAKING US PROUD AGAIN," GERALD FORD, 1976

The Ford campaign tried out this slogan in a couple of advertisements, and while it obviously contrasted him to the disgraced president Richard Nixon, it failed to catch on as a popular sentiment. Ford was certainly a marked improvement over his predecessor, but his pardon of Nixon turned out to be too much for the voting public to overcome. Jimmy Carter narrowly defeated him.

First Ladies

First Ladies play an important ceremonial function, as well as an increasingly political and advocacy role, in their husbands' administrations. In some cases, the First Lady can be a tremendous political asset to the president; in fact, a president rarely has a higher approval or popularity rating than his wife does. And as Hillary Clinton has proven, the role of First Lady can serve as a stepping-stone to elected office.

1. DOLLEY MADISON

Dolley Madison was the first First Lady to consider her role as a highly public position, and she established many of the responsibilities associated with the office. Also interesting, she fulfilled many of the ceremonial and hosting duties of First Lady during widower Thomas Jefferson's administration while her husband, James Madison, was the secretary of state. Dolley Madison organized the first inaugural ball and regularly entertained "society people" with high-profile dinners and events at the White House. She also raised funds for orphaned girls, and by doing so she created the precedent of First Ladies taking on particular causes. Perhaps her noblest gesture—and one of the bravest acts of any First

Lady in history—came as the British Army was burning down Washington during the War of 1812: Dolley refused to leave the White House until its valuable treasures were removed, including important state papers and a large portrait of George Washington. And afterward, when some suggested the capitol should be moved back to Philadelphia, Dolley lobbied ferociously to keep it in Washington.

2. ELEANOR ROOSEVELT

As her husband transformed the powers of the presidency, Eleanor Roosevelt transformed the role of First Lady. She came to the White House with a sense of purpose and used her platform to speak out against social injustices, championing the need for civil rights, more child labor laws, better schools, and access to health care for the poor. She was the first First Lady to write her own daily newspaper column, to host a radio program, and to regularly hold press conferences. She also undertook several tours of the nation without her husband to impoverished and other troubled areas, reporting back to Franklin on her findings, often leading to new policy proposals by the president. In 1935, she helped found the National Youth Administration, a government program that gave thousands of high school and college students part-time work. During World War II, she cochaired a national committee on civil defenses and toured several military and civilian centers to boost morale and observe operations. Following her husband's death, Eleanor Roosevelt became something of an elder statesperson in the Democratic Party and a champion of the underprivileged around the globe. Perhaps Eleanor Roosevelt's most famous quote following her husband's death came in response to Harry Truman's inquiry, "Is there anything I can do for you?" She quickly responded, "Is there any we can do for you? For you are the one in trouble now."

Eleanor Roosevelt visits Sydney, Australia, during World War II.
Franklin D. Roosevelt Presidential Library and Museum

3. JACKIE KENNEDY

Perhaps no First Lady in history captured the imagination of the American people as did Jacqueline "Jackie" Kennedy. A beautiful young mother of two, she was renowned for her grace, elegance, and style, and almost overnight she became the most popular and recognizable woman in the world. Almost immediately upon moving to the White House, she undertook a major restoration of the executive mansion, bringing in the top designers of the day to restore and recreate some of the eloquence, history, and beauty to the living quarters. She successfully lobbied Congress to make all White House furnishings property of the White House (prior to that, they were considered the occupants' property) and to create the position of White House curator so as to protect the mansion's historical integrity. A lover of the arts, Mrs. Kennedy also used the White House as a platform to showcase the arts, hosting ballet and opera concerts, as well as jazz and classical music productions and Shakespearian performances. Her support for establishing a national cultural center ultimately led to the creation of the Kennedy Center for the Performing Arts, the nation's leading performance arts institution. Mrs. Kennedy forever earned the nation's love and affection following President Kennedy's assassination; her strength and courage under extreme duress steadied the nation and helped begin the healing process.

4. HILLARY CLINTON

If Eleanor Roosevelt began the process of transforming the First Lady's role, then Hillary Clinton completed it, making the First Lady's post one of the most powerful in Washington. As one of the nation's most prominent lawyers, Mrs. Clinton had experience in taking on substantive policy issues while she served as First Lady of Arkansas. During the 1992 campaign, Bill Clinton joked that voters would get "two [presidents] for the price of one" should he be elected. President Clinton took the unprecedented step of appointing his wife head of the task force to overhaul the nation's health care system, a move that ultimately backfired when Congress rejected the task forces' recommendations and Mrs. Clinton was openly criticized for her failure to make the process more transparent. Notwithstanding the "Hillary-care" debacle, Mrs. Clinton continued to make access to health care—particularly for children and the disadvantaged—her primary cause, along with global women's rights. Throughout the Monica Lewinsky scandal, Mrs. Clinton remained committed to her marriage, and her political support for the president helped contain the scandal's size and magnitude. In 2000, Mrs. Clinton made history when she became the first First Lady to win elective office and became a U.S. senator from New York.

5. LUCY HAYES

Lucy Hayes is considered the most popular First Lady of the nineteenth century. In fact, the term *First Lady*—though not coined during her tenure—gained widespread acceptance after she undertook a coast-to-coast tour of the United States and was acclaimed the "First Lady of the Land" by the newspapers. She was a gracious and popular White House hostess, and before long women around the country copied her choice in dress and hairstyle. Lucy is probably best remembered for bringing the temperance movement to the White House; she banned all alcohol from the premises and in the process earned the nickname "Lemonade Lucy." It was jokingly written that "water poured like wine" in the Hayes's White House. She's also noted for starting the annual Easter egg roll on the White House lawn, a tradition that continues today, and for commissioning portraits of those presidents who did not have one at the time of her husband's administration. The National First Ladies' Library writes that "no First Lady's leaving was lamented more by the public than hers."

6. EDITH WILSON

Edith Wilson was the second wife of Woodrow Wilson. The two met shortly after Wilson's first wife, Ellen, had passed away, and within a year they were married. Instead of marrying in the White House, however, the ceremony took place in Edith's own home in Washington, D.C. Edith Wilson became First Lady shortly before the United States entered World War I, and as such she was more interested in aiding her husband through stressful times than in performing the traditional hostess role. After President Wilson suffered a debilitating stroke in 1919, Edith Wilson became something of a "temporary president" and ran the administration while hiding the president's illness from the press, Congress, and even cabinet members. According to the National First Ladies' Library, "Edith Wilson decided to somehow continue the Administration by conducting a disinformation campaign, misleading Congress and the public into believing that the President was only suffering from temporary exhaustion which required extensive rest. She became the sole conduit between the President and his Cabinet, requiring that they send to her all pressing matters, memos, correspondence, questions and requests." Edith Wilson served as a gatekeeper to the president, and nothing happened without her consent. Her guardianship of the presidency still rates as one of the oddest moments in presidential history.

7. BETTY FORD

Elizabeth "Betty" Ford was a breath of fresh air in the White House, especially after a closed and dark time for those in

public life. She was outspoken, entertaining, and free spir-
ited. She was not the least bit shy about expressing her point
of view on the hottest issues of the day, including abortion
(she supported legalized abortion) and the Equal Rights
Amendment for women (which she championed)—two policies that the Republican establishment opposed. She also
spoke openly about her battle with breast cancer and her
mastectomy just weeks after becoming First Lady. "Maybe
if I as First Lady could talk about it candidly and without
embarrassment, many other people would be able to as well,"
she said. Seemingly no subject was off-limits with Betty Ford.
She once told *McCall's* magazine that the only topic she
was never asked about was how often she had sex with the
president. She continued: "And if they'd asked me that I
would have told them—as often as possible." Perhaps Betty
Ford's most lasting legacy, however, is the establishment of
the Betty Ford Center to treat chemical dependencies. She
established the center in 1982 after going public with her
own struggles with alcohol and painkillers, and since then it
has helped thousands of people overcome their dependency
problems.

8. NANCY REAGAN

Nancy Reagan will always be remembered for her doting
care of Ronald Reagan during and after his presidency, particularly as he struggled with Alzheimer's disease toward
the end of his life. She was her husband's fiercely devoted
guardian, always putting his well-being ahead of hers, and
unquestionably was Reagan's closest friend (and perhaps
unofficial adviser). Her years in the White House were not
without controversy. She was known to consult an
astrologist, on occasion, to determine "good" and "bad"
days for the president's schedule—a practice she picked
up after he was nearly assassinated. She also maneuvered

behind the scenes on some of the administration's personnel decisions, most notably the firing of White House chief
of staff Donald Regan, who she believed was exercising too
much control over the president. Nancy Reagan is probably best remembered, however, for her highly public "Just
Say No" campaign against teenage drug use. She made
numerous TV appearances touting the program, including
a memorable episode of the television show *Diff'rent
Strokes,* and during the Reagan years drug use among teen-
agers dropped noticeably.

9. LAURA BUSH

While her husband's poll ratings have steadily declined over
the course of his eight years in office, Laura Bush has remained popular with the American public and ranked among
the most popular First Ladies in recent years. Many see her
as a political moderate with commonsense sensibilities and
a steadying influence on the president. President Bush, in
fact, credits Laura with helping him to stop drinking in the
early 1980s and at times with softening his rough edges.
Laura Bush was a source of comfort to the nation following
the September 11 terrorist attacks, and in particular she
spoke about how parents should explain that day's events
to their children. Being a former librarian, it didn't surprise
anyone when she made literacy one of her causes, as well
as women's rights. Following the liberation of Afghanistan,
she spoke openly about the plight of women in the war-torn
country.

10. FRANCES CLEVELAND

Frances Cleveland, the youngest First Lady, was just twenty-
one years of age when she married Grover Cleveland, who
was twenty-seven years her senior and already in the White
House. Hers was the first (and still only) presidential wedding

to take place in the White House. Frances Cleveland was the daughter of Cleveland's longtime law partner, Oscar Folsom, and upon Folsom's death Grover Cleveland became the administrator of his estate, which included guiding Frances's education. When she turned eighteen and entered college, Grover Cleveland asked Frances's mother for permission to correspond with her, and shortly thereafter a romance blossomed. Two years into his term, the two were married in what turned out to be the social event of the year. Newspapers across the country covered every aspect of the wedding, and overnight Frances became an international celebrity. Known for her great sense of style, Frances Cleveland became a frequent cover girl for magazines like *Harper's* and *Leslie's*, and her picture (without her endorsement) adorned all sorts of products such as candy, perfume, and face creams. In fact, her likeliness was misappropriated so often that one member of Congress actually introduced a bill outlawing the use of a woman's likeness for commercial gain without her permission. Frances Cleveland loved mingling with people, and she even had regular Saturday morning receptions during which working-class women who were unable to visit the White House during the week could stop by and chat with her. Frances received so much fan mail that she hired a social secretary to assist with her correspondence, the first time a First Lady had a staff member.

Mistresses

For as long as the nation has had presidents, the presidents have had mistresses. Some presidents have had the good fortune of keeping their private lives out of public view, but others have not fared so well.

1. LUCY MERCER, FRANKLIN D. ROOSEVELT

It is said that the last face Franklin Roosevelt saw was that of his longtime mistress, Lucy Mercer, who was with him in Warm Springs, Georgia, when he suffered a fatal stroke in April 1945. Their romance actually began a quarter century earlier; working as Eleanor Roosevelt's social secretary, Lucy caught the eye of then–assistant secretary of the navy FDR. Eleanor learned of the affair in 1918 and confronted Franklin with a choice: Lucy or her. Roosevelt knew a divorce would sink his political ambitions, so he vowed to never see Lucy again—a promise he kept until 1944, when the two rekindled their romance. Sensing Roosevelt's loneliness and isolation in his waning years, his daughter Anna arranged the clandestine meetings between her father and Lucy, something Eleanor learned only after FDR's death. Many historians believe FDR's affair with Lucy drove a permanent wedge between Franklin and Eleanor and in some respects marked the beginning of Eleanor's independence as a political and social leader.

2. JUDITH CAMPBELL EXNER, JOHN F. KENNEDY

While it's no secret that President Kennedy had many romantic interludes during his three years in office, it's generally believed movie actress Judith Exner Campbell was his most serious relationship. During the 1960 presidential campaign, Exner met Kennedy through Frank Sinatra, who later introduced her to mob boss Sam Giancana as well, and thus began perhaps the oddest love triangle in presidential history. While she was mistress to both Kennedy and Giancana at the same time, it is uncertain if she ever acted as a conduit between the two men as she boasted in a *People* magazine interview years later. Her affair with the president ended abruptly in 1962, after the FBI confronted Kennedy about the relationship. In 1975, Exner testified under oath to her relationship with Kennedy before the Church Committee, a Senate committee that was investigating ties between the CIA and organized crime. Two years later she recounted the entire affair in her best-selling autobiography, *My Story*.

3. CARRIE PHILLIPS, WARREN G. HARDING

Of all the presidential mistresses through the years, Carrie Phillips is believed to be the only one to have successfully blackmailed a major political party—in this case, the Republican Party. Phillips, a family friend of the Hardings', carried on a fifteen-year relationship with the future president that was documented in more than a hundred letters between the two. The affair came to a halt in 1915, when Phillips moved to Germany at her husband's insistence, but it resumed upon her return to the United States. Phillips actually lobbied then-senator Harding to vote against U.S. involvement in the war in Europe and even threatened to go public with their affair if he didn't, but she never followed through with the threat. Harding revealed the affair to the Republican Party bosses shortly after receiving the presidential nomination, telling them that Phillips possessed hundreds of incriminating letters and could potentially black-mail him. During the campaign, Phillips again threatened to go public with the affair, and for her silence the Republican Party gave her $50,000, a trip to Asia, and a yearly stipend for the rest of her life. Shortly before dying, Phillips turned the letters over to author Francis Russell, whose attempt to publish them was blocked by a court injunction; instead, the letters were placed under seal until 2023 (the hundredth anniversary of Harding's death), at which point they will be released to the public.

4. MISSY LEHAN, FRANKLIN D. ROOSEVELT

In addition to Lucy Mercer, Franklin Roosevelt also had a long affair with his personal secretary, Missy Lehand. They met in 1923 while Roosevelt was seeking treatment for his polio in Warm Springs, Georgia. Unlike his previous affair with Lucy Mercer, Roosevelt did little to hide his affection for Lehand; his family came to refer to her as his "second wife." Roosevelt's son, Elliott, would later write about his father's relationship with Lehand that "everyone in the close knit inner circle of father's friends accepted it as a matter of course. I remember being only mildly stirred to see him with Missy on his lap as he sat in his wicker chair in the main stateroom holding her in his sun-browned arms . . . He made no attempt to conceal his feelings about Missy." Lehand suffered a debilitating stroke in 1941 and died a few years later. Upon Roosevelt's death, half of his $3 million estate went to Lehand's heirs, effectively cutting out his five chil-dren from their inheritance.

5. SALLY HEMMINGS, THOMAS JEFFERSON

Rumors that Thomas Jefferson had fathered two children by one of his slaves, Sally Hemmings, first circulated during Jefferson's first presidential term. The *Richmond Recorder* newspaper wrote that it was

> well known that the man, whom it delighted the people to honor, keeps and for many years has kept, as his concubine, one of his slaves. Her name is Sally. The name of her eldest son is Tom. His features are said to bear a striking though sable resemblance to those of the president himself. . . . By this wench Sally, our president has had several children.

Jefferson knew of the gossip about him and Hemmings, but he never confirmed nor denied the relationship in either his public or private correspondences. Rumors about the affair remained just that—baseless speculation—until a 1998 study in the scientific journal *Nature* proved conclusively that, based on DNA testing, Jefferson undoubtedly had fathered Hemming's youngest son, Eston. Ironically, Hemmings wasn't made a free person until 1833, seven years after Jefferson's death.

6. MARIA HALPIN, GROVER CLEVELAND

While running for president in 1884, Grover Cleveland was hit with a rumor that he had fathered a son out of wedlock. The mistress, Maria Halpin, was a thirty-six-year-old widow when he befriended her a dozen years earlier. Cleveland's hometown paper, the Buffalo *Evening Telegraph*, broke the story of his illegitimate child, and the candidate responded with an unusual move: he admitted to the affair and taking responsibility for the child, even though his paternity was in question. The Republicans tried to capitalize on the scandal with the campaign taunt "Ma, Ma, Where's My Pa? Gone to the White House, Ha, Ha, Ha," but many historians believe it may have backfired in light of Cleveland's honesty and forthrightness. Although privately Cleveland had doubts about the child's paternity, he never publicly denied responsibility for him.

7. MONICA LEWINSKY, BILL CLINTON

With eleven simple words—"I did not have sexual relations with that woman, Miss Lewinsky"—President Bill Clinton forever defined his presidency by his sexual affair with twenty-two-year-old White House intern Monica Lewinsky. Like his idol, John F. Kennedy, Bill Clinton had a well-earned reputation as a chronic skirt chaser and philanderer. Throughout the 1992 campaign he was dogged by rumors of infidelity, and both he and his wife, Hillary, famously went on *60 Minutes* to deny an affair with Gennifer Flowers. The Lewinsky affair began during the government shutdown in December 1995 and lasted several years until exposed by Internet gossip Matt Drudge and *Newsweek* magazine. The ensuing scandal paralyzed the presidency, consumed the media for months, and ultimately led to Clinton's impeachment. While Clinton was acquitted of all charges, the affair effectively derailed his second term and, according to some experts, may have cost Vice President Al Gore the 2000 election. Clinton finally admitted to having sexual relations with Monica Lewinsky while testifying under oath before Whitewater special prosecutor Ken Starr and later explained in his autobiography *My Life* that he began the affair simply because "he could."

8. NAN BRITTON, WARREN G. HARDING

Among Warren Harding's many romantic pursuits, his other

well-known mistress was Nan Britton, a local Ohio resident whose father was a friend of Harding's. It is said that Britton developed a crush on Harding while still a teenager growing up in Marion, Ohio, and later consummated the relationship when Harding became a U.S. senator. Britton is credited with writing the first Oval Office kiss–and-tell book, the best-selling *The President's Daughter,* which chronicled in great detail her many encounters with Harding (including one famous episode in a White House closet) and also exposed him as her daughter's father. Though he never saw his illegitimate child, Harding did make generous child support payments to Britton, using the Secret Service as an intermediary. After Harding's death, Britton unsuccessfully sued his estate to win child support payments. Britton dedicated her book "to all unwed mothers, and to their innocent children whose fathers are usually not known to the world."

9. MARILYN MONROE, JOHN F. KENNEDY

It only makes sense that the leading philanderer of his generation would have an affair with the leading sex goddess of her generation, which was the case with John F. Kennedy and Marilyn Monroe. The footage of Marilyn serenading President Kennedy on his birthday is one of the more memorable moments of his presidency. Monroe met Kennedy through the president's brother-in-law, actor Peter Lawford, who helped arrange their secret trysts on the presidential yacht and at the Carlyle Hotel, among other places. The affair lasted two years. After he abruptly dumped her, some believe Marilyn moved on to his brother Bobby and had a romance till the time of her death. Conspiracy theorists have long held that the Kennedys were somehow involved in the legendary actress's untimely death, though there has never been any evidence to substantiate their claims.

10. WILLIAM RUFUS KING, JAMES BUCHANAN

The nation's only bachelor president, James Buchanan, is also generally considered to be the only gay president, though some historians dispute this contention. There is no denying, however, that for sixteen years Buchanan lived with Senator William Rufus King, who later served as Franklin Pierce's vice president. Buchanan took to calling King "Aunt Nancy," a commonly used eighteenth-century expression to describe homosexuals. "I am now solitary and alone, having no companion in the house with me," wrote Buchanan while King served as minister to France.

> I have gone a wooing to several gentlemen, but have not succeeded with any of them. I feel that it is not good for man to be alone; and should not be astonished to find myself married to some old maid who can nurse me when I am sick, provide good dinners for me when I am well, and not expect from me any very ardent or romantic affection.

While in his early twenties, Buchanan was once engaged to the daughter of a prominent industrialist, but she abruptly called off the wedding and then killed herself a few days later.

Offspring

B eing the child of a president has been a blessing for some and a curse for others.

1. JOHN QUINCY ADAMS, JULY 11, 1767–FEBRUARY 23, 1848

John Quincy Adams holds the distinction of being the first presidential offspring to attain the presidency as well as being a member of one of the greatest political dynasties in American history. He's also unique for being the only former president to return to the House of Representatives, where he served nine terms after leaving the White House. Like his father, Adams brought one of the most impressive résumés to the White House: he did stints in the Massachusetts State Senate and U.S. Senate, served as secretary of state in the Monroe administration, and was foreign minister to Portugal, the Netherlands, and Prussia. He actually died in the Capitol Building from a cerebral hemorrhage while doing the nation's business. Most historians contend John Quincy Adams served with more distinction and accomplishment in the House of Representatives than he did in the White House.

2. GEORGE W. BUSH, JULY 6, 1946–

In 2000, George W. Bush became the second presidential offspring to achieve the highest office in the land, following in John Quincy Adams's footsteps. Like Adams, Bush won a controversial election and is also part of a political dynasty: his grandfather Prescott Bush served two terms in the U.S. Senate; his father, George, was the forty-first president; and his brother Jeb served as governor of Florida. Few could have predicted presidential success for Bush, however. After a failed congressional bid in 1978, Bush spent a decade toiling in the oil business and, as part of a consortium, purchased the Texas Rangers baseball team. Bush parlayed the high-visibility owner's position into a run for governor, and in 1994 he pulled an upset victory over incumbent Ann Richards. In 1998 Bush was reelected in a landslide, and two years later he won the presidency in the most contested election in history. In defeating Al Gore by five electoral votes, Bush became only the third president to lose the popular vote but still win the presidency. In 2004, Bush did something his father could not: he won a second term.

3. THEODORE ROOSEVELT, JR., SEPTEMBER 13, 1887–JULY 12, 1944

There is little that Teddy Roosevelt, Jr., didn't achieve or do in his fifty-six years. Like his father, he graduated from Harvard College and charted a successful course in finance before enlisting in the army. He was a highly decorated soldier in World War I, achieving the rank of lieutenant colonel by the war's end. In 1919 he won a seat in the New York State Assembly, and in 1921 President Harding appointed him assistant secretary of the navy, a position his father once held. Under his watch the infamous Teapot Dome scandal occurred, though Roosevelt was never charged with any wrongdoing. Perhaps because of the scandal, Roosevelt was defeated in his bid for governor of New York in 1924, and it appeared his political career was over. In 1929, President Hoover appointed Ted the governor of Puerto Rico, where he won plaudits from the locals for his efforts to ease poverty. He was then appointed governor-general of the Philippines, a post he held until his cousin Franklin replaced him. During most of the Franklin Roosevelt administration, Teddy remained in private business and served on corporate boards, most notably as chairman of the American Express Corporation. At age fifty-three in 1941, he returned to active military duty as a brigadier general and commanded forces in North Africa, Sicily, and Sardinia. On D-Day he led the Fourth Infantry's landing at Utah Beach. At age fifty-seven, he was the oldest American in the first wave at Normandy and the only general on the beaches. He saw some of the most difficult combat conditions, all the while hobbled by decades-old injuries. Though he escaped enemy bullets, he was felled by a massive heart attack in France a month later. When asked about the greatest heroism he had ever seen, Gen. Omar Bradley responded, "Teddy Roosevelt at Utah Beach." General Patton simply called him the "bravest soldier" he had ever known.

4. ROBERT TAFT, SEPTEMBER 8, 1889–JULY 31, 1953

Nicknamed "Mr. Republican" by his Senate colleagues, Robert Taft served three terms in the U.S. Senate and sought the Republican nomination for the presidency in 1940 and 1952. In both attempts, Taft ran as the conservative alternative to the "establishment" candidate—Wendell Wilkie and Dwight Eisenhower, respectively. Though one of the most conservative lawmakers of his generation, members of both political parties greatly admired and respected Taft for his integrity and dedication to public service. In only his first term in the Senate, he was elected chairman of the Republican Conference, the powerful policy steering committee, and when the Republicans regained control of the Senate in 1952, he became majority leader. Shortly after his death, Taft was one of the five senators featured in then-senator John F. Kennedy's Pulitzer Prize–winning book, *Profiles in Courage*. Taft belongs to one of the most enduring political dynasties in American history: his grandfather Alphonso Taft served as attorney general and secretary of war; his father, William Howard Taft, was the only president to also sit on the Supreme Court; his son Robert was elected to the U.S. Senate and another son William Howard Taft III served as ambassador to Ireland; and grandson Robert Taft II was the governor of Ohio.

5. FREDERICK DENT GRANT, MAY 30, 1850–APRIL 12, 1912

The oldest son of Ulysses S. Grant, Frederick Grant had a long and distinguished career in public service. Like his father, he attended West Point, and during two tours in the military, he saw combat in the Bannock War and the Spanish-American War. Though he didn't follow his father into elected office, President Harrison appointed him as the minister to Austria. President Cleveland later nominated him to be secretary of state, but his confirmation was defeated in the Senate. He went on to serve as commissioner of the New York City Police Department, succeeding Teddy Roosevelt in that post, and later in life Grant returned to active duty in the army, where he was promoted to major general in 1906. At the time of his death, he was the second-highest-ranking officer in the U.S. Army.

6. JAMES WEBB COOK HAYES, MARCH 20, 1856–JULY 26, 1934

Webb Hayes is widely considered to be the most powerful

presidential offspring to serve in his father's administration. Though his title was simply "personal secretary," Webb was actually one of his father's closest advisers. He was regarded as his father Rutherford's "eyes and ears" on Capitol Hill and often was a stand-in at important social functions. Popular with the ladies, Webb's social exploits and whereabouts were often chronicled in the press. After his father left office, Webb went into private business and helped found the company that would go on to become the multinational conglomerate Union Carbide. Wealthy, In need of some excitement, and in something of a midlife crisis, Webb joined the military and wound up seeing action in the Spanish-American War, the Russo-Japanese War, the Boxer Rebellion, and World War I, winning all sorts of accolades along the way. His last great achievement was to create the Rutherford B. Hayes Presidential Center, the first ever presidential library.

7. ROBERT TODD LINCOLN, AUGUST 1, 1843–JULY 23, 1926

The only one of Abraham Lincoln's four children to live to adulthood, Robert Todd Lincoln led an extraordinary life of public service and achievement. He left Harvard Law School shortly before the Civil War ended, joined the Union Army, and served on Ulysses Grant's personal staff. After his father's assassination, Robert completed his legal studies at the University of Chicago. He had a thriving legal practice when Democratic president Rutherford B. Hayes offered him the position of assistant secretary of state, which he declined. Four years later President Garfield appointed him secretary of war, and Lincoln served in that capacity through the Arthur administration. Later he was the ambassador to the United Kingdom during the Harrison administration, and from 1901 through 1911 he was the chairman and president of the Pullman Company, one of the largest companies of the day. Upon his death, his widow made the unusual choice of having him buried at Arlington National Cemetery rather than in Lincoln's Tomb (where his father and three deceased siblings were buried), because, as she put it, Robert "was a personage, made his own history, independently [underlined five times] of his great father, and should have his own place 'in the sun'!"

8. JAMES RUDOLPH GARFIELD, OCTOBER 17, 1865–MARCH 24, 1950

Many historians rank James R. Garfield as one of the finest cabinet members in history. Fifteen-year-old James Rudolph was at his father's side when an assassin shot the president; the two were waiting to board a train bound for the president's college reunion. He earned a law degree from Columbia University and practiced with his brother Harry before winning a seat in the Ohio State Senate. It was at the national level where he made his mark, befriending President Teddy Roosevelt and earning an appointment to his Civil Service Commission in 1902. Roosevelt then appointed him commissioner of corporations at the Department of Commerce and Labor, where he played an instrumental role in investigating the meatpacking and steel industries. His final post in the administration was as secretary of the interior, and he pioneered the conservation of natural resources. Roosevelt called his choice the "finest appointment" of his presidency.

9. CHARLES FRANCIS ADAMS, AUGUST 18, 1807–NOVEMBER 21, 1886

Son of President John Quincy Adams and grandson of President John Adams, Charles was the third generation to strive for the highest office in the land. Something of a child prodigy, Adams was fluent in seven languages by his early teenage years, and he graduated from Harvard Law at age seventeen. He served in the Massachusetts State legislature before being elected to the House of Representatives in 1858, where he was an outspoken critic of slavery. He resigned from the House to become President Lincoln's minister to England and played a critical role in keeping the British neutral during the Civil War. In 1872 and again in 1876, Adams's name was put forth as a candidate for the presidency, but both times he failed to win his party's nomination. His second son went on to become the president of the Union Pacific Railroad.

10. JOHN SCOTT HARRISON, OCTOBER 4, 1804–MAY 25, 1878

John Scott Harrison has the distinction of being the only son of a president—William Henry Harrison—who was also the father of a president, Benjamin Harrison. John Harrison served two terms in Congress (1853–57) before retiring to his farm, where he spent the final thirty years of his life. Harrison didn't live long enough to see his son win the presidency. In a strange footnote, shortly after his death, grave robbers exhumed his corpse and sold it to a medical college, where his son the future president actually discovered it.

Vice Presidents: The Powerful and Memorable

As the Founding Fathers debated the Constitution, the vice presidency was hardly even an afterthought. They gave it almost no consideration during the proceedings, and the sole role they devised for the position was to preside over the Senate and cast tie-breaking votes. In fact, the office was held in such low regard that the First Congress actually debated eliminating the position altogether. Franklin Roosevelt's first vice president, John Nance Garner, famously said the office wasn't "worth a pitcher of warm spit," and John Adams, the nation's first vice president, called it "the most insignificant office that ever the invention of man contrived or his imagination conceived." Not surprising, for most of the office's history, it's been filled with less-than-memorable characters—a collection of political hacks, has-beens, and empty suits, more or less—with a few bright lights interspersed. It wasn't until World War II that the vice presidency began to grow in importance, and by the twenty-first century, it has come full circle: it now rates among the most powerful positions in the government.

1. DICK CHENEY—GEORGE W. BUSH

Few politicians in recent memory has aroused as much passion from his defenders and detractors as Vice President Dick Cheney. Love him or hate him, one thing is undisputable:

Cheney is the most powerful vice president in history and maybe the most controversial as well. Cheney came to the office with an impressive résumé, which included stints as the White House chief of staff to Gerald Ford, House minority whip, secretary of defense during the George H. W. Bush administration, and most recently as the chief executive officer (CEO) of the oil conglomerate Halliburton. Ironically, George W. Bush had put Cheney in charge of his vice presidential selection committee following his victory in the 2000 Republican primary but then concluded that Cheney himself was the best person for the job. Before long Cheney established himself as a genuine power broker; Bush entrusted him with the administration's top domestic and foreign policy priorities and admittedly rarely made an important decision without consulting Cheney. Cheney's considerable influence grew following the terrorist attacks of September 11 as he became the administration's point person on the war on terror and as he helped shape the strategy for the incursion in Afghanistan and later the war in Iraq. Many of his critics blame Cheney for "pushing" President Bush into war with Iraq and of knowing full well that Saddam Hussein did not represent an imminent threat. At one point, Cheney's power and influence had grown so unprecedented that many pundits and observers began to view him as "Bush's puppeteer." In light of the stalemate in Iraq and its lack of weapons of mass destruction, the disastrous 2006 midterm elections for Republicans, and the indictment of his Chief of Staff Scooter Libby for perjury in the CIA leak case, some speculate Cheney's influence is on the wane. Even so, Cheney certainly remains among the president's most trusted advisers and will leave office as the vice president with the most impact—by a long shot—in history.

2. AL GORE—BILL CLINTON

Prior to Dick Cheney, it was generally agreed that Vice

President Al Gore was the most influential veep in history. As a junior senator from Tennessee, Gore actually ran for president in 1988 and won six southern primaries before losing the nomination to Michael Dukakis. His selection as Bill Clinton's running mate in 1992 was slightly unconventional in that both were from the South—Tennessee and Arkansas, respectively—and the two were not close friends. Gore proved to be an effective campaigner with Clinton, and upon their victory he was given a broad portfolio in domestic policy. Gore's "reinventing government" initiative is considered his biggest accomplishment; it was the largest government reform program in history at the time. He also led the administration's push for adopting the North American Free Trade Agreement (NAFTA) and took the unusual step of debating NAFTA opponent (and presidential candidate) Ross Perot on CNN's *Larry King Live* program on the eve of the vote in Congress. His thrubbing of Perot helped secure NAFTA's passage and established his bona fides as a major force in the White House. Gore also played a pivotal role in shaping the administration's environmental policy and generally receives high marks for his accomplishments in this arena, though he did suffer a major defeat when the Senate voted against the Kyoto Protocol 95–0. Toward the end of their second term, the president's relationship with Gore had cooled considerably after Gore criticized Clinton's moral shortcomings in the Lewinsky affair; consequently, Clinton did little campaigning for Gore in 2000. Gore's defeat to George W. Bush effectively ended his political career and left many in the Democratic Party wondering how a two-term incumbent vice president with a strong economic record could lose to a two-term governor.

3. WALTER MONDALE—JIMMY CARTER

Walter Mondale is mostly remembered as the guy whom

Ronald Reagan pasted in the 1984 presidential election; instead, he should be remembered as the first vice president to dramatically increase the scope, size, and influence of the position. George McGovern had offered the vice presidential nomination to Mondale four years earlier, but he wisely turned it down. Thus Mondale was known as an accomplished and well-respected senator from Minnesota when Carter made him his running mate, and undoubtedly he harbored presidential ambitions of his own. Mondale had a couple of firsts as vice president—including the first official government residence, namely, the Naval Observatory, and the first vice president's office in the West Wing—and established the tradition of the weekly president–vice president lunch, which is still followed today. Carter mostly used Mondale as a troubleshooter for the administration and relied on his foreign policy experience to help with global flash points, including South Africa and the Middle East. Mondale also played a big role in reorganizing the intelligence community. His defeat to Reagan ended his political career, though he was briefly called out of retirement when Bill Clinton made him the ambassador to Japan. In 2002, Mondale stepped in as a last-minute Senate candidate when Minnesota senator Paul Wellstone died in a plane crash, but Norm Coleman soundly defeated him.

4. RICHARD NIXON—DWIGHT D. EISENHOWER

Given Richard Nixon's tumultuous presidency, it is easy to forget or overlook his eight years as Dwight Eisenhower's vice president. Nixon arrived at the office at age thirty-nine— a wunderkind of the Republican Party. Though Eisenhower did not personally like Nixon, he believed the vice president's role was important and consequently delegated substantial authority to Nixon, particularly when it came to foreign affairs. Nixon traveled to fifty-four countries during his eight years in the office—by far the most of any vice president at the time—for more than just symbolic visits. On three occasions, Nixon also stepped in to temporarily run the country while Eisenhower was ill or incapacitated, representing the first time a veep had taken the reigns of government. Nixon's crowning moment—one of the most memorable for any vice president, for that matter—was his "Kitchen Debate" with Soviet premier Nikita Khrushchev in 1959 at the American National Exhibition in Moscow, where they debated the merits of capitalism versus communism. Unfortunately for Nixon, the most anyone remembers about his time as Ike's vice president is a quote that the president served up at a press conference in 1960: after a reporter asked him what Nixon's accomplishments were, Ike responded, "If you give me a week, I might think of one."

5. AARON BURR—THOMAS JEFFERSON
Aaron Burr holds the distinction of being the only sitting vice president who was wanted in two states on charges of murder after dueling with and killing Alexander Hamilton in New Jersey (dueling was illegal in the state). Burr is one of the most fascinating characters in American political history. In the presidential election of 1800, because of a quirk in the voting process, which was subsequently changed by the Twelfth Amendment, Burr actually tied Thomas Jefferson with seventy-three electoral votes even though he was Jefferson's running mate. Jefferson consequently lost confidence and trust in Burr and excluded him from all deliberations (much as Adams had shut him out during his tenure in that office). Even so, Burr was regarded as a terrific leader in the Senate and was given especially high marks—even by his critics at the time—for his impartial presiding over the impeachment trial of the Associate Justice of the Supreme Court Samuel Chase. Chase was acquitted

on all counts (the charges were mostly about political bias in a particular case), and by his actions, Burr is credited with helping establish the notion of a politically independent judicial system. On his final day in office, Burr delivered what many consider one of the finest speeches of the early republic when he said farewell to the Senate. The oratory was so moving and heartfelt that it left many senators, including some of his detractors, in tears.

6. THOMAS JEFFERSON—JOHN ADAMS

Thomas Jefferson may be the only vice president in history who had no conversations whatsoever with his president, for he and Adams didn't speak a word to each other in their four years together aside from a single exchange on a street corner. He unquestionably is the only vice president to defeat the incumbent in an election, as well as the only vice president to serve two terms as president (Van Buren and George H. W. Bush both failed to win their second term). Jefferson's greatest contribution while vice president was undoubtedly writing the *Manual of Parliamentary Practice,* the first book on U.S. parliamentary procedure. While it's not considered a direct authority on parliamentary procedure, the Senate still defers to Jefferson's manual and treats it as authoritative. The official U.S. Senate website refers to Jefferson's manual as "the single greatest contribution to the Senate by any person to serve as vice president, it is as relevant to the Senate of the late twentieth century as it was to the Senate of the late eighteenth century." In 1837 the House of Representatives also adopted Jefferson's manual as a direct authority for its rules.

7. JOHN C. CALHOUN—JOHN QUINCY ADAMS AND ANDREW JACKSON

John C. Calhoun rates as one of the most accomplished

men to ever serve as vice president. He was a former congressman and James Monroe's secretary of war prior to cutting a deal with John Quincy Adams in the disputed 1824 election: in return for Calhoun's electoral support, Adams made him vice president. Adams soon regretted that deal, as the two had a falling out and Calhoun actively worked against Adams's interests in the Senate. Calhoun then switched parties and agreed to serve as vice president for Andrew Jackson, who had defeated Adams in the election of 1828 (it would be akin to Al Gore agreeing to be George W. Bush's vice president). Jackson and Calhoun also had a falling out, in part because of Calhoun's support of the theory of nullification, which held that states could simply ignore those federal laws they considered against their interests. Jackson vehemently opposed nullification and threatened to invade South Carolina and to arrest Calhoun if the state refused to pay federal tariffs. By this time, Calhoun had resigned from office—he was the first vice president to resign, with the other being Spiro Agnew—and was elected to the U.S. Senate. This time, South Carolina blinked, but it would not do so some two decades later.

8. GARRET HOBART—WILLIAM MCKINLEY

By all accounts, Garret Hobart was one of the nicest and most decent persons to occupy the vice president's office. And he was one of the least experienced. Prior to winning office as McKinley's running mate, Hobart's political experience consisted of several terms in the New Jersey General Assembly and New Jersey State Senate. He was extremely popular with his colleagues in both chambers and had little ambition to extend his reach beyond New Jersey mostly because he had a comfortable law practice there and an intense fear of public speaking. At the 1896 convention, Hobart and twenty other national figures were given vice presidential consideration. In the end political kingmaker Mark Hanna chose him because New Jersey was a critical swing state and Hobart was an exceptional fund-raiser. He reluctantly accepted the vice presidential nomination, writing to his wife from the convention that

> I am heart-sick over my own prospects. It looks to me I will be nominated for Vice-President whether I want it or not, and as I get nearer to the point where I may, I am dismayed at the thought. . . . But when I realize all that it means in work, worry, and loss of home and bliss, I am overcome, so overcome I am simply miserable.

Though Hobart and McKinley didn't know each other prior to the election, they formed a close bond, and Hobart became a trusted adviser and key player in his administration. Moreover, Hobart's wife, Jennie, became dear friends with First Lady Ida McKinley, who suffered from epilepsy and was a recluse in the White House. Jennie Hobart essentially looked after Ida McKinley and performed many of the First Lady's customary social duties in Ida's stead. Hobart passed away toward the end of the term, leaving McKinley to tell the family, "No one outside of this home feels this loss more deeply than I do." Hobart's place in history was almost instantly overshadowed by his successor, Theodore Roosevelt, who came to dominate the era that they shared.

9. GEORGE CLINTON—THOMAS JEFFERSON AND JAMES MADISON

Clinton is best remembered as the longest-serving governor in U.S. history, having been governor of New York for twenty-one years, but he was also the first vice president (and only one of two) to serve for two different presidents as well as the first to die in that office. Ironically, at the

Constitutional Convention, Clinton had opposed the creation of the office altogether, stating that it was unnecessary. It didn't stop him, however, from accepting Jefferson's offer to replace Aaron Burr on the ticket in 1805.

10. JOHN ADAMS—GEORGE WASHINGTON

As the nation's first vice president, John Adams was aware that just as George Washington was setting presidential precedents with each act and gesture, so too was he establishing precedents for the nation's second-highest office. He believed that as the president of the Senate, the vice presidency was primarily committed to the legislative branch, and he was careful not to be viewed as usurping Washington's authority or undermining his leadership in any way. He was neither a close confidant nor a valued counselor of Washington's, and he mostly stayed away from cabinet meetings. When it came to ruling on points of order during Senate deliberations, Adams looked to British parliamentary procedures since there were no guidelines or rules on running the Senate. In that sense, he created many of the precedents that still exist today regarding Senate rules. Adams's view that the office had limited powers and little role in shaping the president's agenda went a long way in shaping how future presidents and vice presidents approached the office.

Vice Presidents: The Forgettable and Regrettable

Throughout the history of the office, there have been more forgettable and regrettable vice presidents than memorable ones. Nineteenth-century veeps proved to be a particularly undistinguished lot—only a few played even a minor role in their administrations, with corruption, illness, and incompetence generally ruling the day—though the modern era has produced a few doozies as well.

1. SPIRO AGNEW—RICHARD NIXON

No politician in the modern era was less qualified to be vice president of the United States than Spiro T. Agnew. Agnew was an undistinguished first-term governor of Maryland when Nixon plucked him from obscurity to be his running mate in 1968, prompting the political punditry to ask, "Spiro who?" If he was known at all outside Maryland, it was because of his hard-line stance against race rioters in Baltimore and his condescending attitude toward black leaders in his state. Nixon most likely put him on the ticket to appeal to southern voters and counterbalance George Wallace's third-party candidacy. Nixon had little use for Agnew as vice president and relegated him to giving speeches attacking the press corps, a role Agnew took to well with the help of Nixon's speechwriter Pat Buchanan. On several occasions during his first term, Nixon quietly plotted ways to get Agnew to resign but ultimately decided not to because he thought it would upset his southern base. He kept his place on the 1972 ticket, but Agnew was forced to resign from office after prosecutors in Maryland unearthed evidence that he had received bribes while governor of Maryland. Agnew pleaded nolo contendere to the charges and quietly left public life. He refused to speak to Nixon for the remainder of his life, though he did attend Nixon's funeral just two years before his own death.

2. SCHUYLER COLFAX—ULYSSES S. GRANT

Colfax is the only speaker of the House to ascend to the vice presidency, and he mostly served without distinction during his four years with Grant. In 1871, Grant took the extraordinary step of asking Colfax to switch positions with Secretary of State Hamilton Fish as a sort of farewell gift to Fish, who intended to retire at the end of the term. "In all my heart I hope you will say yes," Grant wrote Colfax. Colfax refused, however, and not surprisingly was dumped from the ticket a year later. Before his term was up, Colfax was implicated in the Crédit Mobilier of America scandal, one of two scandals that rocked Grant's administration. The House committee investigating the scandal produced solid evidence that Colfax had received $1,200 from Crédit Mobilier in return for his support of their government contracts, a charge he hotly denied. He narrowly averted impeachment and left the office in disgrace.

3. HANNIBAL HAMLIN—ABRAHAM LINCOLN

As Lincoln's first vice president, Hamlin was so bored with presiding over the Senate that he only stayed in Washington long enough to begin and close the Senate session, spending the remainder of his time at home in Maine. Hamlin had zero clout with Lincoln and was summarily dropped from the ticket in the summer of 1864 in favor of Tennessee governor Andrew Johnson. As a lame-duck vice president, Hamlin enlisted as a private in the Maine Coast Guard and served as a cook during the Civil War. "I am the Vice-President of the United States, but I am also a private citizen, and as an enlisted member of your company, I am bound to do my duty," he told the commanding officer.

4. RICHARD JOHNSON—MARTIN VAN BUREN

Johnson was considered something of a scoundrel in his day, a seedy character with few friends or supporters. He made his name in the War of 1812 when he claimed to have personally killed Indian leader Tecumseh during the Battle of the Thames (a claim that is widely disputed). He used his notoriety to win a seat in the Congress and later the Senate, where he spent most of his time advocating for pay raises for elected officials (he was always teetering on bankruptcy) and eliminating debtors prison (he feared going to jail). He also proposed that post offices remain open seven days a week simply because he liked receiving mail. Johnson's personal life was no better; he made his slave his common-law wife, and when she passed away he made another slave his common-law wife, but she escaped. He found her, sold her at a slave auction, and then took her sister as his mistress. Fortunately for Johnson, his one benefactor was Andrew Jackson, and because of this connection, Johnson received the Democratic vice presidential nomination in 1836. Though the Democratic candidate for president, Van Buren, won the election easily, Johnson was so unpopular with members of the Electoral College that he failed to receive a majority of votes. For the first and only time in history the Senate chose the vice president, and Johnson won, thanks to Jackson's arm twisting. On the outs with Van

Buren, however, Johnson spent most of his vice presidency back home in Kentucky, where he tended bar at his hotel and resort. English author Harriet Martineau may have summed up Johnson best when she observed that "if he should become President, he will be as strange-looking a potentate as ever ruled."

5. DAN QUAYLE—GEORGE W. BUSH

Few politicians in the modern era have suffered through more ridicule, jokes, and character assassinations than Dan Quayle. From the moment he was thrust into the national spotlight at the 1988 Republican Convention, Quayle became something of a punch line for the media and Democrats, and he never escaped the caricature of a political lightweight not ready for prime time. If Quayle is remembered for anything, it's two incidents: being on the receiving end of one of the most memorable lines in political history—Lloyd Bentsen's retort, "You're no Jack Kennedy"—and failing to correctly spell "potato" while attending a grade-school spelling bee. He played a small role in the Bush administration. His one moment in the sun came in 1989, when he stepped in for a traveling President Bush and led the Situation Room during an attempted coup in the Philippines. Otherwise, he mostly kept a low profile, aside from an occasional swipe against fictional TV character Murphy Brown, and was nearly dumped from the 1992 reelection ticket. Said Senate Republican leader Bob Dole at the time: "No Vice President took as many shots—unfair shots—as Dan Quayle. And no Vice President withstood those shots with as much grace, good humor, and commitment to not back down."

6. WILLIAM RUFUS KING—FRANKLIN PIERCE

William King is notable for having the shortest tenure of any vice president—he died a little over a month into his term— and for being sworn in from Cuba, where he was recovering from tuberculosis. Congress passed a special law allowing him to be sworn in abroad, the only time in history this dispensation has occurred. In a severely weakened state, King tried to return to Washington but died shortly after reaching his plantation in Alabama. He was also the only bachelor vice president and was rumored to have had a relationship with President Buchanan, though no real evidence of this exists.

7. HUBERT HUMPHREY—LYNDON JOHNSON

Vice President Hubert Humphrey once said, "I did not become vice president with Lyndon Johnson to cause him trouble," and that statement essentially captures his time in office as Johnson's veep. Humphrey had been one of the most distinguished and respected members of the Senate and a trailblazer on important issues of the day, most notably regarding civil rights; Humphrey was twenty years ahead of his time in his support of equal rights for African Americans. He brought little of this fire to the vice presidency, however. He chose instead to be a dutiful supporter of his president's agenda even if he personally disagreed with it, as was the case with the Vietnam War. Prior to becoming vice president, he had opposed the incursion into Southeast Asia, but he changed his tune at Johnson's behest and became one of the administration's leading spokespersons for the war. As the war grew increasingly unpopular, Humphrey continued to speak publicly in favor of it, at one point even calling it "our great adventure." As liberals began to abandon Johnson and the war, Humphrey was left in the unenviable position of having to be loyal to Johnson while acknowledging to his progressive base that Vietnam was a mistake and a lost cause—something he never quite succeeded in doing. The great tragedy of Humphrey's vice presidency is that he had the acumen, courage, and stature to counsel LBJ out of his disastrous Vietnam policy, but for reasons of political expediency he chose not to, leaving a sad legacy.

8. DANIEL TOMPKINS—JAMES MONROE

A leading essayist of the time wrote that Tompkins had a "face of singular masculine beauty" and an unpretentious demeanor. That's about all he had, as it turned out. Tompkins spent his two terms in office mostly drinking heavily and trying to clear his name after financial wrongdoings during his time as governor of New York. He rarely spent any time in Washington, D.C., and preferred to remain in New York, where he meddled in local politics, battled financial and legal problems, and drowned his sorrows. His few attempts at presiding over the Senate were efforts in futility and incompetence, and he generally tried to stay away when it was in session. He managed somehow to survive two terms on the ticket (mostly because Monroe had no challengers) and left the office after eight years a sick and impoverished man.

9. HENRY WILSON—ULYSSES S. GRANT

Wilson was Grant's second vice president, and he narrowly averted implication in the Crédit Mobilier scandal that had forced the previous vice president, Schuyler Colfax, from the ticket. Early in his term, Wilson suffered a stroke that impaired his speech and caused him to lose control of his facial muscles. He spent most of his time recuperating in his home state of Massachusetts and somehow managed to pen a three-volume history of the Civil War. Making little attempt to help Grant as he suffered through one scandal after another, Wilson died in office shortly before his term ended.

10. THOMAS HENDRICKS—GROVER CLEVELAND

Known as the "Vice President of the spoilsmen," Thomas Hendricks and Grover Cleveland disagreed sharply over the role of patronage positions for the Democratic Party. Cleveland, a reformer, believed in expanding the Civil Service at the expense of the spoils system while Hendricks—along with most Democrats who had been out of power for decades—wanted to reward the party's longtime supporters for their loyalty. Hendricks considered Cleveland's behavior treacherous and privately rebuked him to party leaders. The two also held differing viewpoints on government intervention in the economy: Hendricks was a proponent of subsidies and tariffs; Cleveland, a supporter of laissez-faire economics. Hendricks died in office without playing any role in the administration.

Ranking the Presidents: The Great and Near Great

Ranking the presidents is not just for professional historians. Everyone has an opinion about the best and worst officeholders. This ranking is not meant to be a definitive compilation; rather, it's meant to be thought provoking. The rankings have been divided into four groups: the great and near great, the good, the average, and the bad and the ugly. They are not based on any specific criteria, methodology, or ranking system—just on opinion. Two presidents, William Henry Harrison and James A. Garfield, are excluded altogether because their terms were too short to judge them adequately.

1. ABRAHAM LINCOLN

Abraham Lincoln's greatness stems from the simple fact that he refused to allow the nation to dissolve. A generation of presidents were incapable of doing anything to prevent civil war, and Lincoln was left to preserve the Union. Some in the North thought that the country would be better off with the South's secession, but Lincoln roundly rejected that approach. "In *your* hands, my dissatisfied fellow countrymen, and not in *mine,* is the momentous issue of civil war," he concluded his inaugural address. "The Government will not assail *you.* You can have no conflict without being yourselves the aggressors. *You* have no oath registered in heaven to destroy the Government, while I shall have the most solemn one to preserve, protect, and defend it." Lincoln had little reservation about suspending civil liberties, imposing martial law, indefinitely jailing suspected Confederate sympathizers, or blockading Southern ports as part of the war effort, even though these actions stretched the outer bounds of the Constitution. They were all necessary, as he saw it, for the Union to prevail. Lincoln proved to be a highly effective wartime president and never hesitated to replace lackluster generals with better ones, which explained Ulysses Grant's meteoric rise through the ranks. He used soaring rhetoric and oratory—most memorably at Gettysburg—to sustain and nourish the nation's commitment to war, particularly during the early years when the outcome was much in doubt. With the Emancipation Proclamation and later the Thirteenth Amendment, Lincoln made the abolition of slavery an official wartime goal, something it had not been at the outset. Of the proclamation he said, "I never, in my life, felt more certain that I was doing right, than I do in signing this paper." Lincoln's assassination rates among the greatest tragedies in American history.

2. GEORGE WASHINGTON

George Washington's contribution to the creation of the United States is nearly incalculable. It includes his role as a delegate at the First and Second Continental Congress, as commander of the army during the Revolutionary War, as presiding officer at the Constitutional Convention of 1787, and of course as the first president of the United States. His presidency was unique in so many aspects, the most important being the nature of the precedents he set. Virtually everything he did was a first, and as such he measured his actions carefully for future generations to observe.

His cabinet choices reflected both geographical and ideo-logical diversity, and it was an important part of the government's decision-making process. While he sided with Alexander Hamilton about the need for a strong central government, he valued Thomas Jefferson's point of view about guarding states' rights. His putting down the Whiskey Rebellion—he personally led the militia—was critical in establishing federal authority over insurrections and rebellions. On foreign policy, he warned against permanent treaties and overseas entanglements, and he chose neutrality in the war between England and France (much to Thomas Jefferson's dismay, who wanted the country to aid France). He meticulously created the appropriate "pomp and circumstance" of the office, avoiding the grandiose European traditions in favor of modest American values. He settled on "Mr. President" as a title, preferring it over John Adams's suggestion of "His Majesty" or "His Highness." Perhaps his most important act as president—maybe his most important act as an American—was the simple act of voluntarily walking away from power after two terms in office. Washington certainly could have run for a third term, or perhaps even created a permanent presidency or throne, but he believed no single person should accrue too much power. In this unprecedented act, he ensured the republic's survival.

3. FRANKLIN D. ROOSEVELT

Aside from Lincoln, no president faced greater challenges than Franklin Roosevelt. He inherited the worst economic depression in the nation's history and simultaneously dealt with an unrelenting march toward global war. He took advantage of his mandate in the 1932 election to create the most far-reaching (Republicans of the day called it "radical") reformation of U.S. economic institutions and social policy and the constructs of the modern-day federal government. His New Deal program, which redefined the "contract" between the government and the people, remains the single most important legislative agenda in history. At times, he exceeded his authority—most notably with the ill-conceived "court-packing" plan—but his missteps were few and far between. His leadership before and during the war, however, may have been his greatest contribution. Roosevelt understood that U.S. involvement was inevitable and began preparing the nation for war even while the isolationists in Congress were insisting on neutrality. His Lend-Lease program was a brilliant move that allowed for increased involvement without technically violating neutrality, and ultimately it may have kept England in the war. His close relationship with Winston Churchill helped forge a seamless and coordinated Allied effort, a monumental and unprecedented achievement in warfare. He was wise enough to allow his generals to set strategy and skillful enough to keep the Allied nations unified. Some critics contend Roosevelt conceded too much to Joseph Stalin at the Yalta Conference—particularly in Eastern Europe—and underestimated the Soviet threat, and others maintain that Roosevelt's prewar policies in Asia goaded Japan into attacking Pearl Harbor. What few dispute, however, is that Franklin Roosevelt was the most dominant American of the twentieth century.

4. THEODORE ROOSEVELT

Theodore Roosevelt built on Andrew Jackson's and Abraham Lincoln's legacies of activist executives and stretched the outer limits of presidential authority. In many ways, his time in office marked the beginning of the modern presidency. He was the first president to aggressively court the press, and he created the concept of the presidential "bully pulpit" (which in some ways is the most powerful aspect of the office today). Roosevelt touched—maybe a better word is *shaped*—just about every aspect of American life. He practically invented the concept of conservation and did more to preserve America's natural beauty than any president before or since. He used the Sherman Antitrust Act to break up scores of monopolistic trusts and championed all sorts of progressive regulation, including the Pure Food and Drug Act and the Meat Inspection Act. He made the navy into the second-greatest fleet in the world after Great Britain's and used it to enforce the Monroe Doctrine's "Roosevelt Corollary," which held that the United States reserved the right to intervene in Latin America when government corruption made it necessary. He enforced the doctrine to prop up a puppet government in Panama, negotiated a favorable canal treaty, and oversaw the canal's construction. It was perhaps his boldest move while in office. His activism translated into an imperialist foreign policy and the "civilizing," as he saw it, of territories such as Cuba, Puerto Rico, and the Philippines. He won a Nobel Peace Prize in 1906 for helping negotiate a settlement in the Russo-Japanese War and other peace treaties. Roosevelt believed the president should be the steward of the people, and as such he felt he could take any measure so long as it wasn't expressly forbidden by the Constitution. "I did not usurp power," he once wrote. "But I did greatly broaden the use of executive power."

5. HARRY S. TRUMAN

The conventional wisdom regarding the near great Truman presidency has changed dramatically over the past several decades. He left office after a difficult second term and for years was considered a weak president. The new consensus, however, is that he governed during extremely difficult times and established the foundations for U.S. foreign policy for half a century. Upon taking office, Truman was faced with one of the most wrenching decisions in history: either use the atomic bomb to end the war in the Pacific or sacrifice countless American and Allies' lives with an invasion of Japan. The decision had moral and ethical implications as well as pragmatic considerations. In the end, he lived by his motto "The buck stops here," made the tough choice of deploying the bomb, and in the process likely saved tens of thousands of lives. He broke with traditional foreign policy and orchestrated the largest aid package in history (some would say bailout) with the Marshall Plan, which played a critical role in rebuilding Western Europe. His Truman Doctrine—or the policy of containing the expansion of Soviet communism—was a bold and historic new direction for U.S. foreign policy and established the framework for its Cold War policy vis-à-vis the Soviet Union. On the domestic front, he solidified and expanded key New Deal programs, including Social Security and labor rights, and desegregated the U.S. military. He pushed for other civil rights reforms at his own political peril (he practically goaded Strom Thurmond and the Dixiecrats to run a third party), but he was blocked by southern Democrats. During Truman's second term, right wing senator Joe McCarthy attacked his administration for supposedly harboring Communists in the State Department, a patently false and ludicrous charge. Truman's popularity plummeted and took an even bigger hit when he decided to fire Gen. Douglas MacArthur for insubordination in the Korean War. While the decision to fire MacArthur was the correct one, it doomed Truman's prospects for reelection in 1952.

6. THOMAS JEFFERSON

Aside from George Washington, Thomas Jefferson was the most respected and admired Founding Father, and his presidency ensured the institutions of government functioned properly after the transition of power from the Federalists to the Democrat-Republicans (his party). He philosophically disagreed with the Federalists on the federal government's role, yet he didn't let ideology drive his decision making. Sensing a great opportunity, Jefferson authorized the Louisiana Purchase from France, even though he wasn't sure he had the constitutional authority to acquire the land. It turned out to be one of the most important decisions in history and started the nation toward fulfilling its "manifest destiny." Though he was a proponent of a small military and navy, he waged a successful war against the Barbary pirates in Tripoli after they demanded outrageous sums for merchant vessels's safe passage through the Mediterranean Sea. He did away with Adams's odious Alien and Sedition Acts and reduced internal taxes and the number of federal employees, believing the federal government shouldn't become too involved with the economy. (Ironically, though Jefferson was the leading Democrat of his day, modern-day Republicans have come to view him as the symbolic forefather of the Republican Party.) He imposed an embargo on England as punishment for its policy of conscripting U.S. merchant ships for its war against France, but when the embargo harmed America more than it did England, he quickly repealed it. Jefferson proved to be a pragmatic leader; he was guided by philosophy but not blinded by ideology.

7. ANDREW JACKSON

Andrew Jackson was the first officeholder to take an expansive view of the president's role, and as such he greatly enhanced the powers of the office. Unlike his predecessors, Jackson considered the presidency a way in which to advance his agenda; a war hero and populist icon, he knew his base of support resided outside the political system. He practically waged war against Congress over rechartering the National Bank, claiming that it was a tool of the wealthy, and ultimately succeeded in eliminating it. It was probably the right decision (the National Bank was a corrupt institution), but in the short term it resulted in a severe recession, which his successor, Martin Van Buren, inherited. Wanting to reward supporters with plum jobs, Jackson also introduced the spoils system to federal patronage; it would be fifty years before the Civil Service replaced Jacksonian patronage. Further, he showed great leadership in handling the nullification crisis and South Carolina's threat to secede from the Union by sending warships to Charleston to enforce the Force Act, a bill he hastily pushed through Congress that preempted the so-called nullification doctrine. "The Constitution . . . forms a *government* not a league. . . . To say that any State may at pleasure secede from the Union is to say that the United States is not a nation," said Jackson. He showed less leadership on the issue of Indian "removal." He aggressively pushed for treaties with dozens of Indian tribes—more than seventy during his administration—to move them from their rightful land. In total, he acquired 100 million acres of land and relocated 46,000 Indians, sometimes by force, to western territories.

8. RONALD REAGAN

As mentioned in this book, Ronald Reagan went to Washington with three simple mandates: reduce taxes and regulation on business, provide moral leadership, and strengthen the nation's defenses. Reagan had an innate understanding that the nation could only focus on a few challenges at once and communicated his vision directly to the American people. He considered the Cold War a titanic struggle between freedom and communism (or good and evil) in which there could be but one victor. At a time when the public's confidence in government was low, Reagan provided a new direction for the nation. Future historians will determine

Reagan's exact role in winning the Cold War, but it was certainly substantial; his unrelenting arms buildup bankrupted the Soviets and showed its system to be terminally flawed. Reagan reaffirmed America's status as a global superpower and helped restore morale in the military. His tax cuts in 1981 and 1986 laid the foundation for nearly twenty years of uninterrupted economic expansion, though he does share the blame for unprecedented deficits and uncontrolled spending. Reagan undoubtedly tarnished his legacy with the Iran-Contra scandal and did not give enough attention to economic and social inequality. In the end, however, he ranks as one of the towering figures of the twentieth century.

9. DWIGHT D. EISENHOWER

As with Harry Truman's case, over the past few decades, historians have revised their thinking on the Eisenhower administration. In the years immediately following his presidency, the conventional wisdom was that Ike was nothing more than a bumbling caretaker with few real accomplishments. The new thinking, however, is that he was an astute leader who guided the nation through peace and prosperity and enhanced the stature of the United States around the globe. Though a military man all his life, Eisenhower proved to be a gifted politician: he deftly handled Senator Joe McCarthy and his ludicrous attacks against the army by refusing to dignify his charges; consistently produced a balanced budget and, in fact, was the last president to actually *cut* federal spending in real dollars; expanded several New Deal programs, including Social Security; secured $40 billion in funding—one of the largest public works projects of its time—for the Interstate Highway System; and presided over a decade-long economic expansion. Further, on his watch the Korean stalemate ended, with South Korea remaining a free nation. He's been criticized—and perhaps rightly so—for not doing more to enforce the Supreme Court's *Brown v. Board of Education* decision to desegregate public schools; he reluctantly sent federal troops to Little Rock Central High School and only after Arkansas governor Orval Faubus used violence to prevent nine African American students from enrolling. Perhaps most telling about Eisenhower's character was his last televised speech as president: he used the opportunity to talk about the dangers of having a permanent military-industrial complex, warning that "we must guard against the acquisition of unwarranted influence, whether sought or unsought, by the military-industrial complex. The potential for the disastrous rise of misplaced power exists and will persist."

10. JOHN F. KENNEDY

Few presidents have accomplished more in less time than Jack Kennedy did. Kennedy took an activist approach to the presidency and outlined a bold vision for the country in his State of the Union address. After inheriting a deep recession, he proposed tax cuts, new spending, and an increase in the minimum wage, thus setting the foundation for a decade-long economic boom. He created the Peace Corps and challenged the young space program to put a man on the moon by the decade's end. He stood strong against the Soviets during the Cuban missile crisis, taking the country to the brink of war, and forced Nikita Khrushchev to back down. Kennedy had his missteps: he botched the Bay of Pigs invasion of Cuba—a plan carried over from Eisenhower's administration—and made the nation look foolish in the process. He also came late to the cause of civil rights, letting racist southern governors wreak havoc with desegregation mandates and intimidate African American citizens before finally asserting federal authority. By the end of his presidency, he had become a champion of civil rights and deserves much of the credit for the Civil Rights Act of 1964. Finally, during his watch, the number of U.S. troops in Vietnam increased to 16,000, though it's uncertain if he would have continued the escalation. "Camelot" mythology notwithstanding, Kennedy brought glamour and majesty back to the office and gave the country a sense of optimism. The 1960s and '70s would likely have been dramatically different had he not been assassinated.

Ranking the Presidents: The Good

Most of the presidents in this category would have been considered "great" were it not for some kind of flaw. In Woodrow Wilson's case, it was his backward views on race relations; in President Clinton's, it was his public struggle with personal foibles. President George H. W. Bush was a brilliant foreign policy president but fairly hapless on domestic policy.

1. JAMES K. POLK

Polk gets high marks for setting a specific agenda and accomplishing much of it during his four years in office. He campaigned on lowering tariffs; reestablishing an independent treasury system, and thus breaking with his party on the issue; resolving the Oregon boundary dispute with Great Britain; and acquiring the California Territory from Mexico. He accomplished all of it and in the process secured more land—more than 1 million square miles—than any other president in history. His handling of the Mexican-American War proved him to be a more effective wartime president than James Madison was. Although he was a slave owner from Tennessee, Polk privately opposed slavery's expansion into the new territories; however, he didn't make an issue of it publicly. Of all the presidents leading up to the

Civil War, Polk was the only one with the popularity, forceful personality, and acumen to forge a palatable solution to the slavery issue; instead, he decided to take a pass.

2. JAMES MONROE

Most Americans remember Monroe for his eponymous doctrine that asserted European colonization in the Western Hemisphere would be viewed as an act of aggression against the United States. It was a bold declaration, considering that the United States lagged far behind the European powers in military and economic might, and would become the cornerstone of U.S. foreign policy for the next century. The Monroe Doctrine ranks as one of the most important presidential declarations in history. His other big accomplishment was to convince Spain to cede Florida to the United States, a position made tenable by Andrew Jackson's incursion into the territory. On the domestic front, he ushered in the "Era of Good Feelings"—a term coined by a Boston newspaper at the time—with the demise of the Federalist Party and with the country temporarily united. The era ended, however, with the Missouri Compromise, which Monroe supported, and later with the election of 1824. Monroe attempted to create a network of coastal fortifications designed to protect the country's shoreline, but the recession of 1819 greatly curtailed the funding. His presidency marked the beginning of the United States taking its first steps to becoming a hemispheric power.

3. WOODROW WILSON

Though known as a foreign policy president, Woodrow Wilson was actually elected as a progressive reformer, and he zealously pursued large-scale economic reforms, including lowering tariffs, reforming the banking system, and establishing the Federal Reserve System—over massive

Woodrow Wilson presides over his first cabinet meeting, in 1913. *Woodrow Wilson House, Washington, a National Trust Property*

opposition—to regulate the nation's banks and monetary policy. Many historians consider the Federal Reserve System one of the most important pieces of legislation in history. He also strengthened the labor movement with the Clayton Antitrust Act, restricted child labor, and helped farmers with the Federal Farm Loan Board. It was in the realm of foreign policy, however, where he made his most lasting impact. After promising to keep the country out of war, he shifted course following the election of 1916 and declared war on Germany, knowing it would be an unpopular decision (though it turned out to be the right one). U.S.

involvement in the war brought about a swift victory Allied victory and marked the beginning of the country's emergence as a global superpower. Following the war, he championed the creation of the League of Nations, but he failed to convince the Senate to ratify the treaty. Though an honorable institution, the league ultimately proved to be inconsequential.

Wilson's legacy, however, must also include his history as a virulent racist. His support of home rule in the South helped fuel the dramatic growth of the Klu Klux Klan (KKK) and served as the intellectual foundation for the racist Dixiecrat campaigns of Strom Thurmond and, later, George Wallace. He essentially allowed the nation's capital to become a "Jim Crow" territory, and he spoke publicly about the "benefits" of segregation. Wilson was unapologetic about his views on race, telling the *New York Times* "if the colored people made a mistake in voting for me, they ought to correct it." After the release of the movie *Birth of a Nation,* which depicted the KKK as heroic and African Americans as savages, Wilson held private screenings for members of his cabinet, Congress, and the Supreme Court.

4. WILLIAM MCKINLEY

McKinley is one of those polarizing presidents, thus making him difficult to rank. Among supporters, he's considered a decisive leader who helped establish the United States as a global(some would say imperialist) power with attaining victory in the Spanish-American War, annexing Hawaii, and gaining control over the former Spanish colonies of Guam, the Philippines, and Puerto Rico. He also used America's growing influence to establish the so-called Open Door policy with China, which lasted for half a century, and sent troops to that country to quell the Boxer Rebellion. Detractors consider him an unimaginative bully who started the United

States on the course of brazen imperialism. On the domestic front, his only notable act was to continue raising tariff levels to an all-time high, something that he had done throughout his career. At a time when the United States was beginning to become an industrial and economic power, McKinley seized the opportunity to make it a global powerhouse as well and in the process helped lay the foundation for the "American Century."

5. **GROVER CLEVELAND**

Cleveland won the presidency on the strength of his reputation as an honest politician who was not driven by ideology. He believed the president's primary duty was to prevent Congress from enacting misguided laws, and to that end he vetoed more bills—most of which were related to boondoggle spending projects—than any previous president had. In his two (nonconsecutive) terms, he had few legislative accomplishments other than lowering tariffs, which he viewed as nothing more than subsidized wealth transfers to the northeastern states. He tried to repeal the disastrous Sherman Silver Purchase Act, which he believed brought on the economic recession of 1894, but the issue only split the Democrats in Congress. He failed to overturn it. Cleveland's approach to foreign policy was similarly restrained: he repudiated Benjamin Harrison's annexation of Hawaii and used the country's growing naval might for strategic purposes only. In that sense, his presidency stood in sharp contrast to the Republican administrations of the era—notably those of Arthur, McKinley, and Teddy Roosevelt—that took the Monroe Doctrine to mean that the United States had the right to intervene anywhere in the Western Hemisphere. In an interesting footnote, aside from Franklin Roosevelt, Cleveland is the only president to win the popular vote in three consecutive elections.

6. JAMES MADISON

It turns out James Madison was a much better Founding Father than he was a president. He's best remembered—and rightly so—for crafting the Virginia Plan at the Constitutional Convention, penning the Bill of Rights, and coauthoring the *Federalist Papers* with Alexander Hamilton and John Jay. As such, Madison's place in history as one of our nation's greatest figures was settled long before his turn in office. Much of his presidency was consumed by the hostilities leading up to the War of 1812. Madison asked Congress for a declaration of war against England, even though the nation wasn't remotely prepared to do battle, and watched as the country suffered several embarrassing loses, including the burning of the White House and other federal buildings. Madison made for a poor wartime president, and although the United States eventually prevailed (most of England's fighting forces were busy defeating Napoleon), it gained no new territories or boundaries. Nonetheless, America had survived its "Second War of Independence," and the postwar years ushered in the Era of Good Feelings.

7. CHESTER ARTHUR

Chester Arthur is perhaps the most overlooked and underappreciated president in history. He assumed office under extremely trying conditions after a deranged supporter, who felt aggrieved when President James Garfield denied him a patronage position, assassinated Garfield. His entire career, Arthur had been part of New York senator Roscoe Conkling's political machine, so many assumed President Arthur would fall in line with Conkling's wishes, which included opposing patronage reform (something Garfield strongly supported). Arthur, however, turned his back on his old cronies and passed the Pendleton Act, which replaced the spoils system with the Civil Service Commission. And he didn't stop there: he knowingly went against traditional Republican constituencies by supporting tariff reduction, which helped consumers and farmers at the expense of big business, and by vetoing the pork-laden Rivers and Harbor Act of 1882, which Congress overrode anyway. Perhaps Arthur's biggest accomplishment was revitalizing the U.S. Navy and putting the nation on course to become a first-rate naval power. He's sometimes called the "father of the American Navy" for securing funding from Congress for the first all-steel vessels, or the so-called White Squadron. He also gave the White House a much-needed refurbishing, bringing in the young upstart designer Louis Comfort Tiffany to give the run-down executive mansion a dramatic makeover. In the end, Arthur delivered much more leadership than anyone had expected and proved to be an honorable and effective president. Said legendary writer and noted political cynic Mark Twain of Arthur: "It would be hard indeed to better President Arthur's administration."

8. JOHN ADAMS

John Adams spent most of his one term in office focused on foreign affairs, prosecuting a quasi-war with France on the high seas, and successfully avoiding an all-out war in the process. Although he was a great political philosopher, he was equally inept at managing his own cabinet or forging a domestic agenda. His only legislative accomplishment—sort of—was the Alien and Sedition Act, one of the most repulsive laws passed in U.S. history. He deserves credit for establishing the Department of the Navy and for peacefully transitioning power to the opposite party; it was the first time in history such a transfer occurred after Jefferson defeated Adams in 1800. Beyond that he had few notable achievements.

9. BILL CLINTON

Bill Clinton had the political skills and acumen to be one of the great presidents, and his list of major accomplishments includes welfare reform, a balanced budget, NAFTA, the General Agreement on Tariffs and Trade (GATT), and a booming economy, among others. At the same time, he had a couple of flops, most notably his attempt at health care reform, which helped contribute to the Democrats losing control of the House and Senate, and his failure to go after Osama bin Laden or deal with North Korea's growing nuclear threat. But the Clinton era can't be measured by policy wins and losses alone. Scandals—and not just the Lewinsky affair—seemed to loom over his presidency from day one: Travel-gate, Lincoln bedroom fund-raisers, Buddhist temple fund-raisers, personnel file misappropriation, cabinet scandals (including Mike Espy and Henry Cisneros), Kathleen Willey groping accusations, pardon-gate—the list goes on and on. Every time he got past one scandal, another seemed to surface. The final two years of his presidency were bogged down by the Lewinsky scandal and impeachment trial, and though he was overwhelmingly acquitted in the Senate, Clinton had irreparably tarnished his legacy and diminished the office with his boorish behavior. As one pundit put it, "He was the most talented politician of his generation, maybe of any generation," and yet he couldn't overcome his own short-sightedness to fulfill his promise.

10. GEORGE H. W. BUSH

George H. W. Bush had a sort of Jekyll-Hyde presidency—brilliant with foreign policy and feckless on domestic policy. Few presidents achieved more successes in the foreign policy arena than Bush did. In addition to assembling one of the most impressive coalitions in world history for Operation Desert Shield, he also masterfully presided over the fall of

the Berlin Wall and the Soviet Union's collapse and orchestrated the capture of Panamanian dictator Manuel Noriega.
Bush clearly preferred to spend time on international matters instead of domestic priorities, even though the economy
was mired in recession from 1990 to 1991. At the insistence of congressional Democrats, he reneged on his "No
New Taxes" pledge in an effort to bring the budget under
control, and instead he only deepened the economic recession. He also upset his Republican base by passing the
Americans With Disabilities Act, which many of his supporters felt went too far in creating new rights. After his approval ratings hit 90 percent following the Gulf War victory,
Bush had an opportunity to use his newfound popularity to
pass a bold domestic agenda, but instead he squandered it
on a bunch of lackluster proposals. History will likely remember Bush as a transitional president from the Cold War
to the post–Cold War era.

Ranking the Presidents: The Average

By and large, the presidents considered "average" had some redeeming qualities, but for the most part they never mastered the demands of the office. They might not have harmed the country, but in the end they didn't move it forward, either.

1. WILLIAM HOWARD TAFT

Taft had the difficult job of following a legend, Theodore Roosevelt. While he lacked Roosevelt's energy, charm, and vision, he did share his predecessor's progressive view of government, with the only difference being that Taft filtered his beliefs through his vast knowledge and respect for the law. Taft actually prosecuted more cases under the Sherman Antitrust Act than Roosevelt had, though unlike Roosevelt, Taft never used its rhetoric to condemn the business community. He supported the first ever tax on corporations as well as passage of the Sixteenth Amendment, which established an income tax, and the Seventeenth Amendment, which provided direct election of U.S. senators. He let down progressives with his failure to lower tariffs, however, and further angered them with his refusal to aggressively promote conservation. Taft believed Roosevelt had wildly exceeded his legal authority in this area. Were it not for

Roosevelt's quixotic (some would say vain) third-party candidacy in 1912, Taft would have easily won a second term, and history would probably remember him more favorably.

2. CALVIN COOLIDGE
Calvin Coolidge is a difficult president to rank. Political conservatives rate him highly for his limited use of executive power and for the Roaring Twenties' strong economy. Political liberals, however, consider him a caretaker antecedent to Herbert Hoover and the Great Depression and essentially a do-nothing president. Coolidge's major domestic achievements include tax and budget cuts and not much else. He despised regulation and had little interest in social or economic equality. He vetoed farm relief legislation that could have helped farmers during the Great Depression and signed the 1924 Immigration Act, drastically reducing emigration from Latin America, Asia, and India. Undoubtedly, his laissez-faire policies contributed to the economic environment that led to the Great Depression, and he did almost nothing to curb rampant stock market speculation, even though he was warned of a looming problem. Columnist Walter Lippmann may have summed up Coolidge best when he wrote that "this active inactivity suits the mood and certain of the needs of the country admirably. It suits all the business interests which want to be let alone. . . . And it suits all those who have become convinced that government in this country has become dangerously complicated and top-heavy."

3. MARTIN VAN BUREN
There are many similarities between the presidencies of Martin Van Buren and George H. W. Bush. Both were vice presidents to popular, two-term presidents; both were saddled with economic recessions for much of their terms; and both failed to win reelection. Just five weeks into Van

Buren's presidency, he was confronted with the Panic of 1837, one of the worst economic depressions in the nation's history. Most historians agreed that wild land speculation, combined with the demise of the Bank of the United States (thanks to Andrew Jackson), brought about the crisis. A states' rights advocate, Van Buren did little to pull the nation out of recession or to address its causes, other than to blame it on "moneyed interests" overseas. His foreign policy was a bit mixed. On the one hand, he steadfastly refused to annex Texas because he opposed the expansion of slavery and didn't want to risk a war with Mexico; but on the other hand, he sided with the Spanish government in the *Amistad* slave-mutiny trial in a crass attempt to appeal to Southern voters. By the end of his presidency, the opposition had taken to calling him "Martin Van Ruin."

4. JOHN QUINCY ADAMS
Because he won office in a disputed election in 1824, John Quincy Adams was at a disadvantage from day one of his presidency. Andrew Jackson's supporters in Congress, outraged over his "corrupt" deal with Henry Clay, were intent on making Adams a lame-duck president. His American System proposal to Congress—a plan to modernize the country's infrastructure and to connect the regional economies through dozens of road and canal projects—was virtually dead on arrival, as was his proposal for a national university and astronomical observatory. He unwisely signed the Tariff of 1828, otherwise known as the "Tariff of Abominations," which virtually ensured his defeat in 1828. About the only good thing to be said of Adams's presidency is that it was relatively free of scandal and foreign policy crises.

5. GERALD FORD
To judge Gerald Ford's presidency solely by legislative accomplishments or policy initiatives would be a mistake.

The only unelected president in our nation's history, Ford and his presidency should be evaluated more by the circumstances of his ascension than by specific policies or achievements. He took over when the public's faith in the office was at an all-time low and restored the dignity, transparency, and honesty to the presidency that had been missing for more than a decade. He was the polar opposite of Nixon and Johnson—a humble, decent, straightforward man whom members of both parties liked and respected. Pardoning Richard Nixon was an act of pure political courage; Ford knew it was the right decision for the nation, even if it meant political suicide for himself. He attempted to jump-start the economy with his Whip Inflation Now (WIN) campaign, but it was a flop, and on his watch the final withdrawal of U.S. troops from Vietnam and the fall of Saigon occurred. Ford doesn't have a laundry list of achievements from his eight hundred-plus days in office, but he was certainly the right man at the right time for the job.

6. ZACHARY TAYLOR
Though his administration lasted a little more than sixteen months, Taylor had proven himself to be a strong and capable leader. Folks expected the Southerner and slave owner to support the expansion of slavery, but he took the opposite view. When angry Southern legislators threatened secession, Taylor responded that he would personally lead the army against them and hang any traitors. Leaders in the Senate began crafting the Compromise of 1850—a patchwork of slave- and free-state territorial compromises that ultimately deepened the crisis—when Taylor died. Though he opposed the compromise, his successor, Millard Fillmore, signed it into law.

7. BENJAMIN HARRISON
Benjamin Harrison did little to distinguish or embarrass

himself during his one term in office. On the domestic front, his support of high tariffs and the Sherman Silver Purchase Act had the cumulative effect of increasing consumer prices and causing inflation, much to his party's consternation. Harrison did, however, sign the Sherman Antitrust Act into law and lobbied Congress to end racial discrimination at the ballot box. His expansionist foreign policy included a failed attempt at annexing Hawaii, a near war with Chile over an assault on American soldiers, and the modernization and expansion of the U.S. Navy. He is also credited with negotiating several reciprocal trade agreements with Latin America that lasted well into the twentieth century. Thus, Harrison probably rates among the better nineteenth-century presidents.

8. Lyndon Johnson

Lyndon Johnson is one of the most enigmatic characters to occupy the office. He had all the markings of a great president: he knew how to maneuver around Congress, had a vision and agenda for the country, and understood how to wield power. Further, he was responsible for some landmark achievements, most notably the Civil Rights Act of 1964 and 1965 and the Great Society programs of Medicare and Medicaid, Head Start, and the War on Poverty. Yet that's only part of his record, much as tax cuts are only part of George W. Bush's record. Johnson has to receive a lion's share of the blame for the Vietnam War—both for getting the United States involved on a large scale with the fabricated Gulf of Tonkin incident as well as for its escalation and ultimate failure. On his watch, the number of U.S. troops involved increased from 15,000 to 500,000, yet few Americans ever understood the logic behind the war. He manipulated Congress into authorizing the "action" and misled the American people about the results without ever having a game plan to achieve victory. In the end, Vietnam's costs turned out to be much greater than lives and dollars:

Americans lost trust in their government, and a generation lost faith in society.

9. JIMMY CARTER

Some people are destined to be president, others are thrust into the role by circumstances, and still others arrive but just aren't suited for the office. The last was Jimmy Carter. By all accounts, Carter ranks among the most honest, trustworthy, and hardworking men to ever occupy the office. Yet, his character wasn't enough to create a successful presidency. He came to power during difficult times: the nation was still recovering from the aftermath of Vietnam and Watergate; the economy was mired in "stagflation"—that is, high unemployment, inflation, and interest rates; and the Cold War was at a stalemate. Instead of articulating a bold vision for the country or inspiring confidence in the people, however, Carter seemed to revel in the minutiae and administrative aspects of the office. He attempted to rally the nation around the energy crisis, but the best he could do was offer his "malaise" speech (see "Biggest Blunders"). At a time when the nation needed bold leadership, he provided incremental action on the periphery. His presidency wasn't a total loss: Carter helped bring about peace between Israel and Egypt through the Camp David Accords, and the Strategic Arms Limitation Talks (SALT) II Treaty reduced U.S. and Soviet nuclear stockpiles. The 444-day Iranian hostage crisis, and the administration's failed rescue attempt, came to symbolize Carter's time in office and dashed his hope for a second term. Just moments after his successor, Ronald Reagan, delivered his inaugural address, it was announced that the hostages had been freed.

10. JOHN TYLER

As the first vice president to accede to the presidency because of a sitting president's death, John Tyler was considered the "accidental president" or "acting president" by many of his contemporaries, and members of Congress showed him little respect. In fact, his own party, the Whigs, expelled him after he vetoed its agenda, and the cabinet he inherited from Harrison all resigned just months into his presidency. Some even talked of impeaching him for his misuse of the veto, but ultimately Congress decided against it. His only contribution of note was the annexation of Texas, which occurred days before he left office. To top it all off, Tyler joined the Confederacy at the onset of the Civil War and was elected to the first Confederate Provisional Congress in 1862.

Ranking the Presidents: The Bad and the Ugly

The presidents who rank at the bottom earned that distinction one of three ways: corruption, incompetence, or outright malfeasance.

1. RUTHERFORD B. HAYES

A contemporary of Hayes's once described him as "a third rate nonentity, whose only recommendation is that he is obnoxious to no one." That account essentially describes his four years in the White House. He came into office without a mandate, having lost the popular vote by a whopping four percentage points; only after several back-room deals was Hayes able to "liberate" the presidency from Samuel Tilden. As part of his alleged deal with Congress to win the presidency, Hayes formally ended Reconstruction and then did little to stem the ensuing violence and intimidation against African Americans in the South. And since he announced in his inaugural speech that he wouldn't seek a second term, Hayes was a lame duck from day one.

2. FRANKLIN PIERCE

Like Fillmore before him and Buchanan after, Franklin Pierce did little but create a gliding path toward civil war. Pierce was a compromise candidate at the 1852 Democratic

National Convention and was only picked on the forty-ninth ballot after the conventioneers couldn't settle on anyone else. They barely knew his views, and it was a minor surprise to everyone when he actually won the presidency. Pierce lacked firm convictions and was susceptible to persuasion; in some cases, it was merely a matter of who spoke to him last. At the urging of his Secretary of War Jefferson Davis, Pierce went along with Stephen Douglas's Kansas-Nebraska Act, which essentially nullified the Missouri Compromise and allowed incoming states to choose whether to allow slavery. The act was viewed as a huge concession to the South and angered so many Northerners that it led to the creation of the Republican Party. By the end of his term, Pierce was so disliked that he was (and remains) the only elected president in history who was not renominated by his party.

3. **MILLARD FILLMORE**
Millard Fillmore has become synonymous with the term *caretaker president*. In truth, he was more of an accidental president after Zachary Taylor's sudden death. Having served four terms in the House, he had little political experience, and those outside the Whig Party barely knew him. He and Taylor also disagreed on slavery. While Taylor thought newly admitted states should be free states, Fillmore held the opposite view: "God knows that I detest slavery, but it is an existing evil . . . and we must endure it and give it such protection as is guaranteed by the Constitution." The only noteworthy legislation that Congress passed during his administration was the Compromise of 1850, which was a series of laws and compromises designed to appease the South. Fillmore supported the compromise, hoping it would quell regional strife, but it only hastened the path to çivil war. The package included the particularly distasteful Fugitive Slave Act, which mandated the return of runaway

slaves no matter where they were captured. In effect, then, Northerners were legally required to return runaway slaves or face a thousand-dollar fine—something that only further fueled the abolitionists' cause to eradicate slavery altogether. Fillmore wasn't even considered for renomination by his own political party because its members thought so little of him. To put Fillmore in better perspective, note that he opposed Lincoln's policies during the Civil War and supported Johnson's Reconstruction plan.

4. GEORGE W. BUSH

It's too soon to take a serious cut at George W. Bush's place in history, but it's not too soon to call the invasion of Iraq "one of the worst decisions in presidential history." Until the invasion, President Bush had a solid record—made all the more impressive given his lack of a mandate. His handling of the September 11 terrorist attacks was both inspiring and decisive; he simultaneously comforted the nation and girded it for war and defeated the Taliban regime in Afghanistan within months of the attack. He also reorganized and strengthened the nation's homeland defenses, which included such controversial measures as domestic reconnaissance and military prisons. On the economic front, his tax cuts softened the March 2000 recession inherited from President Clinton (and compounded by the terrorist attack) and led to five years of impressive growth. Much to the political establishment's surprise, the Republicans made strong gains in the 2002 midterm elections (the president's party usually loses seats during the midterms), mostly on the strength of Bush's record. And then he invaded Iraq, ostensibly because Saddam Hussein presented an imminent threat to the United States. It turns out Bush rushed into the war based on faulty intelligence and then failed to appreciate the ethnic divisions in the country or to provide adequate resources for a swift and decisive victory with no reconstruction plan after hostilities. At the time of publication, U.S. troops remain mired in policing Iraq's civil war with no end in sight.

5. WARREN G. HARDING

Harding's three years in office were marred by scandal, and his legacy continued beyond his years in office. Harding wasn't personally involved in any scandal, but by appointing so many of his political cronies (the "Ohio Gang," as they were known), he created an environment where bad behavior could flourish. The most notable of the era's scandals was the Teapot Dome fiasco, in which the secretary of the interior sold off the rights to natural resources in exchange for bribes, but his Justice Department was also riddled with corruption (his mentor and closest adviser was acquitted of charges twice), as was the Veterans Bureau and the Office of Alien Property. Harding's philosophy was that of executive restraint: he believed Congress should pass laws, the president should sign them, and the courts should interpret them. As president, then, he spent a good deal of his time on the golf course or playing poker with his buddies. Harding does get high marks for being outspoken against racial inequality—something his predecessor, Woodrow Wilson, completely ignored—but at the end of the day he had little to show by way of accomplishments or achievements.

6. ULYSSES S. GRANT

Grant unquestionably ranks as one of the greatest military leaders in American history and arguably in world history. His rise through the ranks during the Civil War was unprecedented; he went from a colonel with the Twenty-first Illinois Infantry to general of the army in four years. His presidency, however, was another story. While he made some advances in the area of civil rights, he's mostly remembered for the

scandals that occurred on his watch. The two most prominent—the Whiskey Ring and Crédit Mobilier of America—
rank among the worst in history, but there were others: the
Fisk-Gould gold scandal, the Sanborn Incident (a kickback
scheme for Secretary of Treasury Richardson), and something called the "Indian Ring" (a bribery scheme involving
Secretary of War William Belknap). While Grant wasn't directly implicated in any of these scandals, his managerial
style certainly left his administration open to rampant abuses
and misappropriations. Given all his promise as a leader,
Grant's presidency turned out to be a huge disappointment.

7. HERBERT HOOVER

Herbert Hoover was a great businessman, humanitarian, and
commerce secretary but a lousy president. He never fully
understood the depth of the Great Depression until it was
too late, and the policies he did implement—one of the largest tax hikes in history and tariff hikes on thirty thousand
durable items—greatly exacerbated the problem. Moreover,
he refused to infuse the economy with any substantial spending projects (believing that wasn't the federal government's
role), and in desperation he authorized the repatriation of
Mexican American citizens in an effort to ease unemployment. By the time he left office, the economy was in tatters
and unemployment was at 30 percent. One phrase sums up
Hoover's presidency best: wrong man at the wrong time.

8. ANDREW JOHNSON

When running for his second term, Abraham Lincoln dumped
Hannibal Hamlin as vice president and put Johnson on the
ticket because he was impressed with Johnson's loyalty and
fidelity to the Union, even though he was from the Southern
state of Tennessee. At one point during the war, Johnson
even spoke publicly about possibly hanging Jefferson Davis,

the Confederate president. But somewhere along the line his views changed, and after Lincoln's assassination he became something of a Confederate sympathizer. His vision for Reconstruction differed sharply with that of the Republican Congress. Johnson favored a quick, lenient reintegration of the South, which included allowing Confederate states to elect their own members to Congress, but Congress refused to seat them; pardoning thousands of Confederate lawmakers; establishing "Black Codes," which basically made former slaves second-class citizens; vetoing the Civil Rights Act, which Congress overrode; and working against the passage of the Fourteenth Amendment, which Congress again overrode. Many historians believe Johnson's approach to Reconstruction did more to stunt the notion and pursuit of equality than any single act in American history. Congress ultimately impeached Johnson, mostly on the basis of his being so out of step with the rest of the country; however, he avoided conviction by a single vote.

9. JAMES BUCHANAN

James Buchanan was a reluctant candidate for president, and as president he was reluctant to do anything to avert civil war. He tacitly lobbied the Supreme Court in the *Dred Scott* case, siding with the rights of slave owners, and lobbied for the state of Kansas to be admitted to the Union as a slave state. When it became apparent that the seven cotton states would secede from the Union, he said publicly he regretted their decision but felt he could do nothing to prevent it. Buchanan sat idly while the Confederate states took over the federal forts and munitions in their boundaries. It's unfair to say Buchanan could have averted war, but he never even attempted to hold the Union together and ultimately had no business being president.

10. **RICHARD NIXON**

It is hard to consider Richard Nixon as anything but the worst president in history. Notwithstanding his foreign policy feats—including pursuing détente with the Soviet Union and normalizing relations with China—and his fairly progressive domestic agenda (especially in the area of the environment and consumer protection), Nixon abused and disgraced the office, and ultimately that is his lasting legacy. With the release of the Nixon tapes, it has only become more apparent that Nixon was emotionally and psychologically unfit to be president. In retrospect he posed a grave danger to the republic.

Postpresidential Careers

Being a former president is one of the most exclusive clubs in the world. The greatest number of former presidents alive at one time has been five: Nixon, Ford, Carter, Reagan, and George H. W. Bush; then Ford, Carter, Reagan, George H. W. Bush, and Clinton. Most former presidents have retired quietly to private life, though some have remained active in public life. In the case of a few presidents, their postpresidential achievements have actually eclipsed their time spent in office.

1. WILLIAM HOWARD TAFT
Undoubtedly William Howard Taft is the most accomplished former president in history. Taft is the only person in U.S. history to lead both the executive and judicial branches of government, serving as the nation's twenty-seventh president (1909–13) and as the tenth chief justice of the Supreme Court (1921–30). Handpicked by Teddy Roosevelt to be his successor in the White House, Taft's lifelong ambition had actually been to serve on the Supreme Court. After graduating Cincinnati Law School, he served as an assistant prosecutor and Ohio Superior Court judge before President Benjamin Harrison appointed him solicitor general of the United States, and he presented cases on behalf of the

United States before the Supreme Court. He was then made chief judge of the newly created United States Court of Appeals for the Sixth Circuit (the court immediately below the Supreme Court), a position he reluctantly gave up when President McKinley asked him to serve as governor-general of the Philippines in 1901. After leaving the White House, he became a constitutional law professor at the Yale Law School and president of the American Bar Association. Taft finally realized his lifelong dream when President Warren Harding picked him to succeed Edward White (whom Taft had nominated) as chief justice of the Supreme Court in 1921, making him the only president to sit on the high court. The Senate unanimously confirmed Taft, who served in that capacity until his death in 1930. During his tenure as chief justice, he wrote more than two hundred opinions, including the landmark case *Myers v. United States,* which held that the president had the power to unilaterally dismiss (without Senate approval) executive appointments that had been confirmed by the Senate, and *Olmstead v. United States,* which held that the Fourth Amendment's prohibition against unreasonable search and seizures did not include wiretaps. Taft was also instrumental in getting the Supreme Court building constructed. Until that time, the Supreme Court had deliberated in the basement of the Capitol Building.

2. JOHN QUINCY ADAMS

Along with Andrew Johnson, John Quincy Adams is the only president to hold elected office after leaving the White House. Following his defeat to Andrew Jackson in 1828, Adams returned to his home state of Massachusetts, where he was elected to Congress in 1830 and served until his death. Many historians contend it was in the House of Representatives that Adams made some of his greatest contributions to public service. He was an outspoken critic of slavery and fought tirelessly against a series of congressional gag rules that prohibited any debate on the subject; he eventually got the rules repealed. Adams also voted against the Mexican War, arguing it was simply a way for pro-slavery advocates to gain another slave state, and staunchly supported the continuance of the Bank of the United States. In 1841, Adams took up the cause of the slaves who had revolted on the Spanish slave ship *Amistad*—one of the biggest international incidents of its day—and helped win their freedom when he argued before the Supreme Court that their imprisonment violated habeas corpus. Shortly before his death in 1846, Adams oversaw the establishment of the Smithsonian Institution.

3. ANDREW JOHNSON

After coming within one vote of being removed from the presidency, Andrew Johnson spent his postpresidential career seeking redemption by returning to elected office. He believed his impeachment was a political act by a hostile Congress and that the best way to "correct the record" was by returning to that same Congress. After failing to be renominated for the presidency in 1868, Johnson ran for the Senate from Tennessee—a seat he had held a decade earlier—but lost. He tried to win a House seat four years later but failed again. Johnson was finally elected to the Senate in 1874, but he served only a few months before dying suddenly from a stroke. Johnson remains the only president to have served in the Senate after leaving the White House.

4. JIMMY CARTER

While many historians consider Jimmy Carter's presidency largely a failure, his postpresidential career has been quite successful and is a template for future presidents to consider. Shortly after leaving office, Carter established the

Carter Center, a nonprofit organization dedicated to "advancing human rights and alleviating unnecessary human suffering." Through the Carter Center, Jimmy Carter has enjoyed his greatest successes on the world stage by monitoring foreign elections, mediating international crises, bringing awareness to human rights violations, and providing resources to combat deadly diseases in developing nations. In 2002, Jimmy Carter became the first former president to win the Nobel Peace Prize for his "decades of untiring effort to find peaceful solutions to international conflicts, to advance democracy and human rights, and to promote economic and social development." Carter is also the author of twenty books on topics as far ranging as political science, religion, negotiation tactics, outdoor living, historical fiction, and poetry, and he has been a tireless supporter of Habitat for Humanity, a nonprofit organization dedicated to helping the poor build their own affordable housing. In awarding former Jimmy Carter and his wife the Presidential Medal of Freedom, the nation's highest civilian honor, President Clinton said, "Jimmy and Rosalynn Carter have done more good for more people in more places than any other couple on the face of the earth."

5. **RICHARD NIXON**

Though he's the only president to resign from office and is widely regarded among the worst officeholders in history, Richard Nixon had an impressive postpresidential career and even became something of an elder statesman and sought-after foreign policy expert in his later years. Following his impeachment and shameful resignation in August 1974, he spent the next two decades rehabilitating his image, beginning with his 1978 autobiography *RN: The Memoirs of Richard Nixon.* He followed that with several best-selling books on foreign policy, and by the early 1990s leaders of both political parties consulted him for his foreign policy insights. Nixon's two-decade campaign to improve his image may have peaked at his funeral in 1994, when President Clinton eulogized him without ever mentioning Watergate. "He suffered defeats that would have ended most political careers," said Clinton, "yet he won stunning victories that many of the world's most popular leaders have failed to attain." In the years following his death, however, Nixon's rehabilitation has suffered several setbacks with the release of additional unflattering White House tapes.

6 AND 7. GEORGE H. W. BUSH AND BILL CLINTON

It is often said that politics makes for strange bedfellows. Some would say none is stranger than the friendship that has developed between Bill Clinton and the man he defeated in 1992, George H. W. Bush. The two former rivals first came together when President George W. Bush asked them to lead private fund-raising efforts after the Indonesia tsunami disaster and netted more than $1 billion for the Red Cross. The duo reprised their roles following Hurricane Katrina and again raised more than $1 billion for the relief effort. Even hardened cynics concede the two former presidents have formed a unique friendship and partnership that has transcended politics. At the dedication ceremony for President Clinton's presidential library, former President Bush remarked, "When President Clinton experienced his heart trouble recently, there was a tremendous outpouring of affection and support. But in hindsight, perhaps we need not have been too worried. After all, few presidents in recent memory have shown greater resilience and a bigger heart."

8. THOMAS JEFFERSON

Though he was a Founding Father, the author of the Declaration of Independence, and the president of the United

States, Thomas Jefferson considered establishing the University of Virginia his greatest achievement. Jefferson first thought about founding a secular university long before he entered the White House, and he wasted no time bringing it to life once he left office. Jefferson was not a passive founder; he had a hand in every facet of the university, laying out the campus, designing the buildings, selecting the faculty, and choosing the curriculum. Jefferson said of the university, "It is the last act of usefulness I can render, and could I see it open I would not ask an hour more of life." His tombstone contains only twenty-two words: "Author of the Declaration of American Independence, of the Statute of Virginia for religious freedom, and Father of the University of Virginia."

9. HERBERT HOOVER

As with the case of Jimmy Carter, many historians believe Herbert Hoover made greater contributions after his presidency than during his time in office. Of course, the bar wasn't set too high; Hoover had presided over the worst financial collapse in U.S. history, and many believe his policies led to the Great Depression. Following his landslide defeat to Franklin Roosevelt in 1932, Hoover became an outspoken critic of the New Deal, arguing that it would lead to socialism in the United States. He even wrote a best-selling book about it, *The Challenge to Liberty*. In 1940, Hoover quietly put out feelers for the presidential nomination at the Republican National Convention in Philadelphia, but his backroom campaign went nowhere. Shortly after World War II ended, President Truman sent Hoover to the reconstructed Germany to survey the food shortage; Hoover's findings were sharply critical of the Allied occupation. Truman then appointed Hoover to chair the Commission on the Organization of the Executive Branch (which would became known as the Hoover Commission), and he was tasked with making

Herbert Hoover is surrounded by Polish war orphans during his
famine-relief survey of Warsaw on April 2, 1946.
Herbert Hoover Presidential Library

recommendations to streamline the executive branch. The
commission was a huge success: 70 percent of the
commission's findings were enacted into law, such as con-
solidating and eliminating numerous departments and creating the Department of Health, Education, and Welfare. In
1953, President Eisenhower convened a second Hoover
Commission, which made similar recommendations.
Hoover's last official act came in 1958, when the eighty-
four-old was appointed the U.S. representative to the World's
Fair in Belgium.

10. THEODORE ROOSEVELT

Barely fifty years old when he left office in 1909, Teddy

Roosevelt was (and remains) the youngest former president in history. He spent the first year of his retirement in Africa on safari, but he returned to active politics after growing concerned about the Taft administration's direction. He challenged Taft to the Republican nomination in 1912, and after falling a little short he took up a third-party candidacy. Roosevelt ran the strongest third-party campaign in history, and though he easily defeated Taft, he lost handily to Woodrow Wilson. He then spent a couple of years in South America's jungles on an expedition and nearly lost his life. He returned to the United States dramatically weakened and spent the final few years of his life writing books, including his autobiography. He told a friend that the journey to South America probably shaved ten years off his life.

Tourist Destinations

For the inquiring tourist, there are hundreds of presidential locations, museums, and libraries scattered throughout the country. Some are privately administered by foundations and nonprofit organizations, others are part of the National Park Service, and still others fall under the National Archives and Records Administration. For a complete listing of the presidential locations, visit the Smithsonian Institution's website at www.si.edu/RESOURCE/FAQ/nmah/pressite.htm.

1. MOUNT VERNON, GEORGE WASHINGTON

Mount Vernon is George Washington's 5,000-acre plantation estate and where he spent most of his adult life. The estate was actually divided into five working farms, and Washington was considered one of the most successful agriculturalists in the country, as well as the largest whiskey distiller. After he passed away, the estate's ownership went to a series of descendants, and the estate fell into disrepair. After the federal government and the Virginia State government declined to purchase Mount Vernon, a group called the Mount Vernon Ladies Association of the Union bought the mansion and grounds for $200,000 in 1860. It was designated the first National Historic Landmark in the country.

Today, Mount Vernon is the most popular presidential estate and museum in the nation, receiving more than one million visitors a year. In 2006, it underwent a $110 million renovation and added two new museums. Mount Vernon is located about twenty minutes from Washington, D.C., and is open to the public 365 days a year. For more information, visit www.mountvernon.org.

2. MONTICELLO, THOMAS JEFFERSON

Located near Charlottesville, Virginia, about 125 miles from Washington, D.C., Monticello was Thomas Jefferson's plantation estate. Jefferson purchased the land in 1768 and designed the house, which he moved into in 1870. Except for his extended trips abroad, Jefferson spent his entire adult life at Monticello and passed away there in 1826. Upon his death, ownership bounced around to several private citizens until a nonprofit organization, the Thomas Jefferson Foundation, purchased the estate in 1923. The group poured millions into restoring the original home and converted the estate into a Jefferson museum. An image of Monticello appears on the backside of the nickel and two-dollar bill. Today, Monticello is open year round and receives approximately a half million visitors annually. For more information, go to www.monticello.org.

3. HYDE PARK, FRANKLIN D. ROOSEVELT

Situated on the Hudson River in tranquil Duchess County, New York, Hyde Park was the Roosevelt family estate and is now home to the Franklin Roosevelt Museum and Library. Franklin Roosevelt, in fact, was the first president to create an official library, and it is owned and operated by the National Park Service. Roosevelt spent his childhood and adult years at Hyde Park, and he frequently visited the estate while in the White House. "All that is within me cries out to go back to my home on the Hudson River," he said during the 1944 campaign. In the late 1930s, he had a separate house built for Eleanor Roosevelt called Val-Kill (Eleanor and Sara Roosevelt, Franklin's mother, did not get along). Today, Val-Kill serves as the Eleanor Roosevelt Center and is also run by the National Park Service. Hyde Park is open year round and receives hundreds of thousands of visitors annually. For more information on Hyde Park and Val-Kill, visit www.nps.gov/hofr/ and www.nps.gov/elro, respectively.

4. MONTPELIER, JAMES MADISON

James Madison's ancestral home now serves as one of the most popular tourist destinations in Virginia. Located about seventy miles from Washington, D.C., the 3,000-acre estate receives hundreds of thousands of visitors each year. Owned by the National Trust for Historic Preservation, Montpelier is currently undergoing a $60 million renovation to restore the mansion and its grounds to their original condition. For more information, visit www.montpelier.org. The James Madison Museum (www.jamesmadisonmus.org), which is not associated with Montpelier, is located seventy-five miles southwest of Washington, D.C., in the nearby town of Orange, Virginia.

5. THE HERMITAGE, ANDREW JACKSON

Since opening in 1889, more than 15 million people have visited Andrew Jackson's thousand-acre estate, the Hermitage. Located just outside Nashville, Tennessee, Jackson purchased the property in 1804 and made his primary residence there until his death in 1845. Unfortunately, after Jackson's death, his son went into debt and was forced to sell half of it to the state of Tennessee. In 1889, the state chartered the Ladies Hermitage Association (LHA) to purchase the land, repair the estate, and turn it into a Jackson museum. In 1960 the federal government declared it a National Historic Landmark, and since that time the LHA has been purchasing the original acreage that Jackson owned. Today, the LHA manages the entire thousand-acre estate that Jackson left in 1845. For more information, visit www.thehermitage.com.

5. FAMILY HOMES, ABRAHAM LINCOLN

Several historic sites associated with Abraham Lincoln's life and death have become favorite tourist spots. The National Park Service operates two locations in Kentucky—the Birthplace Unit and the Boyhood Home Unit at Knob Creek—where Lincoln spent the first seven years of his life. The Birthplace Unit has a replica log cabin similar to the one he was born in, while the Knob Creek house and its 228-acre farm remain largely intact from the time Lincoln spent there (www.nps.gov/abli). The National Park Service also operates the Lincoln Boyhood National Memorial (www.nps.gov/libo) in Indiana, where Lincoln spent fourteen years (from ages seven to twenty-one) before moving to Illinois, as well as his residence at Eighth and Jackson Streets in Springfield, Illinois, where he lived for seventeen years before moving into the White House. His son, Robert, donated the home to the state of Illinois in 1887, and in 1972 it was conveyed to the National Park Service (www.nps.gov/liho). Ford's Theater, where Lincoln was shot, and the Peterson House across the street, where he died, were designated National Historic Sites and are also administered by the National Park Service (www.nps.gov/foth).

6. ADAMS NATIONAL HISTORIC PARK, JOHN ADAMS AND JOHN QUINCY ADAMS

Located in Quincy, Massachusetts, about ten miles from Boston, visitors can see the birthplace of four generations of Adamses, including the second and sixth presidents. The site contains eleven designated historic structures, including the presidents' birthplaces; the "Old House," where four generations of the family were raised; and the famous Stone Library, where more than fourteen thousand historic volumes are housed. It includes John Quincy Adams's entire book collection. Visit www.nps.gov/adam for more information.

7. EISENHOWER NATIONAL HISTORIC SITE, DWIGHT D. EISENHOWER

Located in Gettysburg, Pennsylvania, adjacent to the Gettysburg Battlefield, the National Park Service has preserved the farm that David Eisenhower used as a weekend retreat during his presidency. Eisenhower purchased the 690-acre farm in 1950 and used it to entertain world leaders and other dignitaries, including Soviet premier Nikita Khrushchev, French president Charles De Gaulle, and Prime Minister Winston Churchill, in a more relaxed setting away from Washington. It was also a working cattle farm and had a golf course on the premises. Visit www.nps.gov/eise for more information.

8. ASH LAWN-HIGHLAND, JAMES MONROE

The College of William and Mary owns and operates James Monroe's historic estate, located in Charlottesville, Virginia, where he lived from 1793 until1826. While Ash Lawn houses the Monroe Museum and has been open to the public since 1931, it remains a 535-acre working farm. Ash Lawn is open year round and hosts a terrific summer music festival every year. For more information, visit www.ashlawnhighland.org.

9. JOHN F. KENNEDY PRESIDENTIAL LIBRARY AND MUSEUM, JOHN F. KENNEDY

In 1979 President Carter dedicated the Kennedy Library and

Museum in Boston, the official repository for the Kennedy administration's papers. Famed architect I. M. Pei designed the library, which contains all sorts of video, artifacts, replicas, photographs, political memorabilia, and correspondences from the Kennedy family and administration. For a virtual museum tour, visit www.jfklibrary.org.

10. SAGAMORE HILL NATIONAL HISTORIC SITE, THEODORE ROOSEVELT

Located in Oyster Bay, Long Island, New York, Sagamore Hill was Theodore Roosevelt's home from 1886 until his death in 1919, and it was considered the "Summer White House" during his presidency (1901-8). The site was first opened to the public in 1953, and in 1962 Congress put it under the supervision of the National Park Service. In addition to his home, the site also contains his official museum and gravesite. For more information, visit www.nps.gov/sahi.

Memorials and Monuments

During the early years of the republic, lawmakers were hesitant to build permanent monuments to the presidents for fear of resembling the European monarchies. As time passed, however, there came a need to honor the nation's heritage and the great leaders who had helped create, defend, and expand the Union, and so the first edifice—the Washington Monument—was constructed. Today, presidential monuments are an indelible part of the landscape, especially in Washington, D.C., and are some of the most popular tourist attractions in the nation.

1. WASHINGTON MONUMENT

The Washington Monument is the most prominent presidential memorial in the United States. At 555 feet, it's the tallest structure in Washington, D.C., and on a clear day is visible some forty miles away. It sits on the west end of the National Mall and every year receives approximately 800,000 visitors. Its history dates back to 1833, the centennial of Washington's birth. In that year a group of private citizens formed the Washington National Monument Society, with the stated goal of raising funds to erect some type of monument for the nation's first president. "It is proposed that the contemplated monument shall be like him in whose honor it is to be constructed, unparalleled in the world, and commensurate with the gratitude, liberality, and patriotism of the people by whom it is to be erected," the society wrote. "It should blend stupendousness with elegance, and be of such magnitude and beauty as to be an object of pride to the American people, and of admiration to all who see it." The first cornerstone was laid in 1848, and it took another four decades before the monument was completed and opened to the public. Construction stopped during the Civil War, and funding ran out several times. An interesting note: the trowel that George Washington himself used when laying the cornerstone of the Capitol Building was used to lay his monument's first slab.

2. LINCOLN MEMORIAL

The Lincoln Memorial is one of the greatest symbols of freedom and democracy in the United States, and since its inception, it has served as a backdrop for scores of speeches, concerts, and rallies associated with the cause of liberty. Congress incorporated the Lincoln Monument Association just two years after Lincoln's death, but ground breaking for a monument didn't take place until 1914. President Harding formally dedicated the monument in 1922 at a ceremony that was attended by Robert Todd Lincoln, the president's only surviving child. The monument is modeled after a Greek temple with thirty-six massive columns, one for each state in the Union at the time of Lincoln's death. Inside the temple is a nineteen-by-nineteen-foot statue of a seated Lincoln looking out at the Reflecting Pool of the Washington Monument, and the chambers feature inscriptions of two of his greatest speeches, the Gettysburg Address and his second inaugural address. Martin Luther King, Jr., chose the Lincoln Memorial as the backdrop for his famous "I Have a Dream" speech in 1963, one of the most inspiring orations of the civil rights movement and perhaps of the twentieth century. The image of the Lincoln Memorial adorns the back-side of the five-dollar bill and the penny, making it the only memorial with such a distinction.

3. MOUNT RUSHMORE

Mount Rushmore is one of the most recognizable edifices in the United States and the most popular presidential memo-rial with more than two million visitors a year. South Dakota State historian Doane Robinson first conceived the idea of building the monument as a way to boost tourism in South Dakota; today tourism is the second-largest industry in the state. Congress approved funding for the project in 1925, and President Coolidge, a Republican, insisted that along with George Washington, the monument should honor two Republicans and one Democrat. The committee settled on Lincoln, Jefferson, and Roosevelt. Washington's face was dedicated in 1934, followed by Jefferson in 1936, Lincoln in 1937, and Roosevelt in 1939. There was some talk at the time of adding Susan B. Anthony as well, but Congress re-jected the notion. Amazingly, for a project of that size, scope, and difficulty, not a single person died during the monument's creation.

4. JEFFERSON MEMORIAL

Shortly after taking office, President Franklin Roosevelt asked Congress to appropriate funding for a memorial dedicated to the nation's third president and author of the Declaration of Independence. Modeled after the Greek Pantheon in Rome, the structure, was officially dedicated on April 13, 1943, the anniversary of Jefferson's 200th birthday and just four years after breaking ground. Because of its location—it's situated on the shore of the Potomac River's Tidal Basin and quite a distance from the National Mall—the memorial does not receive as many visitors as the Washington Monument and Lincoln Memorial. Similar to the Lincoln Memorial, its interior houses a nineteen-foot-high statute of Jefferson. The walls feature engraved quotations from some of his most famous speeches and writings, including perhaps the most powerful line from the Declaration of Independence: "We hold these truths to be self-evident that all men are created equal, that they are endowed by their Creator with certain inalienable rights, among these are life, liberty, and the pursuit of happiness, that to secure these rights governments are instituted among men."

5. FRANKLIN DELANO ROOSEVELT MEMORIAL
Dedicated in 1997, the Franklin Roosevelt Memorial is the most recent presidential monument to be erected on the National Mall. The edifice consists of four outdoor "rooms" to represent Roosevelt's terms in office. Each room portrays various moments from his presidency and the era, such as fireside chats, bread lines, and soldiers. Waterfalls are present in all four rooms as well. In 2001, a statue of Roosevelt in his wheelchair was included at the memorial's entrance after disability groups complained that the memorial ignored his handicap.

6. THEODORE ROOSEVELT ISLAND
Located just off the Potomac River in Washington, D.C., Teddy Roosevelt Island is a fitting memorial for the nation's first conservationist president. The George Mason family owned the ninety-acre island for more than a century before the Theodore Roosevelt Memorial Association purchased it in 1932. Dedicated in 1967, the memorial contains a seventeen-foot-tall statue of Roosevelt, along with four stone monoliths engraved with some of Roosevelt's most famous quotes. The island is a beautiful nature conservancy where

millions of visitors can walk, jog, and picnic every day. Roosevelt Island can only be accessed by footbridge from Arlington, Virginia, even though it is considered part of the District of Columbia.

7. JOHN F. KENNEDY CENTER FOR PERFORMING ARTS

While it is the leading performing arts center in the United States, the Kennedy Center is also considered a living memorial for the thirty-fifth president. The center's planning actually predated Kennedy by a few years and was called the National Cultural Center, but just months after President Kennedy's assassination it was renamed the Kennedy Center. As a living memorial, it receives federal funding for maintenance and operations, but it also raises funds through private donations and ticket sales. The center, which is situated on the banks of the Potomac River, consists of three main theaters: the 2,500-seat state-of-the-art Concert Hall, the Opera Hall, and the smaller Eisenhower Theater. Every year, the center puts on hundreds of performances—everything from opera to jazz, ballet, drama, orchestra, and dance—by some of the most accomplished and talented artists in the country.

8. WOODROW WILSON INTERNATIONAL CENTER FOR SCHOLARS

According to its website (www.wilsoncenter.org), the Woodrow Wilson International Center for Scholars is a living memorial to President Woodrow Wilson. Its mission is "to commemorate the ideals and concerns of Woodrow Wilson by: providing a link between the world of ideas and the world of policy; and fostering research, study, discussion, and collaboration among a full spectrum of individuals concerned with policy and scholarship in national and world affairs." The Smithsonian Institution established the center in 1968, but it has its own independent board of trustees (appointed by the president) and is located in the Ronald Reagan Building in Washington, D.C. According to its website, the center "is not an advocacy think tank developing specific policy recommendations, but a nonpartisan center for advanced study, a neutral forum for free and open, serious, and informed scholarship and discussion." It receives a third of its funding from the federal government, with the rest supplied by grants and contracts, foundations, corporations, individuals, and subscriptions.

9. HARRY S. TRUMAN SCHOLARSHIP FOUNDATION

Like the Wilson Center, the Truman Scholarship Foundation (www.truman.gov/) is a living memorial to honor President Harry S. Truman. Created by Congress in 1975, a thirteen-member board of trustees governs the foundation. Its mission is "to find and recognize college juniors with exceptional leadership potential who are committed to careers in government, the nonprofit or advocacy sectors, education or elsewhere in the public service; and to provide them with financial support for graduate study, leadership training, and fellowship with other students who are committed to *making a difference* through public service." Its endowment is currently $55 million, and it annually awards approximately seventy Truman scholarships to college juniors who show leadership potential and have an interest in government or public service. Ironically, Harry Truman was the last president who did not attend college.

10. ULYSSES S. GRANT MEMORIAL AND JAMES GARFIELD MONUMENT

The Ulysses S. Grant Memorial and James Garfield Monument compromise two-thirds of a sculptural group located on the grounds of the U.S. Capitol at Union Square.

Dedicated in 1922 on the centennial of his birth, Grant's memorial consists of a twenty-two-foot-high pedestal of Grant on his horse alongside Union artillery and Cavalry groups. It is believed to be the tallest equestrian statue in the United States and second in the world only to Italy's King Victor Emmanuel statue in Rome. Not far from Grant's memorial is the James A. Garfield Monument, a pedestal statue of the fallen president that was sculpted by John Quincy Adams Ward. It was funded by both congressional and private donations and erected several years after Garfield's assassination.

Movies

For as long as there have been movies, there have been movies about the most powerful office in the world. Hollywood has tackled it all: serious biopics, conspiratorial fantasies, satires, and thrillers. While the actors, subjects, and genre may change, one thing remains constant: the star is usually the office itself.

1. *SEVEN DAYS IN MAY,* 1964

Adapted by *Twilight Zone* creator Rod Serling, *Seven Days in May* depicts an attempted presidential coup by the chairman of the Joint Chiefs of Staff, played brilliantly by Burt Lancaster. One of the most underrated and underappreciated movies of any genre, it's an absolute thriller. While it may seem a bit far fetched today, the movie has to be viewed in context: when it was released, the Cold War was at its height. It followed on the heels of *Sputnik* and the missile race, the Bay of Pigs fiasco, the Cuban missile crisis, and the presidential aspirations of Arizona senator Barry Goldwater; and some on the political fringe thought the Kennedy administration was "too soft" on the Soviet Union and that a more aggressive posture was needed. Kirk Douglas plays the Marine colonel who uncovers the nefarious plot, and Ava Gardner has a small but pivotal role as Lancaster's ex-girlfriend turned unknowing informant. *Seven Days in May* is one of those movies that often appears on cable late at night, and once it starts, it is nearly impossible to turn away from the screen.

2. *THE AMERICAN PRESIDENT,* 1995

The *American President* takes a unique look into the private life of the most powerful man on the planet. Michael Douglas gives one of his best performances as President Andrew Shepherd, a widower who is simultaneously trying to run the country and court a beautiful environmental lobbyist played by Annette Benning. The stellar cast includes Martin Sheen as Shepherd's chief of staff, Michael J. Fox as presidential adviser, and David Paymer as his slightly neurotic pollster. It's considered one of the most accurate depictions of life inside the modern White House, although some critics contend it was biased in its portrayal of the issues and of the Republican antagonist, a malicious and dumb-witted senator played by Richard Dreyfuss. Ironically, the screenplay's writer, Aaron Sorkin, would encounter that same criticism a few years later for his television show *The West Wing,* which some on the Right took to calling "The Left Wing." Political sensitivities notwithstanding, *The American President* has many memorable scenes and exchanges and has held up nicely over time.

3. *YOUNG MR. LINCOLN,* 1939

Of the 158 movies made about Lincoln, this one is generally regarded as the finest. It's also considered one of the best performances of its star, Henry Fonda. The plot of the movie involves a fictionalized murder trial, in which Lincoln serves as the defense attorney for the accused. It serves to showcase his wit, wisdom, humility, and admiration for the law and politics. It also touches on his romantic pursuits with a comedic touch. *Young Mr. Lincoln* had the misfortune of being released in one of the greatest movie years ever—alongside such classics as *The Wizard of Oz*, *Mr. Smith Goes to Washington*, *Gone With the Wind*, and *Of Mice and Men*—which may account for it being overlooked as a classic in its own right.

4. *DR. STRANGELOVE,* 1964

Although based on the serious Cold War novel *Red Alert* by Peter George, director Stanley Kubrick decided to make it a dark comedy about the hazards of the nuclear arms race and, in doing so, created an all-time satirical masterpiece. Peter Sellers portrays three characters, most notably the weak-kneed president Merkin Muffley, and George C. Scott plays psychotic Gen. Buck Turgidson (some say a precursor to his Patton role). The movie prays upon real fears at the time for the potential of an accidental (or in this case semi-intentional) nuclear attack. The film's release was delayed several months after President Kennedy's assassination, and when it was finally made public, it came with a disclaimer from the U.S. Air Force that their "safeguards would prevent the occurrence of such events as are depicted in this film."

5. *NIXON,* 1995

Director Oliver Stone surprised many critics with his almost evenhanded take on Richard Nixon; it was not the hatchet job audiences widely expected. Perhaps chastened by his experience with the film *JFK,* Stone delved into both sides of Nixon—brilliant and hardworking, insecure and paranoid. The movie spans Nixon's entire life, paying special attention to his presidency and Watergate. Though nothing new was revealed about our thirty-seventh president, Stone's storytelling creates a context to better understand the flawed

leader. Anthony Hopkins captures Nixon's intensity and dis-
comfort around others, though his lack of physical resem-
blance sometimes detracts from the narrative. The large
supporting cast includes a dozen Hollywood stars. Released
shortly after Nixon's death, it was nominated for four Academy Awards.

6. *JFK,* 1991

It has been said that the only thing assassinated in director
Oliver Stone's highly controversial movie about President
Kennedy's death was the truth. Recounting all the inaccura-
cies would be pointless, though dozens of websites itemize
the hundreds of distortions, factual errors, and outright fabrications Stone made. Kevin Costner turns in a typical
"Costnerian" performance as New Orleans district attorney
Jim Garrison, the man who indicted reputed underworld figure and CIA operative Clay Shaw (played by Tommie Lee
Jones) for President Kennedy's murder. The rest of the star-
studded cast serves mostly in the background, save for Joe
Pesci's manic portrayal of David Ferrie, Shaw's paranoid
accomplice. What the film lacks in historical grounding and
evenhandedness, it makes up for in cinematic brilliance.
Stone's interspersion of historical footage with grainy re-
creations has the impact of creating a believable illusion, so
much so that a majority of Americans now accept Stone's
version of reality over that of the Warren Report.

7. *ALL THE PRESIDENT'S MEN,* 1976

While the president isn't depicted on screen at all, *All the
President's Men* might be the most powerful movie about
the office of the presidency. Director Alan Pakula wisely cast
Robert Redford and Dustin Hoffman as Bob Woodward and
Carl Bernstein, the young investigative journalists whose
reporting for the *Washington Post* helped bring down the

Nixon White House. Until recently, the movie may have best been best remembered for its depiction of the secretive government informant known as "Deep Throat," which Hal Holbrook played so brilliantly that he helped spawn three decades of serial identity guessing. Deep Throat's identity remained Washington's best-kept secret until 2005, when the former number two man at the Federal Bureau of Investigation (FBI), J. Mark Felt, came forward. The movie lost out to *Rocky* for the Academy Award for Best Picture in 1976.

8. *WILSON,* 1944

One of legendary producer Daryl Zanuck's most ambitious projects ever, the story of our twenty-eighth president turned out to be a colossal flop at the box office, though it was widely praised by critics and even garnered five Academy Award nominations. The movie chronicles Woodrow Wilson's presidency in a mostly glowing fashion, trumpeting his many accomplishments and soft-peddling some of its more controversial aspects, such as his backward views on race relations and the debilitating stroke (toward the end of his second term) that left his wife essentially running the country. Even so, it still holds up as one of the most robust presidential biopics ever made. Rumor has it that 20th Century Fox employees were forbidden to utter the word *Wilson* in front of Zanuck for years afterward.

9. *WAG THE DOG,* 1997

Although the popular 1997 movie speaks more about the press than the presidency, *Wag the Dog* still rates as one of the best lampoons of politics and the media. The movie's premise—contriving a war to distract the media from a sex scandal in the White House—didn't seem far fetched at the time (it was released a year before the Monica Lewinsky scandal broke). How the plot unravels, however, does require some suspension of disbelief when the reporters don't travel to the war-torn Albania, the United Nations doesn't intervene, and the president suddenly appears in the war zone. With Robert DeNiro as his straight man, Dustin Hoffman turns in one of his most underrated performances as the war's oddball director. Ironically, the phrase "wag the dog" has entered political parlance as shorthand for presidential actions that are meant (in the press's opinion) to distract the media from other news.

10. *ABSOLUTE POWER,* 1997

The only bona fide "thriller" of the bunch, *Absolute Power* is a highly entertaining movie about a philandering president and the grisly murder of his paramour, who happens to be the wife of his closest political benefactor. Clint Eastwood is a small-time crook who happens to witness the murder and ultimately sets in motion a chain of events that leads to the commander in chief's downfall. Gene Hackman is perfectly cast as the reptilian president, and Ed Harris is the detective on the case. The movie is a great way to spend a few hours.

DISHONORABLE MENTION

Air Force One, 1997
Only in a Harrison Ford movie could the most secure plane in the world be taken over by hijackers and then be saved by the super macho president.

Dave, 1993
Kevin Kline stars as both the president of the United States and a guy who looks exactly like him and is asked to take over when the president falls into a coma. Enough said.

Hackers in Chief

S ince the advent of the sport, every president but three—Herbert Hoover, Jimmy Carter, and Harry Truman—has played golf while in the White House. Some had a genuine passion for the sport while others simply used it as a temporary distraction. It can be argued that how they played was a reflection on how they governed: Nixon and Clinton had little regard for the rules, Ford counted every shot, and Eisenhower was methodical and precise.

1. JOHN F. KENNEDY

Though President Kennedy was plagued by a bad back his entire adult life, he was an avid golfer and a very good one at that. Kennedy picked up the game in his youth and had a long, fluid golf swing. At his best he was about a 7-handicap, though he played infrequently while serving as president. According to author Don Van Natta Jr., during the 1960 campaign and while playing with his friend, Paul Fay, Kennedy nearly made a hole in one. Fay rooted for the ball to go in while Kennedy watched in horror. "If that ball had gone into that hole, in less than an hour the word would be out to the nation that another golfer was trying to get into the White House," Kennedy said. A set of Kennedy's clubs sold for $770,000 in an auction of Jackie Kennedy's estate.

2. DWIGHT D. EISENHOWER

Ike may not have been the best golfer in chief, but he certainly was the most passionate. He picked up the game when he was stationed in the Philippines, and he usually played once or twice a week while in the White House. He played so frequently, in fact, that many credit Eisenhower (along with a swashbuckling young pro named Arnold Palmer) with popularizing the sport during the 1950s. Ike even had a putting green installed on the White House grounds and once told a White House gardener, "The next time you see one of those squirrels go near my putting green, take a gun and shoot it!" His favorite venue was the historic Augusta National Golf Course, home of the Masters and founded by golf legend Bobby Jones. Eisenhower made scores of trips to Augusta National, frequently playing with Chairman Clifford Roberts and Palmer. His best round at Augusta was a very respectable 84, though he usually shot in the low 90s. A large pine tree some two hundred yards off the seventeenth tee at Augusta National is known as "Eisenhower's Tree" because he hit it so many times. Ike even tried to have it cut down, but the club ignored his request. At age seventy-seven he recorded his only hole in one.

3. GERALD FORD

Contrary to popular press accounts, Gerald Ford was a terrific athlete—the best of among the presidents by far—and a good golfer. Unfortunately, he is mostly remembered for spraying the galleries at charity golf tournaments. His friend Bob Hope once quipped, "It's not hard to find Jerry Ford on a golf course—you just follow the wounded." Even Ford couldn't resist needling himself, frequently saying, "I know I'm getting better at golf because I'm hitting fewer spectators." Recounting the thirty-plus rounds he played with President Ford, golf legend Jack Nicklaus described him as a "big hitter off the tee and played to about a 13- or 14-handi-cap. And when I say he was a 13- or 14-handicap, I mean he was a real 13 or 14. He would regularly shoot 85." Ford was the first former president to play in a PGA Tour event when he partnered with Jackie Gleason, Jack Nicklaus, and Bob Hope at the 1977 Jackie Gleason Invitational. For twenty-five years Ford hosted his own celebrity golf tourna-ment to raise funds for charity.

4. BILL CLINTON

Bill Clinton's reputation as someone who played fast and loose with the truth followed him to the golf course, where he was dubbed the "cheater in chief" by the press. He pur-ported to shoot in the mid- to low 80s, though many sus-pect he was usually aided by a liberal dose of mulligans (or do-overs) and "eraser math." As a playing companion once said of his game, "It took him 200 strokes to shoot 82." While president, Clinton typically hit the links three to four times a month, and his most frequent playing companion was Washington super lawyer Vernon Jordan. For his birth-day one year, his wife, Hillary, surprised President Clinton with a playing lesson with golf legend and NBC announcer Johnny Miller, and it was at Greg Norman's house in Florida where Clinton famously slipped and tore a knee ligament in 1997. In 1995, President Clinton became the first sitting president to play in a PGA Tour event when he teamed with George H. W. Bush, Gerald Ford, Bob Hope, and tour player Scott Hoch during the first round of the Bob Hope Chrysler Classic. It's also believed to be the only time three presi-dents played a round of golf together.

5. GEORGE H. W. BUSH

George Bush was neither the best nor the most passionate golfer to reside in the White House, but he certainly was the fastest. An erratic high 80s player, Bush typically played a round of golf in three hours. His playing in the White House was mostly restricted to rounds at Kennebunkport while on vacation and to an occasional outing with foreign leaders. You could say golf is in his blood; his grandfather George H. Walker was the president of the United States Golf Association. In 1920 he donated a cup for the amateur team competition between the United States and Great Britain that became known as the Walker Cup (and is still played today). Since leaving office, Bush has been big supporter of the PGA of America and the PGA Tour and has attended numerous Ryder Cup and President's Cup competitions. In 2006 he and President Clinton teamed up for a charity golf tournament to raise funds for the Indonesia tsunami victims.

6. WOODROW WILSON

Woodrow Wilson holds the distinction of playing the most rounds of golf while president—by one estimate, almost twelve hundred. Wilson took up the sport after entering the White House and the doctor ordered him to get some exercise. He tried to play almost every day and refused to let bad weather get in the way; in fact, the Secret Service took to painting balls red so that he could hit balls in the snow on the White House lawn. For all his practice and playing, however, Wilson was pretty horrendous— he never broke 100— and his wife regularly beat him at the game. Wilson was on the golf course when he received notice of the sinking of the *Lusitania*.

7. WILLIAM HOWARD TAFT

William Howard Taft was the first president to play a round of golf, and he is credited with helping to popularize the new sport in the United States. Golf had been played in the United

William Howard Taft was the first president to play a round of
golf. *William Howard Taft National Historic Site*

States for only a decade when Taft first hit the links, and it was mostly considered the province of the affluent. Teddy Roosevelt warned Taft to give up the game while president because it would hurt his public image, but he refused. Taft once canceled a meeting with a dignitary because it conflicted with his golf game. "I'll be damned if I will give up my golf game to see this fellow," he said.

8. WARREN G. HARDING

Like his predecessor, Woodrow Wilson, Harding was also an inept but avid golfer. Back home in Ohio, he frequently played the great Scioto golf course, and he was actually playing golf on election day when he was elected president. He mostly played with the "Ohio Gang"—a group of Ohio cronies who followed him to Washington—and enjoyed high-stakes betting. Don Van Natta writes that a Harding aide once remarked that settling golf wages with Harding was "a job for a Philadelphia lawyer." One sign that his health began to decline in late 1922 was his inability to complete nine holes.

9. RICHARD NIXON

Richard Nixon was probably the least athletic president of the twentieth century, and he only took up the sport while vice president so he could spend more time with Eisenhower. Though he practiced quite a bit, Nixon had little skill, rarely broke 100, and wasn't above moving his ball or shaving shots from his score. While president, his most frequent playing partner was his good friend and businessman Charles "Bebe" Rebozo; the two often played in Palm Beach, Florida, where Rebozo owned an estate. Nixon claimed to have given up the game after shooting a miraculous 79, an account that seems highly improbable.

10. **RONALD REAGAN**

Like his political idol, Calvin Coolidge, Reagan played infrequently—and horribly—while president, but it's purported that he regularly scored in the low 90s while governor of California. Reagan spent most of his recreation time in the White House on horseback and when asked his golf handicap usually replied, "Congress." Reagan made it a point to play nine holes every New Year's Day at the private course of his friend and publishing magnate Walter Annenberg.

Ten Things You Didn't Know About the Presidency

Finally, here's some good information that didn't fit in elsewhere. And it might come in handy if you ever appear on the game show *Jeopardy!* or simply want to be more interesting at your next cocktail party.

1. CHILDREN

Though President James Madison had no biological children, he cared for wife Dolley's son from a previous marriage. Unfortunately for Madison, his stepson had virtually no redeeming qualities. A degenerative drinker, gambler, and womanizer, John Payne Todd amassed more than $40,000 in debts—an astronomical sum in those days—which the president dutifully paid. After the president's death, Todd went so far as to try and sell Madison's priceless papers, but fortunately Congress stepped in to purchase them. When Todd threatened to sue the congressional trustees over the purchase, Dolley Madison wrote to him: "Your mother would have no wish to live after her son issued such threats." She died the following year without hearing from him again. Similarly hopeless, the adopted son of Old Hickory, Jackson Jr. was an incorrigible skirt chaser and flamboyant spender. Throughout his life, he accumulated massive debts, which his father paid. The president charged "Junior" with looking after their Tennessee plantation, the Hermitage, hoping he would mature and settle down. The younger Jackson continued his wild spending, however, and eventually drove the estate so far into debt that the state of Tennessee purchased half of it. Fortunately, the state let Jackson live on the estate rent free until his death.

2. PETS

Over the years, presidents have had some odd pets. John Quincy Adams was the only president to have a pet alligator in the White House; a gift from Marquis de Lafayette, Adams kept it in the East Room. After their famous expedition, Meriwether Lewis and William Clark gave Thomas Jefferson two bear cubs. Calvin Coolidge practically kept a zoo in the White House. His pets included eleven dogs, three canaries, three cats, two raccoons, a donkey, a bobcat, a goose, a bear, an antelope, lion cubs, and a pygmy hippo. Fillmore, Pierce, and Arthur were the only presidents without pets. Spot, a Springer spaniel, was the only dog born in the White House during one administration (George H. W. Bush) and then lived in the White House again during another administration, that of George W. Bush. Jimmy Carter's dog was named Grits the Dog.

3. EDUCATION

Harvard University boasts the most presidents as alumni, seven: John Adams, John Quincy Adams, Rutherford B. Hayes (law school), Teddy Roosevelt, Franklin Roosevelt, John F. Kennedy, and George W. Bush (business school). Yale is second with five alumni, and the College of William and Mary is third with three. Nine presidents, including George Washington and Abraham Lincoln, didn't attend any college, and Harry Truman was the last not to attend college. Twenty-six presidents were lawyers or held law degrees, representing by far the most popular profession among the presidents. Woodrow Wilson is the only president to hold a doctorate, and George W. Bush is the only one with a master of business administration (MBA). Andrew Johnson did not have any formal education; instead, his future wife taught him how to read at age seventeen. She also taught him how to write and do arithmetic.

4. SIZE
The tallest president was Abraham Lincoln, standing 6 foot 4. At 5 foot 4, James Madison was the shortest, as well as the lightest (he weighed a hundred pounds). By far William Howard Taft was the heaviest president, tipping the scales at more than three hundred pounds while in the Oval Office. He was so large, in fact, that the White House staff had to install a new bathtub after he got stuck in the old one; the new tub was large enough to accommodate four adult males. Legend has it that Taft was buried in a piano case. Taller candidates have defeated their shorter counterparts 2 to 1 in the fifty-three contested presidential elections (Washington ran unopposed twice). The tallest major-party candidate to lose was Gen. Winfield Scott, who stood at 6 foot 5. Stephen Douglas was the shortest candidate; according to some estimates he was 4 foot 7.

5. RELIGION
Though 24 percent of the U.S. population is Catholic, there has only been one Catholic president—John F. Kennedy. Though they make up less than 2 percent of the population, Episcopalians include eleven presidents among their ranks, the most of any religion. Presbyterians are second with ten presidents. Dwight Eisenhower's parents were both Jehovah's Witnesses, though Ike became a communicant in the Presbyterian Church just weeks after his first

inaugural. Among vice presidents, Presbyterians lead Episcopalians 12 to 10, and none of the vice presidents have been Catholic. George Washington, Thomas Jefferson, and James Madison considered themselves "Deists," meaning they believed in divine providence but did not believe in divine intervention after creation. Franklin Pierce questioned the existence of God following the tragic death of his twelve-year-old son and refused to kiss the Bible after affirming (he wouldn't swear) the oath of office.

6. ANCESTRY
Everyone knows the Adams and Bush families have had the only father-son combinations to serve in the White House, and the Harrisons are the only grandfather-grandson pair. It's not as well known, however, that James Madison and Zachary Taylor are the only second cousins to hold the office. Franklin and Teddy Roosevelt were fifth cousins; furthermore, Teddy was Eleanor Roosevelt's uncle and gave her away in her marriage ceremony to Franklin. It's been determined that Franklin Roosevelt was related to eleven presidents (by far the most of any president), including George Washington, James Madison, John Adams, John Quincy Adams, and Ulysses Grant. He was also a distant cousin of Winston Churchill's. George H. W. Bush is the eleventh cousin once removed of Gerald Ford, and his wife, Barbara Pierce Bush, is a descendent of Franklin Pierce.

7. WEALTH
George Washington's salary was $25,000; George W. Bush earns $400,000 a year as president. As late as 1946, the vice president earned only $20,000 a year (the president earned $100,000 then). Herbert Hoover is the only president who declined taking any salary; already wealthy, he was probably the most successful businessman to hold the

office. John Kennedy donated his salary to charity. At his death, George Washington was one of the wealthiest Americans by virtue of his enormous estate (though he acquired most of it through marriage). Thomas Jefferson was an uncontrollable spender throughout his life and was virtually bankrupt at the time of his death. Ulysses Grant also faced severe financial hardship following his presidency, and just days before he died, he completed and sold his autobiography for nearly $500,000—an astronomical sum in those days.

8. LOVE AND MARRIAGE
James Buchanan is the only president never to have married. He was briefly engaged while in his twenties, but his

Grover Cleveland, shown here on his yacht, was one of three presidents who married while serving in the White House. *New Jersey Division of Parks and Forestry, State Park Service, Grover Cleveland Birthplace State Historic Site*

fiancée called off the wedding and committed suicide days later. Some historians have speculated that Buchanan was intimately involved with William R. King, for the two lived together for fifteen years while in Washington and before King briefly served as Franklin Pierce's vice president. Three presidents—John Tyler, Grover Cleveland, and Woodrow Wilson—were married while serving in the White House. Ronald Reagan was the only president who had been divorced. Three First Ladies died during their husbands' terms: Letitia Tyler, Caroline Harrison, and Ellen Wilson. Eight presidential daughters have been married in the White House, the last being Tricia Nixon in 1971.

9. CURRENCY

Washington, Lincoln, and Jefferson are the only presidents to appear on both print and coin currency. The Franklin Roosevelt dime was first issued in 1946, the year after his death, and replaced the Winged Liberty Head, or Mercury, dime. John F. Kennedy replaced Benjamin Franklin on the half dollar in 1964. In addition to the current $20 bill, Andrew Jackson's picture also appeared on the Confederate $1,000 bill. William McKinley's portrait appears on the $500 bill, Grover Cleveland on the $1,000, James Madison on the $5,000, and Woodrow Wilson on the $100,000, but these bills are no longer in circulation.

10. RANDOM

Andrew Jackson believed that the earth was flat. He was also the only president to have been held prisoner; at thirteen during the Revolutionary War the British captured him and his brother. Jimmy Carter once reported seeing an unidentified flying object (UFO). The word *OK* is derived from Martin Van Buren's nickname, which was "Old Kinderhook" (after his birthplace). In Van Buren's autobiography, he doesn't mention his wife once. Between 1840 and 1960, every president elected in a year that ended with a zero died in office: Harrison, Lincoln, Garfield, McKinley, Harding, Roosevelt, and Kennedy. John Tyler had the most children—fifteen. Zachary Taylor didn't know he had been elected president until three days after election day because he refused to accept any mail that did not have sufficient postage (including notification that he was elected president). Franklin Pierce was the only president arrested in office, on charges of running over an old woman with his carriage, but the case was eventually dropped because of insufficient evidence. A week before he was assassinated, Lincoln told several close friends that he had had a dream that he had been assassinated. Ironically, Edwin Booth, brother of Lincoln's assassin, John Wilkes Booth, actually saved Lincoln's son Robert from being crushed by a train as the two waited at a rail station in Jersey City, New Jersey. Born Hiram Ulysses Grant, Grant changed his name because he didn't want to enter West Point with the initials H.U.G. The Baby Ruth candy bar was named after Grover Cleveland's baby daughter Ruth and not the baseball player Babe Ruth. Theodore Roosevelt was the first president to ride in an airplane when he spent four minutes in one of the Wright brothers' early creations in 1910; it would be thirty-four years before another president traveled by plane. According to legend, while visiting Andrew Jackson's birthplace, Teddy Roosevelt drank a cup of Maxwell House coffee and commented it was "good to the last drop"—a tag line the company decided to adopt. Harding and JFK were the only two presidents to predecease their fathers.

Selected Bibliography

Birnbaum, Jeffrey, and Alan Murray. *Showdown at Gucci Gulch: Lawmakers, Lobbyists , and the Unlikely Triumph of Tax Reform*. New York: Random House, 1987.

Boller, Paul. *Presidential Wives: An Anecdotal History*. New York: Oxford University Press, 2006.

Brallier, Jess. *Presidential Wit and Wisdom: Maxims, Mottoes, Sound Bites, Speeches, and Asides: Memorable Quotes From America's Presidents*. New York: Penguin, 1996.

Bush, Gregory. *Campaign Speeches of American Presidential Candidates*. New York: F. Ungar, 1948–1984, 1985.

Ferrell, Robert. *Presidential Leadership: From Woodrow Wilson to Harry S. Truman*. Columbia: University of Missouri Press, 2005.

Fornieri, Joseph. *The Language of Liberty: The Political Speeches and Writings of Abraham Lincoln*. Washington, DC: Regnery, 2003.

Friedenberg, Robert. *Notable Speeches in Contemporary Presidential Campaigns*. London: Praeger, 2002.

Gilbert, Robert. *Managing Crisis: Presidential Disability and the Twenty-Fifth Amendment*. New York: Fordham University Press, 2000.

Goldsmith, William. *The Growth of Presidential Power: A Documented History*. New York: Chelsea House, 1974.

Goodwin, Doris Kearns. *Team of Rivals: The Political Genius of Abraham Lincoln*. New York: Simon & Schuster, 2005.

Henderson, Phillip. *The Presidency Then and Now*. Oxford: Rowman & Littlefield, 2000.

Humes, James. *My Fellow Americans: Presidential Addresses That Shaped History*. New York: Praeger, 1992.

Israel, Fred. *Major Presidential Decisions*. New York: Chelsea House, 1980.

Kengor, Paul. *The Crusader: Ronald Reagan and the Fall of Communism*. New York: Reagan Books, 2006.

Lamb, Brian, et al. *Who's Buried in Grant's Tomb? A Tour of Presidential Gravesites*. New York: Public Affairs, 2003.

Marton, Kati. *Hidden Power: Presidential Marriages That Shaped Our Recent History*. New York: Anchor Books, 2002.

Mathis, William. *Presidency of the United States: History, Analyses, Bibliography*. New York: Nova Science, 2002.

Matviko, John. *The American President in Popular Culture*. Westport, CT: Greenwood Press, 2005.

Nelson, Michael. *The Presidency: A History of the Office of the President of the United States From 1789 to Present*. London: Salamander Books, 1996.

North, Robert. *Encyclopedia of Presidential Campaigns, Slogans, Issues, and Platforms*. Westport, CT: Greenwood Press, 2004.

Oshinsky, David. *A Conspiracy So Immense: The World of Joe McCarthy*. New York: Free Press, 1983.

Ragone, Nick. *The Everything American Government Book: From the Constitution to Present-Day Elections, All You Need to Understand Our Democratic System*. Avon, MA: Adams Publishing, 2004.

Rollins, Peter, and John O'Connor. *The American Presidency in Film and History*. Lexington: University Press of Kentucky, 2003.

Schroeder, Alan. *Celebrity-In-Chief: How Show Business Took Over the White House*. Boulder: Westview Press, 2004.

Stanwood, Edward. *A History of the Presidency From 1788 to 1897*. New York: Houghton Mifflin, 1898.

Troy, Gil. *Mr. and Mrs. President: From the Trumans to the Clintons*. Lawrence: University Press of Kansas, 2000.

Van Natta Jr., Don. *First Off the Tee: Presidential Hackers, Duffers and Cheaters From Taft to Bush*. New York: Public Affairs, 2003.

Vile, John. *Presidential Winners and Losers: Words of Victory and Concession*. Washington, DC: CQ Press 2002.

Watson, Robert. *The Presidents' Wives: Reassessing the Role of First Lady*. Boulder: Lynne Rienner, 2000.

Watterson, John. *The Games Presidents Play: Sports and the Presidency*. Baltimore: Johns Hopkins University Press, 2006.

Witcover, Jules. *Crapshoot: Rolling the Dice on the Vice Presidency*. New York: Crown, 1992.

Wright, Russell. *Presidential Elections in the United States: A Statistical History, 1860–1992*. Jefferson, NC: McFarland, 1992.

Young, Donald. *American Roulette: The History and Dilemma of the Vice Presidency*. New York: Viking, 1974.

Young, Jeff. *The Fathers of American Presidents*. Jefferson, NC: McFarland, 1997.

Index

Vinson, Fred, 146

Wag the Dog, 255–56
Walker, George H., 260
Walker Cup, 260
Wallace, George, 39, 141, 147, 210
War of 1812, 62, 63–64, 158
Ward, John Quincy Adams, 250
Warren Report, 254
Washburne, Elihu, 12
Washington, Booker T., 6
Washington, George, 3, 5–6, 14, 25–26, 58–59, 63, 127, 158, 188, 197–98, 201, 238–39, 246, 265, 267, 269
Washington Monument, 244–245, 247
Washington National Monument Society, 244
Watergate, 35, 56, 97–98, 221
Wayne, "Mad Anthony," 62
Weaver, James Baird, 143–44
Weinberger, Caspar, 100
Wellstone, Paul, 183
West Wing, 13, 252
Whip Inflation Now (WIN), 219
Whiskey Rebellion, 198
Whiskey Ring scandal, 98, 227
White, Edward, 231
White Squadron, 213
Whitewater scandal, 101
Whittinton, Harry, 111
Wilkes Booth, John, 67

Wilkie, Wendell, 7, 122, 175
Willey, Kathleen, 214
Wilson, 255
Wilson, Edith, 77, 162
Wilson, Ellen, 269
Wilson, Henry, 194
Wilson, Joe, 103
Wilson, Valerie Plame, 103
Wilson, Woodrow, 1–3, 8, 76–77, 89, 117, 122, 138, 143, 153, 156, 162, 207–9, 226, 237, 248–49, 255, 260, 266, 268–69
Winged Liberty Head dime, 269
Wizard of Oz, 253
Woodrow Wilson International Center for Scholars, 248–49
Woodward, Bob, 97, 254–55
World War I, 162, 174, 176, 209–10
World War II, 32, 158, 175
World's Fair, Belgium, 236
Wright Brothers, 6, 270

XYZ Affair, 102

Yalta Conference, 79, 199
Yom Kippur War, 21
Young Mr. Lincoln, 252–53

Zangara, Giuseppe, 73
Zanuck, Daryl, 255
Zedong, Mao, 35
Zorin, Valerian, 127

About the Author

Nick Ragone is a public relations executive in New York City. He earned a bachelor of arts in history and political science from Rutgers University and is a graduate of the Eagleton Institute of Political Science at Rutgers University and the Georgetown University Law Center. His previous books include *The Everything American Government Book: From the Constitution to Present-Day Elections, All You Need to Understand Our Democratic System*. He lives with his wife and two children in Jersey City, New Jersey, and spends what little free time he has on the golf course or cheering on the New York Mets.